Evolution:
Tech's Transformative Journey

Shen Kuo

Shen Kuo
All rights reserved.

Abstract

Scripting involves an ambiguity. First, it indicates a directive, as in the commands of "scripture"; or, in the disappointment that an apparently spontaneous happening was in fact "scripted." This engages a familiar outlook on computing: code is language operating in a "prescriptive" register. Additionally, however, scripting also hints towards the materiality of graphic "inscription," such as the traces expressed in the written form of a "manuscript." The history of computing presented here is situated at the joints of these two senses. Working between them prompts an archaic image of the computer, far removed from advanced technologies of electronic machinery. It instead suggests its deep historical heritage in clerical labor, affording a perspective on computation as a manual, incorporated, and lived activity—that is, as the product of scribes.

This dissertation elaborates on some consequences of reorienting the histories of computing and graphics around such a schism. Rather than placing computerization at the summit of a media historical lineage—of scribal practices succeeded by print media and leading from printing itself to electronics—it proposes a superimposition of the scribal with the computational. Computing is approached neither as software nor hardware, and beyond its scope as either science or technology. Through close readings of pivotal documents in the development of computing, each of three chapters reconsiders a key concept in computational media and the keen attachments that have consolidated around them: (1) the sequential basis to *algorithms*; (2) the operative dimension in *programming languages*; and, (3) the interactivity of *computer screens*.

Table of Contents

Title Page	i
Copyright	ii
Abstract	iii
Table of Contents	v
Acknowledgements	vii

Introduction: Calculus, Calculation, Calcification (Charles Babbage as Geologist)   1
    Some Comments on Historiography (Deep History and the "Long" 1950s)   21

Chapter 1: Algorithmic Media and Visuality
    §1.1: Graphical Computing: Scopic Regimes of the Algorithmic   34
    §1.2: Threshold Objects: A Detour through Data   52
    §1.3: The Algorithm Concept, 1684-1958   57
    §1.4: Red-Black Trees: or, What Does Color Want?   79

Chapter 2: Turology, An Imaginary History of Computer Programming
    §2.1: Decorative Programming Languages   93
    §2.2: "Rat Theory" (I): Complications in the Behavior Concept   111
    §2.3: "Rat Theory" (II): The Cultural Techniques of Cognitivism   121
    §2.4: "Rat Theory" (III): Crustacean Theologies and an Expanded Bestiary of Animacy   141
    §2.5: The Cultural Politics of Skill: Computer Science as "Procedural Epistemology"   158

Chapter 3: Sphygmography and Screening
    §3.1: Screen Media: A (Non-)Philosophical History of Dots   176
    §3.2: The Altair 8800: "Hackers"   185
    §3.3: The Charatron: "Real Mode"   193
    §3.4: The IBM 740 and 780: "Hulking Giants"   208

§3.5: The Sphygmograph and the Capillary Electrometer:
Rheotomic Physiology 217

§3.6: Crookes's Tubes: Projections of Radiant Matter 241

Acknowledgements

I am deeply grateful to the following:

- Laura Frahm's consistent guidance, encouragement, and support has accompanied this project from before its inception through its completion.
- Giuliana Bruno and Bernhard Siegert have been sources of inspiration and sympathy.
- Others from the Film and Visual Studies program were collegial interlocutors.
- Parts of this dissertation have been presented at conferences and published in journals. The feedback and careful editorial attention it benefited from have reshaped both the final text presented here, as well as my scholarly perspectives more generally. I thank all involved for their interest and insights.

Introduction:

News of his election as the Lucasian Professor of Mathematics at Cambridge left Charles Babbage unimpressed. The chair carried an honor more symbolic than material. Having in the past been held by Isaac Newton, it afforded its occupant some prestige by association. However, it was supported by a rather meagre annual salary of less than £100. Upon the death of his father a year prior, Babbage had inherited an estate worth around £100,000 through which he intended to fund his pursuits. These included the construction of his design for a Difference Engine, a contraption that would mechanize the task of performing calculations. Babbage hesitated in accepting the university position over concerns that it might distract him from complete focus on his machine, only relenting for fear of the offense he might cause should he have declined. Besides, the duties demanded of him as professor were limited: in this capacity, he gave no lectures, took no students, and spent little time in Cambridge.

Still, he was in no hurry to assume the new post. Having entrusted the fabrication of the Difference Engine to his friend John Herschel's oversight, Babbage had set off on a tour of Europe in late 1827 and was in Rome when he learnt of the appointment in the spring of 1828. Although his initial plans of a voyage to Asia were disrupted as the Greek war of independence from the Ottoman Empire had made passage dangerous, Babbage nevertheless continued onwards, reaching the south of the Italian peninsula in May. Volcanic activity did not dissuade him from ascending the summit of Mount Vesuvius, and at Pozzuoli, near Naples, he conducted a rigorous inspection of the Temple of Serapis, taking detailed measurements of its ruins. A subsequent detour to Berlin, where Babbage called on the great naturalist Alexander von Humboldt, further delayed his eventual return to London to the end of 1828. Humboldt was keen for updates on scientific developments from across the Channel ("What are the moving molecules of Robert Brown?"), and in those weeks was engaged in preparations for a grand meeting, conscripting Babbage to resolve "the important question, how they were to dine?"[1]

It would, of course, be the invention Babbage left behind unfinished rather than the itinerary of his travels that accounts for much of the interest he continues to provoke. Despite significant investment over the span of more than a decade, a fully working product would never be completed, and the Difference Engine was definitively abandoned in 1834. Later attempts at constructing an even more ambitious successor with stored memory, the Analytic Engine, were also unsuccessful. These disappointments have become celebrated anachronisms, considered at least in retrospect to have prefigured today's modern computers. In Babbage's lifetime, however, the profit they accrued stemmed primarily from a subsidiary concern that originated as a byproduct of their development process. Introduced as "one of the consequences that have resulted from the Calculating-Engine," his bestselling exposition *On the Economy of Machinery and Manufactures* (1832) was based on findings accumulated from extensive visits to workshops and factories.[2] The enthusiastic reception it received is somewhat ironic given that the outcome of Babbage's endeavors could hardly have recommended his expertise on either the craft of manufacturing or its management.

---

[1] Charles Babbage, *Passages from the Life of a Philosopher* (London, 1864), p. 201, hereafter abbreviated *P*. Naturally, the answer was to be determined through "experiment," i.e., "by dining successively at each of the three or four hotels." As Babbage would recount, this was a responsibility he was deemed well qualified for: "Humboldt put me on that committee, remarking, that an Englishman always appreciates a good dinner." On his appointment as Lucasian Professor, see pp. 29-31.

[2] Charles Babbage, *On the Economy of Machinery and Manufactures* (London: Charles Knight, 1832), p. iii, hereafter abbreviated *E*.

There is a telling anecdote recounted in Babbage's memoirs that neatly lays out the structuring dichotomy running across his interest in computing machinery through his treatment of industrial economics. It takes place on a daytrip to the manufacturing town of Bradford, where Babbage chanced upon a small manufactory and succeeded in obtaining a tour of its works. The particular products it specialized in were of little concern and would escape his memory ("I think it was of door-mats," he suggested). Rather, what Babbage was really after were insights that could be generalized as principles. Of the helpful workmen he spoke to, one possessed an especially impressive depth of knowledge.

> Much pleased by the intelligence and acuteness of this man, I thought it possible he might have read the "Economy of Manufactures." On mentioning that work, I found he was well acquainted with it, and he asked my opinion of its merits. I told him that, having myself written the book, I was not an impartial judge. On hearing that I was its author, his delight was unbounded; he held out his brawny hand, which I cordially grasped. The most gratifying remark to me, however, amongst the many things in it to which he referred with approbation, was the expression he applied to it as a whole. "Sir," said my new friend, "that book made me think."

"To make a man think for himself," Babbage sagely concluded, "is doing him far higher service than giving him much instruction" (*P*, p. 229).

Curiously, then, the celebrated highlight of this excursion to the hinterlands of production involved a suspension of productivity. *Thinking* was considered an end in itself, a virtue that stood apart from—and, indeed, above—the activities that his counterpart's "brawny hand" might otherwise have been engaged in, like *making* or *doing*—that is, the manual tasks associated with *working*. Intelligent conversation interrupts utilitarian efficiency. At the local co-operative, Babbage would encounter more sympathetic comrades: "the secretary, as soon as he heard my name, held out his hand and greeted me with a hearty grasp" (*P*, p. 230). It is almost as if the civility of (thoughtful) dialogue has freed the "hand" from its quotidian attachments to labor.

Supposedly, the convention of the handshake has its roots as a sign of peaceful intent, demonstrating that both parties are not bearing arms; here, however, I am tempted to believe that the "hearty grasp" is rather a demonstration that one has relinquished vice and lathe—not the absence of weaponry but a surrender of workshop tools. The mouth can truly speak only after the hand has set aside its toils.[3]

Of the varied concerns addressed in Babbage's *Economy of Manufactures*, most provide precisely the sort of "instruction" that he would later grade as subaltern. These sober dissertations outlined useful advice to improve output and cannot have been mistaken for anything so scandalous as an incitement to *think*; they are imperatives to get to *work*. There is just one likely candidate for this role. It is closely linked to the ambitions for a calculating engine, conspicuous as a flight of imagination with no discernible immediate application. Babbage even found it necessary to issue a warning that it "may, perhaps, appear paradoxical to some of our readers" (*E*, p. 153) to speak of the "Division" of what he referred to as "Mental Labour" (see *E*, pp. 153-163).

By this, Babbage meant the computing of mathematical tables, a task which required great perseverance if little ingenuity. He described, as proof of the apparent paradox, a three-tiered system that had been used in France to organize procedures of computation. The logarithmic and trigonometric tables of Baron Gaspard Riche de Prony were processed and compiled on such a vast scale that they necessitated the institution of quasi-industrial management techniques.

---

[3] In this regard, it is interesting to consider Babbage alongside ideological traditions which have associated cerebral development and the availability of speech with the "liberation" resulting from the interventions of the hand. See André Leroi-Gourhan, "Brain and Hand" in *Gesture and Speech*, trans. Anna Bostock Berger (Cambridge, MA: MIT Press, 1993), pp. 25-60. Especially noteworthy is the following passage from Gregory of Nyssa's *Treatise on the Creation of Man* (A.D. 379), cited by Leroi-Gourhan: "So it was thanks to the manner in which our bodies are organized that our mind, like a musician, struck the note of language within us and we became capable of speech. This privilege would surely never have been ours if our lips had been required to perform the onerous and difficult task of procuring nourishment for our bodies. But our hands took over that task, releasing our mouths for the service of speech" (p. 25).

Specifically, Prony had adapted Adam Smith's principles on the division of labor, extending it to encompass the mental operation of calculation. As Babbage explained, Smith had cited three dimensions through which the division of labor yielded an increase in productivity: (1) specialization led to the acquisition of skill through repetition; (2) focus on a single task led to efficiencies by eliminating time lost to adjustments required in the change from one occupation to another; and, (3) limiting attention to a single process fostered a familiarity that might prompt the invention of tools to facilitate that task, leading to the development of machinery.

To this relatively well-established canon, however, Babbage added a fourth factor which he considered yet more vital:

> *That the master manufacturer, by dividing the work to be executed into different processes, each requiring different degrees of skill and force, can purchase exactly that precise quantity of both which is necessary for each process; whereas, if the whole work were executed by one workman, that person must possess sufficient skill to perform the most difficult, and sufficient strength to execute the most laborious, of the operations into which the art is divided.* (*E*, pp. 137-138)

Unlike the amplifications of competency that Smith had specified, this newly identified advantage suggested a process of deskilling. Decomposing complex procedures into their elementary components would lower the cost of training, allowing even those with limited domain-specific expertise to be mobilized as productive contributors: "the greater the number of distinct processes, the longer will be the time which the apprentice must employ in acquiring it. ... If, however, instead of learning all the different processes for making a needle, for instance, his attention be confined to one operation, a very small portion of his time will be consumed unprofitably at the commencement" (*E*, p. 132).

Prony's workshop was especially useful as an example that could highlight the sort of economies Babbage sought to introduce, readily lending itself to interpretation in such terms: "we avoid employing any part of the time of a man who can get eight or ten shillings a day by his skill in tempering needles, in turning a wheel, which can be done for sixpence a day; and we equally avoid the loss arising from the employment of an accomplished mathematician in performing the lowest processes of arithmetic" (*E*, p. 162). Handled in quantities appropriate to an industrial age, calculation would no longer be the province of a solitary savant. Under Prony's charge, the orchestration of computing was directed by "five or six of the most eminent mathematicians" who expended little effort on "actual numerical work" (*E*, p. 156), instead fully devoting their talents to investigating which expressions were most amenable to simple numerical calculation. Having established their selections, they would be assisted by a slightly larger second section comprising of "seven or eight persons of considerable acquaintance with mathematics" (*E*, p. 156) responsible for translating these expressions into numerical terms. Finally, at the base of the pyramid was a larger class of sixty to eighty who supplied the bulk of the labor but needed only the most rudimentary arithmetic skill, their tasks limited solely to addition and subtraction. It was this last group—the numerical counterparts to the "sixpence a day" wheel turners—whom Babbage sought to replace with the Difference Engine, determining that the tedious work they undertook "may almost be termed mechanical" (*E*, p. 157). His goal in recruiting machinery was to refurbish the analogy of this "almost" into literal functional equivalence.

Whereas Babbage's other examples were characterized by their relative fungibility—a reference to tempering needles could, for instance, be substituted with a description of making door-mats without inducing too much confusion—the distinction of "Mental Labour" was its difficulty. Reconciling this irregularity with familiar procedures required a triumph of the imagination; it was the sort of challenge that would "make a man think for himself" (*P*, p. 229). Historian Lorraine Daston has identified the inflection of this exceptional status as a point on which

Babbage subtly shifted the stakes of Prony's project. For the latter, the extravagant precision of the cadastral logarithms was antithetical to efficiencies. His regime of specialization, in Daston's estimation, should not be mistaken for the factory system but rather approximated practices of fine craftsmanship that "could not compete successfully against small domestic ateliers unless shored up by large government subsidies. Costs were otherwise too high and labor supply too uncertain to undercut the prices of an efficient family business. Only the demand, small but highly placed, for certain exquisite products—for example, fabrics fit for a king's coronation robes or palace upholstery—could justify the extra expenditure for enterprises that meshed the labor of so many workers in so unprofitable a fashion."[4] Prony's tables were intended as a one-of-a-kind achievement that defied any resemblance with standard practice.

Babbage, on the other hand, precisely drew parallels between the role of an industrialist in the manufacturing process and the mathematician's responsibilities under conditions of mass production. He concluded his discussion of Prony's administrative feat by highlighting its resonance with customs from other spheres of production, noting how it "much resembles that of a skillful person about to construct a cotton or silk-mill":

> Having, by his own genius, or through the aid of his friends, found that some improved machinery may be successfully applied to his pursuit, he makes drawings of his plans of the machinery, and may himself be considered as constituting the first section. He next requires the assistance of operative engineers capable of executing the machinery he has designed, some of whom should understand the nature of the processes to be carried on; and these constitute his second section. When a sufficient number of machines have been made, a multitude of other persons, possessed of a lower degree of skill, must be employed in using them; these form the third section: but their work and the just performance of the machines, must be still superintended by the second class. (*E*, pp. 157-158)

---

[4] Lorraine Daston, "Enlightenment Calculations," *Critical Inquiry* 21, no. 1 (Autumn 1994): 199.

When establishing this comparison, Babbage undoubtedly had in mind a more concrete point of reference than the hypothetical textile mill operator, namely, his own venture as an entrepreneur of symbolic goods. The steps outlined in the passage quoted above would be echoed in his later recollections of efforts undertaken to construct the Difference Engine: "The drawings and the experiments [for the Difference Engine] were of the most costly kind. Draftsmen of the highest order [that is, a second section] were necessary to economize the labour of my own head; whilst skilled workmen [that is, a third section] were required to execute the experimental machinery to which I was obliged constantly to have recourse" (*P*, p. 112).

It was not so much that Babbage lacked an appreciation for artisanal competencies that Prony held in esteem; neither maintained a particularly egalitarian outlook towards the diversity of responsibilities, clearly considering certain roles superior and others inferior. Instead, two styles of social ranking might be distinguished. The order specified by Prony expressed an aristocratic conservatism in which each position was fixed in its place, and excellence attained by refining the pursuit of that assignment. In the more bourgeois patrician sensibility that Babbage espoused, a hierarchical disposition was instead directed towards a process of self-betterment: the "sixpence" worker turning a wheel could not advance their station by enhancing their aptitude at wheel-turning but upgraded their returns to the rank of "shillings" by aspiring towards worthier commissions. Or, at any rate, what was assessed to be worthier. Economy was the basis for edification that culminated in the freedoms of *thinking*, the vocation Babbage deemed most proper. His Difference Engine was conceived as a contribution to these (supposed) dignities of industry not through an acknowledgement of the virtues in labor but by providing relief from the exertions of menial chores. Even the "brawny hand" would be left with no duties more onerous than the courtesy of a "hearty grasp"—manual activity would amount to the symbolism of a handshake.

What I find most striking in Babbage's schema is thus neither the genius of the first section nor the exertions of the third, but what lies between; neither the mathematicians nor the workmen, but the draftsmen. The medial function of drawings occupies a queer status as the third component in a dichotomy, positioned between intellect and labor; skill and force; design and implementation; plans and execution; idea and application; mind and mechanism—that is, between *thinking* and *working*. Babbage had long taken an interest in inscription as a mathematical tool. As a student, he risked controversy by extolling the superiority of a differential calculus based on the Leibnizian *d*-notation (more popular on the Continent) over fluxional methods using Newtonian dot-notation (privileged by the British mathematical establishment). His earliest published writings from 1815 and 1816 had focused on "the calculus of functions," proposing a "new calculus" which "comprehends questions of the greatest generality and difficulty."[5] Such commitments were intensified rather than dampened by the prospect of machinery that would mechanically complete the operations of calculation. In a paper "On a method of expressing by signs the action of machinery" (1826), he explained the limitations of existing diagrammatic practices premised on the representation of a single state, outlining an alternative system of notation more compatible with the expression of motion across numerous states. Although the animation of simple machinery could be depicted through a quasi-cinematographic succession of drawings corresponding to each state occupied in a course of action, Babbage considered this ill-suited especially in cases involving more complicated movements. Instead, he proposed a "language of signs" through which one might grasp the process in its entirety "at a glance of the eye."[6]

---

[5] Charles Babbage, "An Essay towards the Calculus of Functions," *Philosophical Transactions of the Royal Society of London* 105 (1815): 389; and "An Essay towards the Calculus of Functions, Part II," *Philosophical Transactions of the Royal Society of London* 106 (1816): 179-256.

[6] Charles Babbage, "On a Method of Expressing by Signs the Action of Machinery," *Philosophical Transactions of the Royal Society of London* 116 (1826): 250.

The Difference Engine is perhaps best understood as a contributor to this graphic *dispositif*, not so much as an instrument that augments or replicates existing capacities but rather as a medium that constitutively engenders the higher faculties of thinking.[7] The associations that the medium concept maintained with the occult are useful here. It is no exaggeration that for Babbage the Difference Engine was a medium that revealed divine providence. His unofficial (and unsolicited) *Ninth Bridgewater Treatise* (1837) was written as a rejoinder to eight texts that had been commissioned by the Earl of Bridgewater to appraise the implications that scientific studies posed for religion. Here, Babbage set about reconciling mechanistic operation with discontinuities which appeared to leave no explanation but the miraculous. The centerpiece of his argument was a brief skit starring a calculating engine as its protagonist:

> Let the reader imagine that such an engine has been adjusted; and that it is moved by a weight; and that he sits down before it, and observes a wheel, which revolves through a small angle round its axis, at short intervals, presenting to his eye, successively, a series of numbers engraved on its divided circumference.[8]

The turning of this wheel required no effort whatsoever, such that even the services of the "sixpence" day laborer could be dispensed with; its engine was fueled by a reader's imagination alone.

1, 2, 3, 4, 5, ...

The process of accumulation would be rather uneventful until it reached the unfathomably large milestone of one hundred million. At this point, an unexpected twist occurs: ... ...,

---

[7] On this distinction of a media function from instrumentation, see Joseph Vogl, "Becoming-media: Galileo's Telescope," *Grey Room* 29 (Fall 2007): 14-25.

[8] Charles Babbage, *The Ninth Bridgewater Treatise* (Cambridge: Cambridge University Press, 2009), p. 34.

99,999,999, 100,000,000, 100,000,001, 100,010,002, 100,030,003, 100,060,004, 100,100,005, 100,150,006, 100,210,007, 100,280,008, ... To the unsuspecting onlooker, this departure from a predictable sequence might appear to suggest the novelty of an intervention, reflecting a change in the underlying mechanism. Yet, sophisticated designs like the Difference Engine were capable of just this sort of metamorphosis, configured from the outset to incorporate dormant patterns.

For Babbage, a mechanism that "received at its first formation the impress of the will of its author, foreseeing the varied but yet necessary laws of its action, throughout the whole extent of its existence" was an accomplishment far superior to another that required a "restoring hand" to adjust its work.[9] Miracles were akin to the latter, suggesting a deficiency in the initial design arising from limitations in foresight. The significance of the calculating engine in this parable was not that such a machine was itself capable of possessing intelligence. Rather, Babbage considered its complexity a testament to the abilities of its creator. In the case of the Difference Engine, this referred of course to Babbage himself. But, more crucially, the reasoning also suggested an analogy with geological processes, where evidence of the divine plan was to be found. Babbage's *Ninth Bridgewater Treatise* furthered its theological claims with an intervention into the controversy between Catastrophism and Uniformitarianism. The former had taken gaps in the fossil record as evidence of supernatural intercession, i.e., as a miracle of God's "restoring hand." His commitment to prove otherwise—i.e., that changes of the past could be explained solely through entirely natural forces still at work in the present—provided Babbage with an opportunity

---

[9] Ibid., p. 33.

to revisit an investigation he had opened during his adventures on the Continent in 1828, but which thus far remained incomplete.

Pozzuoli's Temple of Serapis had been known amongst proponents of the Uniformitarian cause even before it was propelled to iconic status upon its selection as the frontispiece for Charles Lyell's influential 1830 exposition on the *Principles of Geology*. Briefly commenting on the ancient ruin's condition in 1802, John Playfair had already surmised from the location of a pavement well below the high water mark an obvious clue that "it cannot be supposed that this edifice when built was exposed to the inconvenience of having its floor frequently under water."[10] Subsequent accounts would repeat this observation as evidence of fluctuations in the terrain over the intervening centuries. For Lyell, the special appeal of the Temple was its highly visible "memorials of physical changes, inscribed on the three standing columns in most legible characters by the hand of nature."[11] These pillars were defined by three "zones" with distinct features: (1) a "smooth and uninjured" lowest segment; (2) a "weathered, but not materially injured" highest segment; and, (3) between these, a middle segment where the marble suffered from deep and large perforations by marine *Lithodomus* (literally, "stone-dwelling") mollusks, suggesting "a long-continued immersion of the pillars in sea-water, at a time when the lower part was covered up and protected by strata of tuff and the rubbish of buildings, the highest part at the same time projecting above the waters."[12]

---

[10] John Playfair, *Illustrations of the Huttonian Theory of the Earth* (London; Edinburgh: Cadell and Davies and William Creech, 1802), p. 450.

[11] Charles Lyell, *Principles of Geology: Being an Attempt to Explain the Former Changes of the Earth's Surface, by Reference to Causes Now in Operation*, vol. 1 (London: John Murray, 1830), p. 453.

[12] Ibid., pp. 453-454.

Taking the columns as a yardstick of geological change, Lyell's account drew on historical documentation of environmental turbulence in the area to formulate an explanation. First, he proposed, earthquakes preceding a volcanic eruption (at Solfatara in 1198) likely caused the subsidence of the ground on which the Temple stood, partially submerging it. Falling debris would have protected the lowest third of the columns from the ravages of time, leaving a middle segment (above the sedimentation but below the waterline) exposed to assault from the mollusks over an extended period. Subsequently, seismic activity associated with another eruption (leading to the formation of Monte Nuovo in 1538) resulted in changes in land elevation along the shoreline, lifting the Temple above sea level and thus accessible to curious geologists. A visit to Pozzuoli in November 1828 allowed Lyell to affirm his suspicions, paving the way for canonization in Uniformitarian theory.

However, in the decades that followed, an alternate theory would become prevalent, and as a consequence the engraving which Lyell had decided on for the 1830 printing had to be retired. The casualty of Lyell's hypothesis was self-inflicted. As Brian P. Dolan has noted, it had been upon Lyell's urging that his friend, Charles Babbage, focused attention towards developing a coherent theory of geological change.[13] Although largely in agreement with Lyell, Babbage had on his own excursion to Pozzuoli just a few months earlier in May 1828 noticed a "calcareous coating" on the columns' lower third corresponding to a "dark incrustation" and a "great incrustation" found on the Temple's inner walls.[14] As these deposits could not have been the

---

[13] Brian P. Dolan, "Representing Novelty: Charles Babbage, Charles Lyell, and Experiments in Early Victorian Geology," *History of Science* 36, issue 3 (1998): 299-327.

[14] Charles Babbage, "Observations on the Temple of Serapis, at Pozzuoli, near Naples, with remarks on certain causes which may produce Geological Cycles of great extent," *The Quarterly Journal of the Geological Society of London* 3 (1847): 186-217, here p. 187, p. 191, and p. 192.

product of seawater, he assessed their probable source to be the attached hot springs. Analysis by Michael Faraday, to whom Babbage sent samples taken from Pozzuoli for examination, further noted a similarity in chemical composition between the "great incrustation" and samples found at an inland freshwater reservoir, strengthening the thesis that the sea did not hold (sole) responsibility for the Temple's defacement. From this, Babbage surmised that Lyell's account had missed a phase: rather than an abrupt collapse which would have immediately flooded the site with seawater, he ascertained that "the ground on which the Temple stood gradually and slowly subsided"; likewise, the re-elevation of the Temple was also determined to have been "gradual."[15] This apparently minor amendment carried deep repercussions. Given that the concentrated tumult Lyell focused on (namely, the months or at most years around a volcanic eruption) could not explain a protracted process of subsidence (occurring over centuries), Babbage suggested in its place a series of conjectures that linked flux in the ground level to heat from the earth, in effect presenting a novel theory not just of the Temple of Serapis but of geology in general. In recognition of this correction, the seventh edition of Lyell's *Principles of Geology* would sport a new depiction of the Temple, a more accurate tracing that had been completed with the aid of a camera obscura—it was the illustration that Babbage had chosen for his "Observations on the Temple of Serapis," finally published in 1847.

Geology would remain a persistent interest for Babbage. Subsequent work built on the groundwork laid by the Pozzuoli study, deepening its propositions in texts "On the Action of Ocean-currents in the Formation of the Strata of the Earth" (1856) and "Observations on the

---

[15] Ibid., p. 197 and p. 203.

Parallel Roads of Glen Roy" (1868).[16] The latter sought quite explicitly to defend his thesis on heat, maintaining that its explanatory value had not been adequately appreciated in an account of the Scottish loch by John Lubbock, the banker and amateur archaeologist who had recently popularized the concept of a "pre-historic" era. Yet, what I find most striking here is not the conclusions that Babbage reached regarding geological change or the impact that he had within this field of research but the computational methodology he deployed.

Unlike the sharp incision of a grand historical event, the gradual process of accretion that led to an incrustation of calcareous matter proceeded without incident, evading notice within the annals of civilization. Rather than the "most legible characters" Lyell had found clearly "inscribed," the inscription systems that Babbage appealed to functioned within a different discourse network. To substantiate his geological theories, Babbage drew on the findings of an experiment that had determined the effects of heat on the expansion of stone, extrapolating from its results to chart a "*Table showing the Expansion, in feet and decimal parts, of Granite from 1 to 500 miles thick, for various additions of temperature.*"[17] By compiling this data, Babbage was able to show that even reasonable estimates of these parameters would imply "a change of level above twenty-five feet—an alteration greater than any of the observed facts at the temple of Serapis require."[18] The challenge in pursuing this methodology, however, was its substantial computational demands, a problem that Babbage was uniquely well positioned to address. Having received a scaled-down but still functional prototype of the Difference Engine in 1833, he was able

---

[16] See Charles Babbage, "On the Action of Ocean-currents in the Formation of the Strata of the Earth," *Quarterly Journal of the Geological Society of London* 12 (1856): 366-368; and Charles Babbage, "Observations on the Parallel Roads of Glen Roy," *Quarterly Journal of the Geological Society of London* 24 (1868): 273-277.

[17] Babbage, "Observations on the Temple of Serapis," p. 215.

[18] Ibid., p. 204.

to put his principle "On the Division of Mental Labour" to practice, delegating this burden to machinery. An early draft was presented to the Geological Society of London in 1834, and more details would be appended to his *Ninth Bridgewater Treatise* in 1837.[19]

Much in this schema hinged on the compatibility of computational and geological processes, to the extent that they might be conceived of as twinned movements. "For Babbage," Dolan argues, "the earth was a calculating engine. It produced its own record of its activities in the form of the fossil record."[20] It is thus perhaps quite apt that Babbage was driven to pursue this study on the insistence of "calcareous" matter: his unusual attention to the *calculus* of mathematics found a parallel in the accumulation of *calculus*—that is, these interventions into the mechanization of *calculation* proceeded in tandem with investigations of *calcification*. The nuance to this pairing is often missed in critical accounts that approach Babbage's deployment of calculation without attending to its sensitivity towards systems of inscription practices, eliding its eccentricity amidst tendencies towards industrialization. It is clear, however, that the Difference Engine did not augment or extend existing practices. The device was not a more efficient means of implementing procedures Lyell had undertaken, and certainly could stake no claim to have replaced work accomplished through the efforts of human labor. Rather, Babbage's earth-engine introduced a distinct regime of evaluation; computing machinery was not deployed as an instrument but as a medium.

This dissertation charts a media history of computing in this sense: its interest in computation is oriented neither around mathematicians nor workmen, but draftsmen. The graphic

---

[19] See Charles Babbage, Abstract of "Observations on the Temple of Serapis at Pozzuoli, near Naples; with Remarks on certain Causes which may produce Geological Cycles of great Extent," *Proceedings of the Geological Society of London* 2, no. 36 (1833-1834): 72-76; and Babbage, *The Ninth Bridgewater Treatise*, pp. 182-240.

[20] Dolan, "Representing Novelty," p. 313.

function of calculi has received limited attention in histories of computing. Yet, it has been a persistent anchor for basic frameworks like the Boolean algebra of binary logic (a project George Boole initiated "to give expression to [fundamental laws of reasoning] in the symbolical language of a Calculus"[21]) and the neural networks increasingly prominent today (the "nervous nets" proposed by Warren McCulloch and Walter Pitts as "A Logical Calculus of the Ideas Immanent in Nervous Activity"[22]). Chapter 1 further fleshes out these neglected episodes in the deployment of computational calculi by tracing its close entwinement with a now-obscured sense of the algorithm concept which stresses its proximity with notation systems. This history elucidates some of the concerns that might have motivated Babbage's interest in the Newtonian and Leibnizian differential calculus. Indeed, his *Ninth Bridgewater Treatise* responded specifically to attacks on analytic methods that extended a longer tradition initiated by Bishop Berkeley in the 1730s in which the "algorism" of the fluxional calculus was a focal point of controversy.[23] Having plotted this trajectory of drafting, the chapter then proceeds in a more speculative fashion: If the algorithmic has historically been aligned with an idiom of drawing, how else might it be figured in other modes of visuality? What if algorithms were not constituted through line but color?

The hierarchy of capacities assumed in the projects of Prony and Babbage enact a political ontology that expresses the moral and political stakes to Mel Y. Chen's theorization of a "calculus of animacy." As opposed to, for instance, *intelligence*, Chen's heading of *animacy* more

---

[21] George Boole, *An Investigation of the Laws of Thought, on which are founded the Mathematical Theories of Logic and Probability* (London: Walton and Maberly, 1854), p. 1.

[22] W. S. McCulloch and W. Pitts, "A Logical Calculus of the Ideas Immanent in Nervous Activity," *Bulletin of Mathematical Biophysics* 5 (1943): 115-133.

[23] Specifically, Babbage's indignation had been provoked by one of the eight official Bridgewater Treatises, William Whewell's *Astronomy and General Physics Considered with Reference to Natural Theology* (London: William Pickering, 1833).

adequately captures the ideological dimensions inherent in a scale that leads from necessity (*labor*) to freedom (*thinking*). Chapter 2 elaborates on how the sustained development of these tendencies in the discourse of twentieth-century evolutionary psychobiology underpinned an amalgamation of programming languages, cognitive science, and software that precipitated the formation of computer science.

Chen's phrasing is suggestive. As they point out, stones (i.e., *calculi*) are customarily targeted as the "'bad' verbal subjects" that exemplify the *in*animate:

> How does animacy work linguistically? To take one popular example involving relative clauses, consider the phrase "the hikers that rocks crush": what does this mean? The difficulty frequently experienced by English speakers in processing this phrase has much to do with the inanimacy of the rock (which plays an agent role in relation to the verb *crush*) as compared to the animacy of the hikers, who in this scenario play an object role. "The hikers that rocks crush" thus violates a cross-linguistic preference among speakers. They tend to prefer animate head nouns to go with subject-extracted relative clauses (the hikers *who ___ crushed the rock*), or inanimate head nouns to go with object- extracted relative clauses (the rock *that the hiker crushed ___*). Add to this that there is a smaller plausibility that rocks will agentively crush hikers than that hikers will agentively crush rocks: a conceptual order of things, an animate hierarchy of possible acts, begins to take shape. Yet more contentious examples belie the apparent obviousness of this hierarchy, and even in this case, it is within a specific cosmology that stones so obviously lack agency or could be the source of causality. What if nonhuman animals, or humans stereotyped as passive, such as people with cognitive or physical disabilities, enter the calculus of animacy: what happens then?[24]

Considered especially amidst recent critical investments into the nonhuman realms of animality and the vegetative, the mineralogical functions as a limit point of sorts in the possibilities of worlding: "The stone is worldless," Martin Heidegger proclaimed.[25] Of course, as Chen points out,

---

[24] Mel Y. Chen, *Animacies: Biopolitics, Racial Mattering, and Queer Affect* (Durham; London: Duke University Press, 2012), p. 5 and pp. 2-3.

[25] Martin Heidegger, *The Fundamental Concepts of Metaphysics: World, Finitude, Solitude*, trans. William McNeill and Nicholas Walker (Bloomington; Indianapolis: Indiana University Press, 1995), p. 184.
Heidegger is of course not alone in this assessment; he builds on a long and firmly established intellectual tradition. See, for example, Johann Gottfried Herder, *Outlines of a Philosophy of the History of Man*, vol. 1, trans. T.

other cultures of stone are not uncommon across non-European perspectives.[26] But perhaps still more germane to the schism between calculation and calcification are the ruminations on stone that build up to another key Heideggerian dictum: "Color shines and wants only to shine."

> A stone presses downward and manifests its heaviness. But while this heaviness exerts an opposing pressure upon us it denies us any penetration into it. If we attempt such a penetration by breaking open the rock, it still does not display in its fragments anything inward that has been opened up. The stone has instantly withdrawn again into the same dull pressure and bulk of its fragments. If we try to lay hold of the stone's heaviness in another way, by placing the stone on a balance, we merely bring the heaviness into the form of a calculated weight. This perhaps very precise determination of the stone remains a number, but the weight's burden has escaped us. Color shines and wants only to shine. When we analyze it in rational terms by measuring its wavelengths, it is gone. It shows itself only when it remains disclosed and unexplained. Earth thus shatters every attempt to penetrate it.[27]

A crucial point of reference for media theory,[28] Heidegger's (non-)worlding quite precisely splits the two senses of calculus, distinguishing the affordances of "number" (i.e., calculus *qua* calculation) from "heaviness" (i.e., calculus *qua* calcification). This highlights a subtlety implicit in the paradoxical formulation of a "calculus of animacy," i.e., the exceptional status that calculus

---

Churchill (London: J. Johnson, 1803): "What in the World has the greatest promptitude? The falling stone; the blooming flower. That falls, this blooms, *according to it's nature*. The crystal shoots with more promptitude and regularity, than the bee constructs it's comb, or the spider her web. In the stone it is only a blind organic instinct, that is infallible: in the insect it is organized to the employment of several limbs and organs, and these may fail. The healthy, powerful consent of these to one end constitutes promptitude, as soon as the perfect creature exists. Thus we perceive why the higher creatures rise, the more their incessant propensity and infallible promptitude decrease. The more, namely, the one organic principle of nature, which we here term *plastic*, there *impulsive*, here *sensitive*, there *artful*, yet which is at bottom but one and the same organic power, is subdivided into several organs and various limbs; and the more it has in each of these a world of it's own, whence consequently it is exposed to particular errours and obstacles: so much the weaker is it's propensity, so much the more is it subject to the command of the will, and therefore of errour" (pp. 108-109).

[26] See Carolyn Dean, *A Culture of Stone: Inka Perspectives on Rock* (Durham; London: Duke University Press, 2010).

[27] Martin Heidegger, "The Origin of the Work of Art," in *Martin Heidegger: Basic Writings*, ed. and trans. David Farrell Krell (New York: HarperCollins, 1993), p. 172.

[28] See Friedrich Kittler, "Thinking Colours and/or Machines," trans. Geoffrey Winthrop-Young, *Theory, Culture & Society* 23, issue 7-8 (December 2006): 39-50.

occupies as the inanimate measure against which animacy is determined. Theoretical interest in the political standing of non-human entities tends to involve elaborations of their (under-acknowledged) agential potential. Indeed, Chen engages such a maneuver, insisting "that stones and other inanimates definitively occupy a *scalar* position (near zero) on the animacy hierarchy and that they are not excluded from it altogether and are not only treated as animacy's binary opposite"—that is to say, stones may be ""bad" verbal subjects," but are still subjects nonetheless.[29] By contrast, a media theoretical approach to calculus suggests another way to circumvent this binary opposition of animacy/inanimacy, instead attending to a medial function which queers the distinction between subject and object.

As such, rather than advocating for reassessments within a normative scale, this other style of inquiry offers an examination of the function of cultural-technical operators in establishing this distinction. Chapter 3 concludes the dissertation with such an account of the technologies of screening through which computation was extricated from a calculus of inscription, and in particular the context of corporate management in which this took place. Contrary to historiographies of invention which assume technical limitations presented a bottleneck that had to be overcome in the adoption of interactive screens, closer attention to historical detail suggests the opposite: modern computing's earliest expressions of graphics were directed towards limiting sites of contact. The computer's screen was the medium through which the executive function of a managerial class was ensconced from the materialities of technical labor. This was especially apparent at the International Business Machines Corporation (IBM), the dominant firm of the

---

[29] Chen, *Animacies*, p. 5.

computing industry by the early 1950s. Their slogan succinctly preserved the legacy of Babbage's sensibility: *Think*.

***

Some Comments on Historiography **(Deep History and the "Long" 1950s)**

Charles Lyell demarcated the scope of geology not just with reference to the subject matter it claimed privileged expertise over, but also through its relations to another discipline with which it would simultaneously be differentiated and entwined: "Geology is intimately related to almost all the physical sciences, as is history to the moral."[30] Although geology and history are perhaps unlikely to be confused today, both fields practicing markedly distinct methods and norms, Lyell considered them enterprises linked by their shared investments in the study of the past. The first, however, was restricted to the positive sphere, leaving the normative issues of civilized societies to the other; history begins at the limits of geology.

And yet, despite the clarity with which this distinction was framed, the permeability between the two—the ineradicable contingency of one upon the other—would remain a nagging source of difficulty. Repeatedly, geology would be summoned to bear witness to matters of historical concern, and history offered as the telos in which geological processes culminate. Consequently, Lyell would himself find it problematic to properly extricate the "physical" from the "moral." Referring to the controversy sparked by Charles Darwin's theses *On the Origin of*

---

[30] Lyell, *Principles of Geology*, vol. 1, pp. 2-3.

Species (1859), Lyell's discussion of *The Geological Evidences of the Antiquity of Man* (1863) began by euphemistically acknowledging that: "No subject has lately excited more curiosity and general interest among geologists and the public than the question of the Antiquity of the Human Race."[31] By "curiosity and general interest," Lyell really meant the crises and anxieties that arose from placing humanity on a biological continuum with the rest of animate (and even inanimate) nature. His response was to affirm human exceptionalism by sketching "a picture of the ever-increasing dominion of mind over matter."[32] According to Lyell (and, indeed, many of his contemporaries), a capacity for morals was the factor that "separates Man from the brutes."[33] In his racialized "doctrine of progression," the "improvable reason" of the former—possessed even by "the lowest races"—was believed to lie beyond the "unprogressive intelligence of the inferior animals."[34]

Debates regarding anthropogenesis were a symptom of a revolution in time that had escalated over the eighteenth and nineteenth centuries, prompted precisely by research into geology. Darwinian theories of evolution might be thought of as the byproduct of such a geological approach as it resonated within other fields like biology. Citing Lyell as his principal influence, Darwin's early writings based on observations from the voyage of the HMS *Beagle* had addressed the formation of coral reefs (1842), volcanic islands (1844), and the terrain of South America (1846)—that is, they pursued studies of geology.[35] Subsequent work extended this sensibility: in

---

[31] Charles Lyell, *The Geological Evidences of the Antiquity of Man* (London: John Murray, 1863), p. 1.

[32] Ibid., p. 506.

[33] Ibid., p. 495.

[34] Ibid., pp. 395-406 and p. 492.

[35] Charles Darwin, *On the Structure and Distribution of Coral Reefs; also Geological Observations on the Volcanic Islands and Parts of South American Geology Visited during the Voyage of H. M. S. Beagle*, first published separately in three parts in 1842, 1844, and 1846 (London: Ward, Lock, & Co., 1910).

his *Origin of Species*, Darwin would describe the "slow and gradual modification [of species] through variation and natural selection" as "the geological succession of organic beings," depicting a relatively smooth transition between inanimate and animate spheres.[36]

Until geological theories, in particular Lyell's *Principles of Geology*, established conclusions that contradicted orthodox chronology, it had been standard belief that the earth was roughly 6,000 years old, and that its age coincided with that of humanity's. Little wonder then that limited interest had been directed towards what occurred before the supposed advent of human civilization. The concept of a "pre-historic" era was popularized in an 1865 book by John Lubbock, a fervent Darwinian.[37] Written in the aftermath of the publication of Darwin's *Origin of Species*, Lubbock's intervention was positioned in the chasm that Lyell had outlined between history and geology:

> Archaeology forms, in fact, the link between geology and history. It is true that in the case of other animals we can, from their bones and teeth, form a definite idea of their habits and mode of life, while in the present state of our knowledge the skeleton of a savage could not always be distinguished from that of a philosopher. But on the other hand, while other animals leave only teeth and bones behind them,

---

[36] Charles Darwin, *On the Origin of Species by Means of Natural Selection, Or the Preservation of Favoured Races in the Struggle for Life* (London: John Murray, 1859), p. 312.
Nor was Darwin unique in forging such cross-disciplinary connections. In later editions, he offered a survey of existing work on the topic of evolution, noting that "of the thirty-four authors named in this Historical Sketch who believe in the modification of species, or at least disbelief in separate acts of creation, twenty-seven have written on special branches of natural history or geology." *Origin of Species*, 6th ed., vol. 1 (New York: American Home Library Company, 1902), 22.

[37] See John Lubbock, *Pre-Historic Times, As Illustrated by Ancient Remains, and the Manner and Customs of Modern Savages* (London: Williams and Norgate, 1865).
Their alliance grew out of a longstanding association. In Lubbock's youth, Darwin had moved to a village about a mile away from the Lubbock family's estate at High Elms. Already at that time a figure of quite some repute, at least amongst scientific circles, Darwin became a mentor to the teenager, encouraging his interest in biology and introducing him to eminent scientists, including Lyell. Lubbock recalled this good fortune in later reflections: "My father came home one evening in 1841, quite excited, and said he had a great piece of news for me. He made us guess what it was, and I suggested that he was going to give me a pony. 'Oh,' he said, 'it is much better than that. Mr. Darwin is coming to live at Down.' I confess I was much disappointed, though I came afterwards to see how right he was" (quoted in Horace G. Hutchinson, *The Life of Sir John Lubbock, Lord Avebury*, 2 vols. [London: Macmillian and Co., 1914], 1: p. 15).

> the men of past ages are to be studied principally by their works; houses for the living, tombs for the dead, fortifications for defence, temples for worship, implements for use, and ornaments for decoration.[38]

For Lubbock, the "pre-historic" interests of archaeology entailed a shift from the evidence of material remains ("bones and teeth") to relics which exhibited the products of technique ("works"), in effect providing proxies for the distinction between the natural (i.e., "physical") and the cultural (i.e., "moral").

Lubbock's archaeological studies made legible an evolutionary scale that ascended from the "savage" to the "philosopher," exemplifying Lyell's "doctrine of progression." In a follow-up text on *The Origin of Civilisation and the Primitive Condition of Man* (1870), he sought to illustrate "the earlier mental stages through which the human race has passed," reaching the conclusion: (1) "That the primitive condition of man was one of utter barbarism," and (2) "That from this condition several races have independently raised themselves."[39] The goal of this racist discourse was not to justify the hierarchy that placed one race over others; to thinkers like Lubbock and Lyell, this seemed self-evident. Rather, disputes over "progression" were directed against competing theories based on "regression," which posited that the "inferiority" found in other societies was a product of "deterioration" from an originally civilized state. Although Lubbock believed that not every race could be said to be "advancing," he found it "an almost invariable rule that such races [that have 'fallen back'] are dying out, while those which are stationary in condition are stationary in numbers also; on the other hand, improving nations increase in numbers, so that they always

---

[38] Lubbock, *Pre-Historic Times*, p. 2.

[39] John Lubbock, *The Origin of Civilisation and the Primitive Condition of Man: Mental and Social Condition of Savages* (London: Longmans, Green, and Co., 1870), pp. 322-323.

encroach on less progressive races."[40] This was considered cause for optimism about the future: "The history of the human race has, I feel satisfied, on the whole been one of progress."[41] The process of *natural* selection could in this way be adapted for the *cultural* sphere, i.e., *geological* movements of evolutionary succession were believed to shape *historical* drive.

Against such tendencies, recent efforts by scholars to articulate a brand of history writing that responds more adequately to the implications of geological or "deep" time have argued for an eradication of the sharp boundary between the two domains, nature and culture, as a corrective to models tied to suspect notions of civilization. Historian Daniel Lord Smail notes, for example, and not without a sense of regret, how during the decades in which "the great historical sciences—geology, paleoanthropology, biology—were made or remade as the bottom dropped out of time, exposing a nearly endless vista … the discipline of history recoiled from that vista, fashioning instead a view of history that begins with the rise of civilization."[42] His colleagues, Andrew Shryock, Thomas R. Trautman, and Clive Gamble, describe prehistory—the measure taken in order to preserve the sanctity of the civilized—as "a conceptual innovation that functioned as a protective barrier," depicting it as a sort of coping mechanism.[43] Understood this way, the impact of remote antiquity might be taken as a form of conceptual trauma necessitating disciplinary

---

[40] Ibid., p. 322.

[41] Ibid., p. 362.

[42] Daniel Lord Smail, *On Deep History and the Brain* (Berkeley, CA: University of California Press, 2008), p. 1.

[43] Andrew Shryock, Thomas R. Trautman, and Clive Gamble, "Imagining the Human in Deep Time," in *Deep History: The Architecture of Past and Present*, eds. Andrew Shryock and Daniel Lord Smail (Berkeley, CA: University of California Press, 2011), p. 21.

repression, an event displaying the structural traits of an "incapacity to respond adequately" to an excessive influx.[44]

Their enterprise takes another course: what these scholars refer to as "*deep* history" is what "*pre*-history" should have been but wasn't. In this approach, claims to civilization are viewed as pretexts for the unfounded dismissal of others as uncivilized. For Smail, "deep history is a natural extension of historiographical trends that began in the mid-twentieth century. The goal of the social history of this era, after all, was to uncover the world of the people without history."[45]

The impetus to this reappraisal of the defining contours of history was a crisis in the conditions by which the past is mediated. A consistent feature in contemporary discussions of the problematic status of deep time is suspicion towards the privileged role of written documentation as a standard for evidence. This point of contention makes the centrality of media to historical inquiry apparent. In the absence of textual sources, the conventional methods deployed by historians provide inadequate insight; engagement with "deep" periods necessitates making less familiar material legible. Deep historians are thus characterized by their catholic approach toward media: "Histories can be written from every type of trace, from the memoir to the bone fragment and the blood type."[46]

Rather than a simple expansion of scope, deep history proposes a challenge to fundamental assumptions that have had a constitutional role in the maintenance of historiographical standards,

---

[44] Jean Laplanche and Jean-Betrand Pontalis, *The Language of Psycho-Analysis*, trans. Donald Nicholson-Smith (London: Karnac Books, 1988), p. 465.

[45] Smail, *On Deep History and the Brain*, p. 54.

[46] Andrew Shryock and Daniel Lord Smail, "Introduction," in *Deep History: The Architecture of Past and Present*, p. 13.

both ideological and practical, but which may be of dubious legitimacy. At its most compelling, it does not apply existing techniques onto hitherto unclaimed territory; it instead presents a reflexive interrogation of their limits and implications, questioning the horizon of existing archives.

"Bringing these arguments into the open, we can appreciate how we no longer need to be bound by their logic," Smail has rather optimistically suggested regarding these impediments.[47] I am sympathetic to the goals of deep history (e.g., for a more complex interplay between nature and culture), and do not dispute the claims forwarded (e.g., that "humanity's natural history persisted after the rise of civilization"[48]). Yet, Smail's suggestion that explicitly addressing what was maintained implicitly suffices to dispel the hold of such logic is less convincing. It is especially suspicious that a belated willingness to consider "every type of trace" occurs only amidst a diminished conviction in speech as the primary manifestation of reason under an ascendance of other forms of rationality, specifically quantitative analysis. (Perhaps it is no coincidence that Lubbock's "pre-history" was a contemporary to the calculating engines of Charles Babbage.) Deep history requires non-textual capacities for sense-making, but can this mean anything other than the blank import of methods from the natural sciences? Can deep history avoid the mere replacement of one dominant with another? I suspect that simply exposing (already faltering) arguments risks offering little else.

Here, if the contemporary crisis of deep time is really a crisis of mediation, more direct consideration of the function of media and its relation to the problem of civilization is key. Doubt over writing's monopoly as a vehicle for cultural transmission has clarified that projects of

---

[47] Smail, *On Deep History and the Brain*, p. 6.

[48] Ibid., p. 11.

"general history," purporting to articulate the history of civilization, implicitly express histories of media. Historiographical norms based on textual documents equate civilized being with writing. As a symptom of its discursive conditions, such attempts are hardly "general" but in fact merely a history of literacy. It might thus also be said, vice versa, that histories of media function as proxies for histories of civilization—i.e., that media process the boundaries between savage and civilized, and the articulation of media histories performatively enact such distinctions.

Archaeology, according to Lubbock, was inherently media archaeology; it was occasioned by a lapse in media: "It is evident that history cannot throw much light on the early condition of man, because the discovery—or, to speak more correctly, the use—of metal has in all cases preceded that of writing."[49] Geological revisions thus functioned as a historical *a priori* across a range of sciences over the nineteenth century, establishing and naturalizing a new basis for reasoning. The stakes to deep time here derived less from the specifics to planetary chronology than the nexus between disciplines that it instigated, an epistemic compound in which revisions from one field (an expanded timeframe in geology) shattered the conditions of possibility in another (the plausibility of evolutionary theories in biology).

Likewise, in media studies, the provocative introduction of geological time as a critical point of reference was also prompted by secondary epistemic effects. Siegfried Zielinski's media archaeological studies mobilize such a conceptual abstraction when articulating a "deep time of the media." His proposal of "variantology" as a methodological ethos extracts the evolutionary implications of a long chronology to sketch an alternate schema to models rooted in "sacred history." Extending the frame of temporal reference removes the origin myths that media might

---

[49] Lubbock, *Pre-historic Times*, p. 426.

otherwise be bound to, rescuing them from what he calls a "divine plan," the simplistic approach to media history that treats it as "the product of a predictable and necessary advance from primitive to complex apparatus" (such as the teleological descriptions of nineteenth-century optical toys as "pre"-cinematic devices, which restrict their significance to a "pre"-history of cinematic media, thereby treating the contingent formation of cinema as an inevitability).[50] Zielinski's emphasis on variants—evolutionary offshoots that may or may not have stood the test of time—rejects such a transcendent ideal against which specimens are supposed to aspire in favor of deviance and fluctuation. Just as deep historians do not direct their attention away from civilization but reformulate what is encompassed by the concept, Zielinski's media archaeology is not an abandonment of the concern with media, in spite of his seeming aversion to what is most commonly referred to by the term. Instead, media ceases to take a stable set of objects as its referent.

Like Smail, Zielinski approaches this hiccup through a belief in discursive deregulation (i.e., that lifting restrictions offers adequate correction to past blinders). Studies of media as "cultural techniques" address this more pointedly. The hinge between "pre"-symbolic activity and conceptualization proper is a key problem in cultural-technical approaches to media. As described in Thomas Macho's seminal definition, "cultural techniques are always already older than their media…. People wrote long before any notions of writing or the alphabet were conceived; pictures and statues did not inspire the idea of a picture until thousands of years later; to date, some people still sing and make music without any conception of tone or a system of notes."[51] Bernhard Siegert,

---

[50] Siegfried Zielinski, *Deep Time of the Media: Toward an Archaeology of Hearing and Seeing by Technical Means*, trans. Gloria Custance (Cambridge, MA: MIT Press, 2006), p. 7.

[51] Thomas Macho, "Second-Order Animals: Cultural Techniques of Identity and Identification," trans. Michael Wutz, *Theory, Culture & Society* 30, no. 6 (November 2013): 44-45.

echoing Macho, has influentially reiterated: "cultural techniques are conceived of as operative chains that precede the media concepts they generate."[52] If a prehistoric era does not so much refer to a well-defined chronological period but a conceptual disposition, and deep history likewise operates on normative territory, the switch between pre- and deep histories is precisely what is at stake in cultural-technical studies of media: an emphasis on cultural techniques targets the significance of what is said to be "older than," have occurred "long before," and which "precede" media historical conditions.

This affinity is perhaps clearest in a collection of Siegert's essays published simply under the title, *Cultural Techniques*. The overarching sweep of the book offers a shadow history of civilization, covering what might be deemed its greatest hits, i.e., the topics that one would expect to be featured in a standard textbook on "general history." Initial selections from "pre"-historical anthropology lead into episodes from Spanish Imperialism, the Italian Renaissance, the Dutch Golden Age, and industrial modernity. "Insignificant, unprepossessing technologies" on the cusp of congealing into symbolic media are points of entry into reading these famed episodes against their grain.[53] Siegert lists numerous examples of such cultural techniques, but the specific instances are perhaps less consequential than a general inclination to foreground acculturation as process. (Culture, rid of its lofty overtones, is processual in the same sense that one might speak of the processing of meat: media churn out trained subjects, filtered to meet standards of cultivation.)

Media theoretical considerations draw attention to an impasse encountered in the practice of deep history, specifically in the connotations of *depth*. Given that the chronological period

---

[52] Bernhard Siegert, *Cultural Techniques: Grids, Filters, Doors, and Other Articulations of the Real*, trans. Geoffrey Winthrop-Young (New York: Fordham University Press, 2015), p. 11.

[53] Ibid., p. 3.

encompassed by *deep* history coincides with that addressed by *pre*history, and depth functions not so much as a quantitative measure than an indication of qualitative revaluation, the project of historiographical revision suggests an attempt to incorporate a broadened scope within the domain of historical inquiry. Yet, its descriptive excess also reveals a failure to close a rift between the sphere of history and what had been deemed extra-historical. For if such a reconciliation had been successful, these studies would no longer require the modifying label *deep* history, but could simply proceed as history *without qualification.* Deep history thus preserves the insistence of received sensibilities, even as it points towards other possibilities; that is to say, it is an expression of ~~pre~~-history, written under erasure.

My interest in the deep history of computing follows this inflection, and may perhaps be more accurately described as a focus on computing's deep historical dehiscence: it pokes at the scarring of a wound that has not properly healed. As such, the subject matter of this dissertation and the form of its approach is quite unusual in eschewing the well-defined contours and analytic consistency conventional in good scholarship, instead orbiting around an absent center. I think of this passage—between the development of the first modern (i.e., electronic, digital, programmable, etc.) computers in the late-1940s and the establishment of computing's institutions (e.g., the analysis of algorithms, the linguistic conception of programming, the discipline of computer science, and even the interactive computer screen) circa 1958—as the "long" 1950s.

The historiography of modern computing's early years could learn a great deal from the maneuvers of scholarship on early cinema. This dissertation follows the latter in displacing critical emphasis from moments of invention in favor of latencies between the introduction of a technical apparatus and the consolidation of institutional norms and spaces. Yet, whereas film historians tended to parse an alien logic through intricate readings of objects paradigmatic *within* that regime, the style of criticism I adopt here instead gravitates *beyond* the extents of discursive coherence; it works through adjacencies and allusions. An expanded framework addressing this "deep time of the media" carries a strong degree of skepticism towards the self-sufficiency of appraisal.

In this regard, what I'm calling the "long" 1950s is less like Eric Hobsbawm's (flexibly) "long" nineteenth century than Giovanni Arrighi's (interminably) "long" twentieth century. The distinction is conceptual. For the former, the question of "how far back into history the analyst should go—whether to the mid-seventeenth century English Revolution, to the Reformation and the beginning of European military world conquest and colonial exploitation in the early sixteenth century, or even earlier, is for our purposes irrelevant, for such analysis in depth would take us far beyond the chronological boundaries of this volume."[54] Hobsbawm thus amends the arbitrary criteria of "chronological boundaries" (1800 and 1900, i.e., milestones based on empty, mechanistic time) with more reasonable markers based on significant events (1789-1914, i.e., a coherent era spanning the French Revolution and World War I). On the other hand, Arrighi presents a challenge towards periodization on a different order of severity in that he casts doubt on the legitimacy of delimitation altogether, insisting that the signatures of an era can only be properly evaluated when set against a grand sweep of developments which do not belong to its moment yet nevertheless continue to cast structural echoes. In his account, the story of financialization in the twentieth century would be lacking if it was not contextualized alongside (lengthy) explications of the development of capitalism over the preceding centuries, thus stretching the narrative of *"the Origins of Our Times"* into the early fourteenth century.[55]

---

[54] Eric Hobsbawm, *The Age of Revolution: 1789-1848* (New York: Vintage Books, 1996), p. 2.

[55] Giovanni Arrighi, *The Long Twentieth Century: Money, Power, and the Origins of Our Times* (London; New York: Verso, 1994).

I've concentrated the crux of this dissertation into a mere decade but the ambitions here are no less imposing than Arrighi's "long" century. Over the 1950s, computing's attachment to its graphic calculus was severely reconfigured, such that it would no longer be associated with scribal activity (computing's "*pre*"-history) but with the imperceptible operations of machinery (computing's *history*). A deep history of this schism (computing's ~~pre~~-*history*) is anchored to this shift, but also necessarily departs from it, ranging across the multiple spheres that stake the conditions for this transformation.

Chapter 1: Algorithmic Media and Visuality

§1.1: Graphical Computing: Scopic Regimes of the Algorithmic

Introducing *Volume 1* of his canonical texts on *The Art of Computer Programming* (1968), computer scientist Donald Knuth warns: "the reader should *not* expect to read an algorithm as if it were part of a novel. ... An algorithm must be seen to be believed."[1] But how can one see an algorithm, an entity almost exclusively discussed in terms of the inclination towards abstract understanding, or even hostility towards empirical factors? And, further, what is the role of belief in algorithmic operations? Convention today might lead one to conclude that algorithms result in automation independent of human agents; they are said to work whether or not you believe that they do:

> When a process on the Web or inside a machine happens automatically, a pithy explanation often comes with it: "It's an algorithm."[2]

> In information societies, operations, decisions and choices previously left to humans are increasingly delegated to algorithms, which may advise, if not decide, about how data should be interpreted and what actions should be taken as a result.[3]

> So why does this all matter? It matters because authority is increasingly expressed algorithmically. Decisions that used to be based on human reflection are now made automatically.[4]

---

[1] Donald E. Knuth, *The Art of Computer Programming, Volume 1: Fundamental Algorithms* (Boston: Addison-Wesley, 1997), p. 4, hereafter abbreviated *TCP*.

[2] Christopher Steiner, *Automate This: How Algorithms Came To Rule Our World* (New York: Portfolio/Penguin, 2012), p. 5.

[3] Brent Daniel Mittelstadt, et al., "The ethics of algorithms: Mapping the debate," *Big Data & Society* 3, issue 2 (December 2016), p. 1.

[4] Frank Pasquale, *The Black Box Society: The Secret Algorithms That Control Money and Information* (Cambridge, MA: Harvard University Press, 2015), p.8.

> Part of the challenge of understanding algorithmic oppression is to understand that mathematical formulations to drive automated decisions are made by human beings.[5]

Suspicion towards the detrimental effects of computing on the mind is hardly a novelty. Bishop Berkeley's 1734 pamphlet attacking the Newtonian method of fluxions, *The Analyst*, questioned "whether the Difference between a mere Computer and a Man of Science be not, that the one computes on Principles clearly conceived, and by Rules evidently demonstrated, whereas the other doth not?":

> It is with the Method of Fluxions as with all other Methods, which presuppose their respective Principles and are grounded thereon. Although the Rules may be practised by Men who neither attend to, nor perhaps know the Principles. In like manner, therefore, as a Sailor may practically apply certain Rules derived from Astronomy and Geometry, the Principles whereof he doth not understand: And as any ordinary Man may solve divers numerical Questions, by the vulgar Rules and Operations of Arithmetic, which he performs and applies without knowing the Reasons of them: Even so it cannot be denied that you may apply the Rules of the fluxionary Method: You may compare and reduce particular Cases to general Forms: You may operate and compute and solve Problems thereby, not only without an actual Attention to, or an actual Knowledge of, the Grounds of that Method, and the Principles whereon it depends, and whence it is deduced, but even without having ever considered or comprehended them.

His misgivings led him to ponder if adherents indulge in such methods "to save themselves the trouble of thinking."[6]

Berkeley's contempt for the mere application of arithmetic rules with pen and paper raises much the same concerns as may be found in the flood of recent critical literature on the topic of algorithms. The latter, although more concerned with advanced electronic machinery, are similarly

---

[5] Safiya Umoja Noble, *Algorithms of Oppression: How Search Engines Reinforce Racism* (New York: New York University Press, 2018), p. 1.

[6] George Berkeley, *The Analyst; or, A Discourse Addressed to an Infidel Mathematician* (London: J. Tonson, 1734), p. 88, pp. 52-53, and p. 17.

premised on an absence of understanding. Algorithms have been termed "objects of ignorance"[7]; they are likely to be discussed in terms of "opacity"[8] and "impenetrability."[9]

Media theorists have broached the ground covered in Berkeley's arguments as well—but with distinctly divergent conclusions. Sharing (somewhat anachronistically) the early modern philosopher's preoccupation with the written signs of mathematics, Sybille Krämer discusses the "operational notational system" effected through "a cultural technique of spatialization." Like Berkeley, Krämer recognizes that with the introduction of symbolic algebra, "the *knowing how* of an operative procedure is separated from the *knowing that* of its justification. In order to be able to calculate correctly, it is not necessary to be able to justify why the calculation algorithms are correct or know something about the complex nature of numbers behind their numerical appearance." In her account, however, this is a prompt for the revision of fundamental assumptions on cognition, the senses, and their medial conditions. "The calculus," she observes, "is a 'language' not speaking to the ears, but to the eyes."[10] Rather than a straightforward outsourcing of thinking onto practical application, Krämer takes the function of this media *a priori* as constitutive of the relation between sensuous and non-sensuous domains:

> Thoughts, when considered alone, are treated as non-perceptual and non-spatial entities. But when placed on a simple sheet of paper or on the surface of a

---

[7] Ana-Christina Lange, Marc Lenglet, and Robert Seyfert, "On studying algorithms ethnographically: Making sense of objects of ignorance," *Organization* 26, no. 4 (October 2018): 598-617.

[8] Jenna Burrell, "How the machine 'thinks': Understanding opacity in machine learning algorithms," *Big Data and Society* 3, issue 1 (January 2016), p. 1.

[9] Tarleton Gillespie, "The Relevance of Algorithms," in *Media Technologies: Essays on Communication, Materiality, and Society*, eds. Tarleton Gillespie, Pablo J. Boczkowski, and Kirsten A. Foot (Cambridge, MA: MIT Press, 2014): "But there may be something in the end impenetrable about algorithms. They are designed to work without human intervention, they are deliberately obfuscated, and they work with information on a scale that is hard to comprehend (at least without other algorithmic tools)" (p. 192).

[10] Sybille Krämer, "Mathematizing Power, Formalization, and the Diagrammatical Mind or: What Does 'Computation' Mean?" *Philosophy of Technology* 27, no. 3 (2014): p. 349 and p. 348.

> blackboard, thoughts acquire a place in the most literal sense of the word: spatio-temporally situated, they become not only thinkable, but also visible and tangible. Once they are embodied in a medium, they can be fixed, observed, altered, re-arranged and erased. It goes without saying that science owes its very existence to such devices, which give spatial form to the non-spatial. ... The surface of the inscription not only builds a representational space for thought, but it also constructs a space of operation: within this space we can—to formulate a paradox—undertake empirical investigation with non-empirical objects. The surface of a sheet of paper becomes a kind of thought-laboratory.[11]

If inscription surfaces are indeed "a kind of thought-laboratory," just what kind is it? Of what relevance, if any, are their medial functions under conditions shaped by contemporary technologies of "opacity"? In such graphical calculi, the varied permutations of the visible, the operative, and the knowable configure computation as a crucial signature of modernity. Algorithmic media arise as cultural techniques in this historical situation, the afterimages of which still linger in stances like Knuth's.

Knuth elaborates on his surprising take, explaining: "the best way to learn what an algorithm is all about is to try it. The reader should always take pencil and paper and work through an example of each algorithm immediately upon encountering it in the text" (*ACP*, p. 4). As he describes it, the algorithmic is not opposed to but informed by lived experience—perhaps even the function of a mimetic faculty; it is something the prospective student should (*and can!*) "try." The algorist is a medium to an occult, otherworldly realm, the process of becoming one deriving from the rituals of incorporation. To be such a "reader," one cannot remain distanced from the object of study but must behave like it, embody its operations.

---

[11] Sybille Krämer, "Is there a diagrammatic impulse with Plato? 'Quasi-diagrammatic scenes' in Plato's philosophy," in *Thinking with Diagrams: The Semiotic Basis of Human Cognition*, eds. Sybille Krämer and Christina Ljungberg (Boston; Berlin: Walter de Gruyter, 2016), 163-164.

Further, from the perspective of the computer scientist, algorithms are a byproduct of drawing. Set in opposition to the cultural techniques of hermeneutic interpretation fostered through the reading of novels, they are a practice based on mark-making and an effect of graphical inscription.

In what ways do algorithms participate in the emergent scopic regimes of the late-twentieth century? What forms of vision are installed by their ascendance as cultural artifacts? Can they even be said to play any part in the shifting logics of visuality, i.e., do they at all shape "sight as a social fact ... how we are able, allowed, or made to see, and how we see this seeing or the unseen therein"?[12] It might easily be assumed that the algorithmic simply results in the complete foreclosure of sight as a legitimate epistemic enterprise in favor of sublimated logic. If Western culture has been marked by a privileging of sight as "the noblest of the senses," and its modern era only occasioned an intensification of ocularcentrism, algorithmic processing seems to herald an end to this lineage, basing evidence instead on non-visible procedures. Close attention to the discourse of computer science suggests otherwise. More specifically, algorithms belong to a historical tradition privileging *disegno* as the distillment of form. What Knuth dubbed "the analysis of algorithms" would be swiftly supplemented to reflect this, as in the title of Alfred Aho, John Hopcroft, and Jeffrey D. Ullman's textbook from 1974: The *Design* and Analysis of Computer Algorithms.[13] Knuth's advice extends a deep history of practices that emerge contemporaneously with and subsequently run alongside the more familiar scopic subcultures of modernity studied by scholars of visual culture including geometricized Cartesian perspective and the observational "art

---

[12] Hal Foster, "Preface," in *Vision and Visuality*, ed. Hal Foster (Seattle: Bay Press, 1988), p. ix.

[13] Alfred V. Aho, John E. Hopcroft, and Jeffrey D. Ullman, *The Design and Analysis of Computer Algorithms* (Reading, MA; Menlo Park, CA: Addison-Wesley Publishing Company, 1974).

of describing."[14] Contemporary fascination with so-called algorithmic culture does not delimit a clean break from the preceding centuries but follows currents of fluctuations and reversals. Further, its disposition is not itself a harmoniously unified scheme; I am keen on highlighting the tints at its extremities. To that end, this chapter is committed to microhistories of the anecdotal, building up to considerations of an instance of algorithmic thinking proposed instead in terms of *disegno*'s counterpart, color: Leo J. Guibas and Robert Sedgewick's elaboration of "red-black trees."

Primarily, the sort of algorithmic visuality I am speaking of does *not* involve what is commonly referred to as data visualization, the modular separation of graphical display from the manipulation of information. More pertinent here are the functions of what Ursula Klein has called "paper tools." Referring to the notation system for describing the composition of chemical compounds introduced by Jacob Berzelius in 1813 (such as, H_2O for water), Klein's study of the semiotics of scientific formulas explains how graphical symbolization was germinal to developments in organic chemistry of the 1830s.[15]

The direction taken in this study is perhaps best described in contradistinction to the former, which treats the process of making visible as an appendage to analytic interpretation. As defined by visualization guru Edward Tufte, criteria of "graphical excellence" in these displays "consists of complex ideas communicated with clarity, precision, and efficiency." Tufte's practice is also committed to a moral code of "graphical integrity," preaching against misleading distortions of

---

[14] On the latter, see Svetlana Alpers, *The Art of Describing: Dutch Art in the Seventeenth Century* (Chicago: University of Chicago Press, 1983). See also Martin Jay, "Scopic Regimes of Modernity," in *Vision and Visuality*, pp. 3-27.

[15] See Ursula Klein, *Experiments, Models, Paper Tools: Cultures of Organic Chemistry in the Nineteenth Century* (Stanford, CA: Stanford University Press, 2003).

"underlying data" which "make it hard for the viewer to learn the truth."[16] Such ideals would be misapplied in considerations of the inscriptions processed with paper tools. It is, of course, not the case that the latter should be *un*clear, *im*precise, and/or *in*efficient; nor should they be deemed *im*moral. Rather, these traces invite evaluation along other lines. Discussing paper tools in those terms, while perhaps not false (H_2O is a clear, precise, and efficient annotation for water), would miss the point entirely. Klein emphasizes this when challenging the received view "that Berzelian formulas were merely a shorthand for names," arguing instead that "chemists began applying chemical formulas not primarily to represent and to illustrate preexisting knowledge, but rather as productive tools on paper." Thus, while the visualizations discussed by Tufte encourage a separation of cognition from the affordances of graphic form, Klein's paper tools are rooted in an attitude towards knowledge practices grasped as embodied experiments with instruments, albeit symbolic ones. Understood this way, theorization is materially grounded in the manual activity of mark-making. It is inappropriate to subject the workings of paper tools to trials regarding misrepresentation as they are "resources whose possibilities are not exhausted by the knowledge and intentions of their inventors and by scientists' attempts to achieve preset goals but rather whose application generates new goals, objects, inscriptions, and concepts linked to them"—that is to say, Klein's argument is precisely *against* the correspondence between graphics and ideas that Tufte swears by, instead thinking through what arises in the gap between the two.[17]

In his study of the rise of mathematical physics at Cambridge over the eighteen and nineteenth centuries, Andrew Warwick has shown that the use of such tools in research is indelibly

---

[16] Edward R. Tufte, *The Visual Display of Quantitative Information* (Cheshire, CT: Graphics Press, 2001), p. 13 and pp. 55-57.

[17] Klein, *Experiments, Models, Paper Tools*, p. 11, p. 2, and p. 3.

intertwined with cultures of pedagogy, describing a shift from oral lectures and Latin disputations, to private coaching on solving model-problems evaluated through written examinations. The latter were performed with what James Clerk Maxwell called the "apparatus of pen, ink, and paper." Practice through such media inculcated future scholars in standards of argumentation which would restructure the presentation of their "research as a sequence of problems, solutions, and applications."[18] Thus, it shaped both the content expressed as well as the form of expression possible in journal articles, becoming a key strand of visuality in scientific institutions.

Knuth's advocacy of drawing is aligned with this sensibility, perhaps even a direct descendent of the style of training developed in the Cambridge described by Warwick. *The Art of Programming* partakes in the genre of mathematical textbooks, providing students with a supply of sample exercises to be manually performed. Computing is especially interesting to consider from this angle as it is not merely one further instance amongst a myriad of paper tools, but the very name of the procedures this concept refers to, i.e., working formulas out on paper is precisely what is meant by the term, *computation*.

Or, in any case, what *was* meant by the term: any discussion of computers today is stained by the prevalence of complex electronics on which algorithms are supposed to run. Indeed, it is perhaps due to such machinery that computation is even legible as a subject of study in its own right, rather than considered an adjunct to proper disciplines, a mere method (and not a particularly prestigious one at that). The persistence of graphical practices in computing suggests that the

---

[18] Andrew Warwick, *Masters of Theory: Cambridge and the Rise of Mathematical Physics* (Chicago: University of Chicago Press, 2003), p. 24.

archaic sense of *computers*, referring to symbolic laborers, has not been rendered obsolete in an age of electronic technology but merely been transposed into a different register.

Warwick's rigorous attention to historical detail complements Krämer's more philosophically-oriented approach, sketching out the space between the potential manipulation of signs through graphic notation and their actualization as a functional *dispositif*. Paper tools, as an experimental apparatus, generate shared competencies through immersion in local contexts; the sense they maintain is specific to their milieux of inhabitation.[19] This is not merely a matter of implementation but has especial urgency today in nuancing the vacillating states that characterizes today's algorithmic culture as a superimposition of computational media systems, between their operation as paper-based *techniques* and electronic *technologies*. If these exercises of inscription retain some sort of significance to algorithmic mediation today, it is not only by virtue of their formal attributes (e.g., two-dimensionality, tangibility) but through their situatedness within an environment of knowledge practices; the materiality of the symbolic is not reducible to physical properties.

In thinking through the vicissitudes of automation brought on by algorithmic processing, I find it more compelling to couple this with the role of algorithmic reasoning in making knowable than to address this solely in terms of "opacity" or "impenetrability" alone; that is, not just as straightforward symptoms, but as playing out potential contradiction. Thus, in vernacular discourse, the algorithmic portends an elimination of subjective judgment and reason resulting from an application of technology. Within computer science, however, this colloquial sense is not shared. A key subfield in the discipline referring to the categorization of computational procedures,

---

[19] See also, on the "dispersion" of drawings, David Kaiser, *Drawing Theories Apart: The Dispersion of Feynman Diagrams in Postwar Physics* (Chicago: University of Chicago Press, 2005).

it names techniques of making otherwise inscrutable phenomena legible within analytic comprehension. The former carries firm associations with the effects of machinery; the latter, in direct contrast, seeks to articulate machine-independent descriptions. Algorithms are not simply an "object of ignorance," but also simultaneously the opposite, a sense-making tool.

At stake in addressing the deep histories of graphical practices as a scopic regime of algorithmic media are the specificities and displacements of their sites. The introduction of highly specialized symbolic languages gave rise to concerns that it would limit membership in the scientific community to experts, imposing a restriction to participation at odds with ideals of civil society.[20] Prerequisite skills and competencies exerted their impact both on what was written, as well as what could be reasonably omitted. Warwick explains that familiarity with "examination problems served to generate a community in which many of the steps in the solution of a new problem could be left as implicit exercises to the implied reader."[21] These are key features of graphical calculi: rendering "visible and tangible" does not obviate tacit practices of knowing by making the implicit explicit but realigns their arrangements. Unlike the subjects treated by Klein and Warwick, computing is further complicated by an extreme prominence within cultural imaginaries. One can imagine getting by relatively untroubled with the legibility of Berzelian formulas and Maxwell's theories, esoteric products of scholarly learning; although demanding equally focused training, it is more difficult to avoid algorithms. Writing for the popular magazine *Scientific American* in 1977, Knuth noticed the sudden entry of his professional vocabulary into quotidian discourse, remarking that "ten years ago, the word 'algorithm' was unknown to most

---

[20] See Steven Shapin, *A Social History of Truth: Civility and Science in Seventeenth-Century England* (Chicago: University of Chicago Press, 1994), esp. pp. 335-338.

[21] Warwick, *Masters of Theory*, p. 24; see also pp. 30-32.

educated people; indeed, it was scarcely necessary."[22] His attribution of this cultural shift to "the rise of computer science, which takes the algorithm as its focal point," is compelling to me. An abrupt reconceptualization of the algorithm concept follows its establishment and institutionalization in the late-1950s, coming into focus as it acquires prominence over the 1960s.

My interest in pursuing the history of computer science is less in examining the discipline itself, than in following the diffusion of its localized developments into other environments. Not only, in other words, have the effects of computing technologies as such exerted pressure across innumerable spheres. In addition, the terminology of computer science (imbued with their contemporary meaning as byproducts of these technologies) has leaked well beyond the discipline's scope, becoming a means of cognitive mapping.

Hans-Jörg Rheinberger's investigations of experimental systems may be read as an exemplary instance of this. Redirecting attention from the "literary technologies … of rhetorical enhancement, persuasion, and dissimulation" to the "scrips and scribbles" of laboratory notes, Rheinberger elucidates the effects of operative writing at work in the provisional "process of graphematic tracing."[23] Indeed, his distinction between "epistemic things" and "technical objects" seems eminently suited to mapping the tensions between computational techniques (paper tools) and computational technologies (electronics) at stake here. Epistemic things, referring to the open process of scientific research "enacted at the frontiers between the known and unknown,"[24] appropriately denotes the continuum of pedagogy-research addressed by Klein and Warwick; the

---

[22] Donald E. Knuth, "Algorithms," *Scientific American* 236, no. 4 (April 1977): 63.

[23] Hans-Jörg Rheinberger, "Scrips and Scribbles," *MLN* 118, no. 3 (April 2003): p. 622 and p. 635.

[24] Hans-Jörg Rheinberger, *Towards a History of Epistemic Things: Synthesizing Proteins in the Test Tube* (Stanford, CA: Stanford University Press, 1997), p. 25.

algorithmic scribbling favored by Knuth likewise does not merely transcribe what one already understands, but functions as a portal to what is not yet understood. Technical objects, on the other hand, are the "sufficiently stabilized" result of findings which have become routine to experimentation.[25] As the assumed conditions from which future research departs, they "need not be definitely stable but ... are reliable and resonant enough to carry the burden to some next step."[26] The resemblance Rheinberger's concept of the technical object bears to the most recognizable traits of contemporary algorithmic culture is no coincidence:

> Within these complex, tinkered, and hybrid settings of emergence, change, and obsolescence, scientific objects continually make their appearance and eventually recede into technical, preparative subroutines of an ongoing experimental manipulation.[27]
>
> Epistemic things turned into technical objects become integrated as stable subroutines into other, still growing experimental systems and may help produce unprecedented events in different contexts.[28]
>
> How are such events [the "unprecedented events" of experimental discoveries] brought about? Because they cannot be foreseen, there is no logical prescription, no algorithm to make them happen.[29]
>
> We have to cope with and envisage the in-principle impossibility of an algorithm or a logic of scientific development that in its historical course is causally grounded.[30]

---

[25] Ibid., p. 29.

[26] Ibid., p. 65.

[27] Ibid., p. 21.

[28] Ibid., p. 80.

[29] Ibid., p. 134.

[30] Ibid., p. 182.

His generous employment of computational metaphors in defining this typology leaves the impression that "subroutines" are not just apprehended by his theoretical framework but the very basis of his theorization; the "algorithm" is the image against which scientific activity gets defined. Despite its somewhat oblique place within Rheinberger's accounts of experimentation, I find it productive to think of computation as a key element of the project and to interpret his work as itself a form of algorithmic (counter-)practice. A distinction between epistemic thing and technical object is a response to and only become possible within the milieu of a certain kind of algorithmic culture—it derives its stakes as a critical position from this epistemic ecology.

The word, "algorithm," has become the default descriptor for anything vaguely computational, to the extent that it appears synonymous with computing itself. It has become the master signifier under which a spectrum of sense has become subsumed, less a well-defined and stable expression than a site upon which numerous concerns are projected. Historian of science Massimo Mazzotti has termed it "a site of semantic confusion." Rather than "engaging in a taxonomic exercise to norm the usage of the word," however, he has proposed that a more generative approach would "consider its flexible, ill-defined, and often inconsistent meanings as a resource: a messy map of our increasingly algorithmic life"—that is, would take "the omnipresent *figure* of the algorithm as an object that refracts collective expectations and anxieties."[31]

Similarly, this chapter has no fondness for semantic discipline. Although what follows is an attempt at conceptual clarification, it is not elaborated with the intention of arriving at a definitive understanding, establishing the precedence of one proper use over others, but rather to highlight the contingency involved in appropriations of this term. Unlike Mazzotti, my focus is

---

[31] Massimo Mazzotti, "Algorithmic Life," *LA Review of Books*, 22 January 2017, https://lareviewofbooks.org/article/algorithmic-life/.

primarily historical. *How did the algorithm come to be such an "omnipresent figure"? What was at stake in aligning the computational with the algorithmic?* Suggesting that the algorithm concept is liable to historical reconditioning runs against the challenge of thoroughly naturalized assumptions regarding its referent. When the dimension of history is invoked in relation to the algorithmic, this tends instead to entail an anachronistic application of current conceptions into antiquity. According to these approaches, "algorithms have been around since the beginning of time and existed well before a special word had been coined to describe them."[32]

At least since the publication of Knuth's *Art of Programming*, it has become customary to begin a discussion of algorithms with a detour into medieval Arabic mathematics. This rhetorical maneuver tends not to be conducted out of any deep concern for insights offered by historical perspective, however, but effectively naturalizes the concept by planting it within an extended pedigree, smoothing over discontinuities between instances. It is "assumed that words had kept their meaning, that desires still pointed in a single direction, and that ideas retained their logic."[33] Knuth, to his credit, acknowledges that it is "the modern meaning for algorithm" (*ACP*, p. 4) that he addresses, a distinction more often elided. Yet, the assumption remains that modes of reasoning expressed by the term are commensurable, if not immediately equivalent: it is supposed that Euclid's algorithm *now* is equivalent to Euclid's algorithm *then*, never mind that this word did not exist in Euclid's time.[34]

---

[32] Jean-Luc Chabert, "Introduction," in Chabert et al., *A History of Algorithms: From the Pebble to the Microchip*, trans. Chris Weeks, ed. Chabert (New York, 1999), p. 1.

[33] Michel Foucault, "Nietzsche, Genealogy, History," in *Language, Counter-Memory, Practice: Selected Essays and Interviews*, trans. Donald F. Bouchard and Sherry Simon, ed. Bouchard (Ithaca, NY, 1980), p. 139.

[34] See Donald E. Knuth, "Ancient Babylonian Algorithms," *Communications of the ACM* 15, issue 7 (July 1972): 671-677. For a more circumspect approach to the application of the algorithm concept, cf. Jens Høyrup, "The Algorithm Concept—Tool for Historiographic Interpretation or Red Herring?," in *Logic and Theory of Algorithms:*

I intend to pursue the opposite. "Method," "Rules," "Principles," "Operations": all these terms deployed in Berkeley's criticisms may be reasonably associated with the algorithmic. But where these are connected, why an "algorithm" would be invoked, and when the term may be properly applied are all less clear, even if it is well-defined. In historicizing rather than naturalizing the algorithm concept, I will be following it as a signifier, not presupposing an underlying significance—examining *how* it can be used, rather than definitively establishing *what* is meant. Just as Michel Foucault's genealogies of single words indicate a consistent problem as it unfolds over a range of deployments (such as *parrēsia*: "truth-telling"),[35] here too following a concept's movement reveals agitation across fields of subject positions, modes of address, and distributions of knowledge; the availability of language yields the basis for a reconstruction of these investments. Whereas more chronologically focused accounts might run the risk of projecting a misleading sense of immutability and inevitability by adopting a single historical moment as their frame of reference, a genealogical approach engages with the unstable conditions of possibility through which concepts are rendered animate. In other words, my insistence on historicization foregrounds disparity amidst the algorithm concept as it is displaced across heterogeneous sites. Do such displacements constitute decisive breaks? "Clearly not, but rather a shift, a change of orientation, a difference in emphasis."[36]

The premise adopted here is thus *not*, as Mazzotti suggests, that of an "increasingly algorithmic life," a truism implying the preconstituted division between an algorithmic domain on

---

4th Conference on Computability in Europe, CiE 2008, Lecture Notes in Computer Science, vol 5028, eds. Arnold Beckmann, Costas Dimitracopoulos, and Benedikt Löwe (Berlin: Springer, 2008), pp. 261-272.

[35] See Michel Foucault, "*Parrēsia*," trans. Graham Burchell, *Critical Inquiry* 41 (Winter 2015): 219–53.

[36] Michel Foucault, *The Care of the Self*, vol. 3 of *The History of Sexuality*, trans. Robert Hurley (New York, 1988), p. 67.

the one hand and lived experience on the other, the latter being reshaped in the image of the former. Not only does such an assessment suppose an unpolluted cultural sphere (what Mazzotti calls "life") threatened by an external interloper, it further essentializes the algorithmic intrusion by treating it as a stable entity. This study instead focuses on demonstrating that neither should be taken as givens but are constitutive of the other: culture has long incorporated an algorithmic dimension; conversely, the concept of an algorithm—as currently understood, or otherwise—only acquires its sense in relation to the cultural position it occupies.

Of interest in examining how the current situation has come to be, then, is less the explanatory narration of a chain of causal succession, than an elucidation of how things might otherwise be. Algorithmic histories of this sort—that is, histories written in the modality of the possible rather than the actual—are prompted as much by an absence of coherence ("semantic confusion"), as by the production of regularities, that is, the formation of an unspoken consensus regarding the proper use of concepts. Specifically, amidst the multiple implications in circulation today, a single conception of the algorithm is prevalent:

> a sequence of computational steps that transform the input into the output[37];
>
> a recipe, an instruction set, a sequence of tasks to achieve a particular calculation or result, like the steps needed to calculate a square root or tabulate the Fibonacci sequence[38];
>
> a sequence of instructions telling a computer what to do[39];

---

[37] Thomas H. Cormen, et al., *Introduction to Algorithms* (Cambridge, MA: MIT Press, 2009), p. 5.

[38] Ed Finn, *What Algorithms Want: Imagination in the Age of Computing* (Cambridge, MA: MIT Press, 2017), p. 17.

[39] Pedro Domingos, *The Master Algorithm: How the Quest for the Ultimate Learning Machine Will Remake Our World* (New York: Basic Books, 2015), p. 1.

a process, a program with clearly defined limits, a finite instruction sequence.[40]

This essential accord maintained over a *sequential* and *step-based* nature of algorithms only attained prominence relatively recently, contemporaneously to the emergence of computer science as an academic discipline. Entrenched in both specialist and popular vocabularies through its seminal texts such as Knuth's *The Art of Computer Programming*, this particular conception has since served as the unquestioned and defining basis in discussion of anything algorithmic. It has perhaps even become difficult to envision an algorithm as anything but an ordered series of if-then statements, a failure of critical imagination most easily remedied through careful historicization.

Consider, as a particularly sharp point of contrast to current orthodoxy, the following passage from psychoanalyst Jacques Lacan's 1957 text on "The Instance of the Letter in the Unconscious":

> To pinpoint the emergence of the discipline of linguistics, I will say that, as in the case of every science in the modern sense, it consists of an algorithm that grounds it. This algorithm is the following:
>
> $$\frac{S}{s}$$
>
> It is read as follows: signifier over signified, "over" corresponding to the bar separating the two levels.[41]

Regardless of any controversy over validity in Lacan's deployment of mathematical formalisms, the quote is useful as a demonstration of historicity in the ordinary use of concepts. My interest here is not in the veracity of psychoanalytic claims regarding subjectivity and linguistics, but in

---

[40] William Uricchio, "The algorithmic turn: photosynth, augmented reality and the changing implications of the image," *Visual Studies* 26, no. 1 (March 2011): 26.

[41] Jacques Lacan, "The Instance of the Letter in the Unconscious: or Reason Since Freud," in *Écrits: The First Complete Edition in English*, trans. Bruce Fink (New York; London: W.W. Norton, 2002), pp. 414-415.

how the word, "algorithm," can be applied in the mid- to late-1950s. An attempt to read "signifier over signified" strictly as "a sequence of instructions" would result only in perplexity: *where is the "sequence"? what are the "instructions"?* Just around a decade before the publication of Knuth's book, any suggestion of step-based operation is completely missing (an omission especially conspicuous given Lacan's interest in "logical time").[42] Neither is the list of synonyms supplied in *The Art of Programming* helpful: "*recipe, process, method, technique, procedure, routine, rigmarole*" (*ACP*, p. 4). Algorithm here means something closer to *formula* or *formalization*; that is, as the article's title clearly states, the factor of importance is the "*letter*," a term that Lacan employs to "designate the material medium [*support*] that concrete discourse borrows from language."[43]

Lacan's is perhaps an extreme but by no means an eccentric nor uniquely French use of the algorithm concept in the 1950s. Even in this relatively recent period, a strong connotation gravitates towards the acquisition of literal form—materialization *à la lettre*, as symbols. An additional prerequisite in order to conceive of the algorithm as a "recipe" (perhaps the most viable of the suggested synonyms), is a gap between plan and performance, between design and execution. A recipe must be followable, already suggesting models of subjectivity, arrangements of being; an entire apparatus must be called up and set to work in order to maintain the simple disposition that algorithms today are inclined towards today. Computational technologies function as a media *a priori* in this regard, not as crude hardware determinism, but by injecting themselves

---

[42] Jacques Lacan, "Logical Time and the Assertion of Anticipated Certainty: A New Sophism," in *Écrits*, pp. 161-175.

[43] Lacan, "The Instance of the Letter in the Unconscious," p. 413.

into shifting nuances in foundational configurations of sense, establishing the conditions under which today's conception becomes possible.

§1.2: Threshold Objects: A Detour through Data

Clearly, the Lacanian sense of an algorithm is not entirely illegible; it does not indicate a complete rupture. His application intersects sufficiently, even if only barely, with today's normative use of the term that it should not spark complete bafflement: the algorithms that Knuth speaks of also require *spelling out* some sort of formula. My focus in this chapter is on the concept's capacity for robustness that allows it to function as a *threshold object* that holds together schisms in epistemic cultures.

What I mean by this may be clarified through a detour into a proximate—yet distinct—concept, "data." Scholars have noted that as the plural of the Latin, *datum* ("to give"), this word used to refer to "something given in an argument, something taken for granted."[44] As Daniel Rosenberg clarifies, although it may have been used in the context of quantitative figures, the concept did not indicate the *quaesita* (or, "quantities sought"), but was part of the definition of a problem; it would have been nonsensical to have spoken of *gathering* data, as one might today. They were part of the "Conditions" to proceed from, as John Colson put it in his commentary appended to Isaac Newton's belatedly published explanation of *The Method of Fluxions* in 1736:

> Indeed it is required on the part of the Master [or, "Instructor"], that the Conditions he proposes may be consistent with one another; for if they involve any inconsistency or contradiction, the Problem will be unfair, or will become absurd and impossible, as the Solution will afterwards discover. Now these Conditions,

---

[44] Daniel Rosenberg, "Data before the Fact," in *"Raw Data" Is an Oxymoron*, ed. Lisa Gitelman (Cambridge, MA: MIT Press, 2013), p. 18.

52

these Points, Lines, Angles, Numbers, Equations, &c. that at first enter the state of the Question, or are supposed to be chosen or given by the Master, are the *data* of the Problem, and the Answers he expects to receive are the *quaesita*. As it may sometimes happen, that the *data* may be more than are necessary for determining the Question, and so perhaps may interfere with one another, and the Problem (as now proposed) may become impossible; so they may be fewer than necessary, and the Problem thence will be indetermin'd, and may require other Conditions to be given, in order to a compleat Determination, or perfectly to fulfil the *quaesita*.

Colson's account, an intervention in the aftermath of Berkeley's criticisms from two years earlier, is particularly helpful for us as he goes on to specify how the concept should be used:

> Indeed the word *datum* is often used in a sense which is sometimes different from this, but which ultimately centers in it. As that is call'd a *datum*, when one quantity is not immediately given, but however is necessarily infer'd from another, which other perhaps is necessarily infer'd from a third, and so on in a continued Series, till it is necessarily infer'd from a quantity, which is known or given in the sense before explain'd. This is the Notion of *Euclid*'s *data*; and other Analytical Argumentations of that kind. Again, that is often call'd a *given quantity*, which always remains constant and invariable, while other quantities or circumstances vary; because such as these only can be the given quantities in a Problem, when taken in the foregoing sense.[45]

It is not so much that Colson is simply adopting the same signifier for another referent. Rather, his explanations take place in discursive conditions incommensurable with our own; his "data" is situated in a different conceptual milieu than today's. Empirically collected information could hardly have been legible as evidence in a controversy over geometric demonstration (or the lack thereof) in the method of fluxions.

How did one sense of the word evolve into the other? If, in the past, a certain understanding of the term was recognized, how did another, entirely distinct conception, take over its territory? To have used the current interpretation then would have been as awkward as anachronistically

---

[45] John Colson, "The Method of Fluxions and Infinite Series; or, A Perpetual Comment upon the foregoing Treatise," appendix to *The Method of Fluxions and Infinite Series*, by Isaac Newton (London: Henry Woodfall, 1736), pp. 321-322.

applying the archaic meaning of the word today. Neither seems easily mistaken for the other. Foucault's investigations, which may be thought of as slices of genealogical strata, raise these questions as well: Euripides's *parrēsia* differs from Plato's *parrēsia*, and both of theirs from those of Quintilian, Gigante, and so on—but what accounts for the slippage in sense between these instances? How and where do these shifts in emphasis and orientation occur?

The threshold object works in this interstitial space, where a smooth transition between the two may take place. Compare the following statements from *Volume 1* of philosopher and psychologist William James's *Principles of Psychology* (1890), written at a moment of uncertainty regarding disciplinary territorialization:

> But Psychology is a mere natural science, accepting certain terms uncritically as her data, and stopping short of metaphysical reconstruction.[46]

> We may immediately call it right and intelligible so far as it posits a past time with past thoughts or selves contained therein—these were data which we assumed at the outset of the book.[47]

He also writes:

> But the data for calculation are too inaccurate for use, and, as Wundt himself admits, the precise duration of stage 3 must at present be left enveloped with that of the other processes, in the total reaction-time.[48]

> To be conscious of a time interval at all is one thing; to tell whether it be shorter or longer than another interval is a different thing. A number of experimental data are on hand which give us a measure of the delicacy of this latter perception.[49]

---

[46] William James, *The Principles of Psychology*, vol. 1 (New York: Henry Holt, 1890), p. 137.

[47] Ibid., p. 332.

[48] Ibid., pp. 89-90.

[49] Ibid., p. 615.

And further:

> The enemies of evolution have been quick to pounce upon this undeniable discontinuity in the data of the world, and many of them, from the failure of evolutionary explanations at this point, have inferred their general incapacity all along the line.[50]

> In sense-perception, we have results in abundance, which can only be explained as conclusions drawn by a process of unconscious inference from data given to sense.[51]

> To sum up the chapter, Psychology assumes that thoughts successively occur, and that they know objects in a world which the psychologist also knows. These thoughts are the subjective data of which he treats, and their relations to their objects, to the brain, and to the rest of the world constitute the subject-matter of psychologic science. Its methods are introspection, experimentation, and comparison.[52]

> The highest and most elaborated mental products are filtered from the data chosen by the faculty next beneath, out of the mass offered by the faculty below that, which mass in turn was sifted from a still larger amount of yet simpler material, and so on. The mind, in short, works on the data it receives very much as a sculptor works on his block of stone.[53]

James moves across different senses of "data" with ease. In the first set of quotes I cite, the concept indicates the "assumed" givens, without great concern for any informatic associations. By contrast, in the second set, it refers to the "experimental" results useful "for calculation," applying the term in a way which, I suspect, would have been quite illegible to Colson but perhaps comfortable to readers today. Finally, in the last set, it is deployed in ways quite irreducible to either former or current uses, perhaps meaning both or neither. These varied applications do not appear to result

---

[50] Ibid., p. 146.

[51] Ibid., p. 168.

[52] Ibid., p. 197.

[53] Ibid., p. 288.

from selective interpretations; for James, the term dwells in an epistemic milieu affording appropriate conceptual mutability that what appears to us as insurmountable barriers are instead quite porous.

A threshold object is a semantic operator that works *in-between*—it mediates between potentially incongruent senses within a single concept. As such, it is more of a historiographical lens than a sociotechnical actant. Not that it does not perform the work of the latter. However, its success as a medium would have resulted in its transparency when it was working well. This dimension thus only becomes apparent retrospectively, such as when an antiquated sense of "data" is no longer seen to be compatible with its current proper use; from the perspective of a resident like James, inhabiting the apparent epistemic schism, association across these variations occurs with immediacy. Thus, if the threshold object cannot be isolated within either one sphere or the other, neither can it properly be said to simply include both. It instead marks an indeterminacy puncturing the clarity of distinction between the two. When James writes, for example, of "data given to sense" or "subjective data," I think he pushes the concept into an uncanny zone which is all the more uncomfortable due to its proximity to familiar use despite an incoherence against current normative standards—*isn't "subjective data" simply a contradiction? but isn't it also perfectly clear what James means there?* The promise I find in reading concepts as threshold objects is historicization's capacity to deform seemingly obvious and deeply naturalized conceptions. Despite a primarily empirical focus on the collection of statements, this methodological inclination is above all a speculative enterprise, rooted in contingency, and invested in how things might otherwise be—*in what world, for example, is "subjective data" possible?*

§1.3: The Algorithm Concept, 1684-1958

It has been said that "algorithms and databases are conceptually conjoined." Are algorithms really "inert, meaningless machines until paired with databases on which to function?"[54] And, if "data" was only attached to its "-base" relatively recently, what did algorithms do without their alleged partner? Antiquated usage of the algorithm concept is profoundly alien, requiring a recalibration of sensibilities to come to terms with. An early definition is offered in John Harris's *Lexicon Technicum* (1704):

> ALGORITHM, sometimes call'd *Logistica Numeralis*, is the Sum of the Principal Rules of Numeral Computation; of which they commonly reckon Five, *Numeration, Addition, Substraction, Multiplication* and *Division*; to which may be added *Extraction of Roots*.[55]

He was not the first to afford the term attention. Edward Phillips's dictionary on *The new world of English words* (1658) had included a schematic entry which associated it with a (now-obsolete) term for the numeral zero: "*Algorithme*, (a word compounded of *Arabick* and *Spanish*,) the art of reckoning with Cyphers."[56]

Harris's elaboration preserves a more precise indication of how he and his contemporaries could work with such a concept. It echoes Joseph Raphson's slightly earlier *Mathematical Dictionary* (1702): "*Algorithm*, otherwise called *Logistica Numeralis* is the Foundation of Numeral Computation, and contains the six Principal Rules thereof, viz. *Numeration, Addition,*

---

[54] Gillespie, "The Relevance of Algorithms," p. 169.

[55] John Harris, *Lexicon Technicum: or, An Universal English Dictionary of Arts and Sciences*, 2 vols. (London: Dan Brown, 1704), 1:[51].

[56] Edward Phillips, *The new world of English words, or, A general dictionary containing the interpretation of such hard words as are derived from other languages* (London: E. Tylor, 1658), p. [22].

Subtraction, Multiplication, Division, and *Extraction of Roots*."[57] Raphson's dictionary was itself based on the French *Dictionnaire Mathematique* (1692) by Jacques Ozanam, which had named the first and principal rules for the art of effective and easy calculation, *"Algorithme,"* differentiating this vulgar or practical arithmetic from algebra due to its emphasis on numerals: "L'Arithmetique Vulgaire, ou *Pratique*, est l'art de bien & facilement supputer. Elle a fix Regles premieres & principals, sçavoir la *Numeration*, l'*Addition*, la *Soustraction*, la *Multiplication*, la *Division*, & l'*Extraction de Racines*: & tout cela ensemble se nomme *Algorithme*, ou *Logistique Nombreuse*, pour la differencier de la *Logistique Specieuse*, dont nous parlerons dans l'Algebre."[58] Several decades later, the first edition of Edmund Stone's *New Mathematical Dictionary* (1726) simply duplicated Harris's text word-for-word, but Stone's revision in a second edition (1743) presented a more succinct articulation: "ALGORITHM, the four chief Rules of Arithmetick, *viz.* Addition, Subtraction, Multiplication, and Division."[59]

Taken in the sense these early treatments indicate, *algorithm* could be used almost interchangeably with *arithmetic*, such as in John Wilson's textbook, *An Introduction to Arithmetic* (1742): "These four Rules, viz. *Addition*, *Subtraction*, *Multiplication*, and *Division*, I call the *Algorithm*, or *Arithmetick* of *Numbers*." However, despite an explicit focus on arithmetic rules, remnants of Phillips's link between "Algorithme" and "Cyphers" continued to inflect the specific spheres in which the algorithm concept could be appropriately used. Wilson, for example, did not

---

[57] Joseph Raphson, *A Mathematical Dictionary: or, A Compendious Explication of All Mathematical Terms, Abridg'd From Mosieur Ozanam, and Others* (London: J. Nicholson, 1702), p. [47].

[58] Jacques Ozanam, *Dictionnaire mathematique, ou Idée generale des mathematiques* (Paris: Estienne Michallet, 1692), p. 52.

[59] Edmund Stone, *A New Mathematical Dictionary* (London: J. Senex, 1726).

write of an "Algorithm" in reference to just any "Arithmetick" but solely mobilized this word in the context of explaining decimal numerals:

> Seeing *Finite Decimals* have an *Algorithm* of their own, which is full and complete, as being the same with that of *Integers*, due regard being had to the place of the *Decimal* point; likewise *Infinite repeting Decimals* have their *Algorithm* fully as complete, and yet *Infinite Circulates* can be wrought by neither of these *Algorithms*, we have all the reason in the world to conclude that they too have an *Arithmetick* of their own.[60]

Likewise, Benjamin Martin only invoked this concept in *Pangeometria* (1739) when elaborating "The Rudiments of Decimal Arithmetic": "But as to *Decimal Arithmetic*, as also the Art of *Logarithms* and *Algebra*, they must be premised in the *Algorithm*, or fundamental Rules of each."[61]

In this regard, the eighteenth century's algorithm concept was closely related to that of the *algorism*, a word with which it shared etymological ties. Knuth cites the latter, correctly noting that it referred to "the process of doing arithmetic with Arabic numerals. During the Middle Ages, abacists computed on the abacus and algorists computed by algorism" (*ACP*, p. 1). Both words, *algorithm* and *algorism*, trace their origins to the name of a ninth-century Persian scholar, al-Khwārizmī (Latinized: *Algorithmi* or *Algorismi*). Initially referring to the translated books that began with the words *Dixit Algorithmi* (So said al-Khwārizmī), the algorisms came to include the genre of arithmetic treatises explaining the use of the (decimal or cypher-based) Hindu-Arabic numeral system, primarily of interest for practical calculations in the mercantile world. Eventually, it would refer to the numeral system itself.[62]

---

[60] John Wilson, *An Introduction to Arithmetick* (Edinburgh: R. Drummond and Company, 1742), pp. viii-ix and p. xii.

[61] Benjamin Martin, *Pangeometria* (London: J. Noon, 1739), p. 1.

[62] See David Eugene Smith, "The Influence of the Mathematical Work of the Fifteenth Century Upon Those of Later Times," *Bibliographic Society of America* (1932), pp. 143-168, esp. pp. 147-148.

I find the hypothesis that our current preference (algori*th*m) succeeded and replaced an outmoded spelling (algori*s*m) unlikely. In fact, Harris's *Lexicon* included a separate entry:

> ALGORISM, is the Practical Operation in the several Parts of *Specious Arithmetick*, or *Algebra*; and sometimes the Word is used for the Practice of Common Arithmetick by the Ten Numeral Figures.[63]

His assessment that they deserved individual specification indicates the contemporaneity of these two cognates, and also suggests at least a minimal degree of difference between them.

But it is difficult to locate where exactly one should mark this distinction. "Algorism," the medievalist Robert Steele wrote in 1922, "is distinguished from Abacist computation by recognising seven rules, Addition, Subtraction, Duplation, Mediation, Multiplication, Division, and Extraction of Roots, to which were afterwards added Numeration and Progression. It is further distinguished by the use of the zero, which enabled the computer to dispense with the columns of the Abacus."[64] His explication recalls archaic descriptions of *algorithm*. Further complicating Harris's categorization, Steele notes a veritable multitude of possibilities in English alone: *agram, algorisme, algorym, algram, augrim, augrym*.

Arithmetic rules? Decimal numerals? If these deployments of the algorithm-algorism(-algorym-etc.) concept seem unrecognizable, it is not because the algorithms of today no longer retain Harris's definition of an algorithm as "the Sum of the Principal Rules" that must be obeyed over the course of computation. This remains a legitimate and perfectly accurate description of an algorithm. Rather, the assembly of such "Rules" with their associated concepts (including:

---

[63] Harris, *Lexicon Technicum*. See also, Stone, *A New Mathematical Dictionary* (1st ed.), which duplicates this definition.

[64] Robert Steele, "Introduction," in *The Earliest Arithmetics in English*, ed. Robert Steele (London: Oxford University Press, 1922), pp. xiv-xv.

operation, numeration, notation, method, and computation) has since been reoriented, leading to shifts in expectations and emphases in the algorithm concept's proper use; to reiterate, we are not confronted with an injection of the algorithmic into culture today (that is, Mazzotti's "increasingly algorithmic life" wherein faculties of judgment and reason are increasingly subject to rule-bound systems), but instead we confront the question of what kind of culture the algorithm concept is situated within (that is, a reconfiguration of relations tying judgment and reason to rules as adjacent components of a meaningful and functional conceptual assemblage).

How should one understand the affirmation in Henry Clarke's *The Rationale of Circulating Numbers* (1777), which states that within certain astronomical tables, "the Arabian Algorithm of Numbers was better accommodated than the Greek or Roman literal Notation"?[65] What does Clarke's "Algorithm" mean here? Does it still refer to the rules of arithmetic? Or does it, as the passage seems to suggest, instead correspond to the numeral "Notation," i.e., the algorism? When reading such statements from the eighteenth century, it would be a mistake, I think, to insist on a firm conceptual separation between an orthography of notation and the rules by which it is operated. Their algorithm concept, unlike today's, cuts across both: it operates as a threshold object, wherein a distinction that appears clear in retrospect is blended in a single entity. However discrete these two domains may appear to us now—syntactic form hardly necessitating semantic rules—one is immediately the other in texts like Clarke's. Algorithm and algorism could be effectively substituted, not because etymological perversions gave rise to confusion, but because this shared heritage is indicative of a conceptual milieu in which the abstraction and isolation of one from the other was barely, if at all, thinkable: the algorism (numeral system) makes it possible

---

[65] H. Clarke, *The Rationale of Circulating Numbers* (London, 1777), p. vii.

to animate an algorithm (rules); vice versa, without an algorithm (method of operation), any algorism (orthographic scribbling) would be meaningless; for early eighteenth-century arithmetic, a calculus of inscription cannot be detached from the sense it inhabits.

That the algorithm concept would depart ever further from its strict reference to al-Khwārizmī's bequest is perhaps indicative of the declining grip such a culture maintained. Like his contemporaries, Harris would reserve this unusual word for descriptions of a special domain. However, in *A New Short Treatise of Algebra* (1702), he neglected to make use of it in chapters on "Addition," "Subtraction," "Multiplication," and "Division"—the very arithmetic rules with which he would define it in terms of just two years later. Instead of referring to the Hindu-Arabic notation, it appears in his treatment "Of Fluxions," Isaac Newton's name for what is today known as the differential and integral calculus.[66]

Harris's discussion of "The main Business of the Algorithm or Arithmetick of Fluxions" is typical.[67] In other instructional texts on fluxions from the period, one finds: a section devoted to "The Algorithm or Arithmetick of Fluxions" in Charles Hayes's *A Treatise of Fluxions* (1704);[68] a chapter with definitions "Of the Algorithm of Fluxions" in Nicholas Saunderson's posthumously published lectures on *The Method of Fluxions* (1756);[69] and an explanation "Of the Algorithm of Fluxions" in James Hodgson's *The Doctrine of Fluxions* (1758).[70]

---

[66] See John Harris, *A New Short Treatise of Algebra* (London: J.M., 1702).

[67] Harris, *A New Short Treatise of Algebra*, p. 118.

[68] See Charles Hayes, *A Treatise of Fluxions: or, An Introduction to Mathematical Philosophy* (London, 1704), p. 5.

[69] See Nicholas Saunderson, *The Method of Fluxions* (London, 1756), pp. 1–2.

[70] See James Hodgson, *The Doctrine of Fluxions* (London, 1758), p. 55.

More precisely, an algorithm in this context further connoted an absence of geometric proof, indicating a style of presentation. Edmund Stone's introduction to his translation of Marquis de L'Hospital's *Analyse des infiniments petits* (1696; translated as the first volume of Stone's *The Method of Fluxions*, 1730) is especially useful in demonstrating this subtlety in expression. Published just before Bishop Berkeley's attacks on the rigor of the fluxional method (1734–1735), it extolled the utility of L'Hospital's text by differentiating it from homegrown alternatives like Humphry Ditton's *An Institution of Fluxions* (1706):

> *That of our Author is much easier, tho less Geometrical, who calls a* Differential *(or* Fluxion*) the infinitely small Part of a Magnitude; not deterring his Readers at first from proceeding, by dwelling long on the Explication of an intricate Definition, but comes immediately to the Algorithm, or Arithmetick of the Art; and thence to plain Examples of Solutions by it.*[71]

It would surely no longer have been possible to cite this lack of "long . . . Explication" as a virtue in the aftermath of Berkeley's vicious criticisms. Amongst his numerous doubts regarding "the Algorism of Fluxions,"[72] Berkeley was specifically concerned with the possibility of its application by those lacking a sound understanding of foundational principles, comparing this "easier, tho less Geometrical" approach with that of sailors (who merely practically apply astronomy and geometry without understanding their principles), and in particular with the "ordinary Man" making use of "the vulgar Rules and Operations of Arithmetic ... without knowing the Reasons of them." Hence his accusation that adherents indulge in such methods "to save themselves the trouble of thinking."[73]

---

[71] Edmund Stone, "The Translator to the Reader," translator's note to *The Method of Fluxions*, by Marquis de L'Hospital [Guillaume François Antoine], trans. Stone (London, 1730), p. xvi.

[72] George Berkeley, *A Defence of Free-Thinking in Mathematics* (Dublin, 1735), p. 53.

[73] Berkeley, *The Analyst*, p. 17. See also Niccolò Guicciardini, *The Development of Newtonian Calculus in Britain, 1700–1800* (New York, 1989), pp. 38–51.

Even in the nineteenth century, as Maxwell's "apparatus of pen, ink, and paper" was gaining traction at Cambridge, Berkeley remained a crucial point of reference. A review published in 1815 of Olinthus Gregory's textbook of mathematical physics, *A Treatise of Mechanics*, had little regard for its employment "of mechanical maneuvres of symbols and abstract quantities," arguing that "instead of being intuitive and elementary truths," it was founded on "obscurity":

> Such are all those pretended demonstrations by the differential calculus, generally used by the continental mathematicians of Europe, and now without judgment attempted to be introduced among the English population throughout the world. To us there appears as much of sanity in this new fangled mathematics for demonstrations, as in endeavoring to lay the foundation of a structure at its top, or to prove obvious truths by deductions from which are the most remote and recondite. It was against this system principally that the learned and acute Berkley raised his voice. ... These, it must be allowed, are excellent tools in the hands of the mathematicians, for the investigation of new truths, since they save much time, and enable him to proceed to vastly greater extent than he otherwise could do; but in delivering and demonstrating to learners, propositions of the mathematics already known, the process which leads to the result must be explained step by step, whether we assume the analytical or synthetical method of reasoning. It is not against either of these methods logically considered, that we contend, but against what may be called the algorithm or complicity of symbolical terms and expressions, maneuvered according to the rules of algebra, and assumed as mathematical reasoning and demonstration.[74]

While the anonymous reviewer admitted their utility as "tools" for mathematicians, an extension of their purview into theatres of proof was deemed less tolerable. Graphical traces of pen and paper were actants in a controversy around regimes of visual evidence. If, as Knuth will note centuries later, "an algorithm must be seen to be believed," the further question of just *what kind* of seeing is necessary to compel belief remains. Ironically, it is an absence of "step by step" explanation that

---

[74] Review of "O. Gregory's *Treatise on Mechanics*," *American Journal of Science and Arts* 7, no. 1 (January 1824): 77.

the reviewer is especially disappointed with. While today a defining trait of algorithms, in the early nineteenth century, this was a property that they could be characterized precisely as lacking.

It was perhaps precisely the association with practical calculations—the symbolic tools of vulgar commoners—that Gottfried Wilhelm Leibniz intended when coining the "differential" calculus in conjunction with the algorithm concept. In his "Nova Methodus Pro Maximis et Minimis" (1684), he wrote:

> Knowing thus the *Algorithm* (as I may say) of this calculus, which I call *differential calculus*, all other differential equations can be solved by a common method.

Adding slightly later:

> For any other quantity, not itself a term, but contributing to the formation of the term, we use its differential quantity, to form the differential quantity of the term itself, not by simple substitution, but according to the prescribed Algorithm.[75]

The "prescribed Algorithm," as Leibniz puts it, once again refers to rules. But as he uses this concept, it is curiously detached from al-Khwārizmī's decimal numerals and instead more comparable to the use of an abacus. Thus, while one may be tempted to define the skills of an algorist through a distinction from those of the abacist, each processing incommensurable cultural techniques of counting, Leibniz seems to indicate otherwise. From early in the sixteenth century, textbooks on computation with the aid of counters, or *calculi* (pebbles), were printed under headings such as *Algorithmus linealis* and *Enchiridion nouus algorismi*. These commercial arithmetics were especially popular in Germany following commercial customs.[76] In the

---

[75] Gottfried Wilhelm Leibniz, "A New Method for Maxima and Minima," in *A Source Book in Mathematics, 1200–1800*, trans. and ed. Struik (Princeton: Princeton University Press, 1986), p. 276.

[76] See Smith, "The Influence of Mathematical Work of the Fifteenth Century," pp. 148-151.

Leibnizian calculus, traces scribbled on a page were no less material than such counting stones; an algorithm imbues them with sense.

Leibniz's text set the customary format in which algorithms were articulated. Having defined the "data" that he would work with, he declared—"Under these assumptions we have the following rules of the calculus":

> If a is a given constant [*quantitas data constans*], then $da = 0$, and $d(ax) = a\,dx$. If $y = v$ (that is, if the ordinate of any curve *YY* is equal to any corresponding ordinate of the curve *VV*), then $dy = dv$. Now *addition* and subtraction: if $z - y + w + x = v$, then $d(z - y + w + x) = dv = dz - dy + dw + dx$. ...[77]

It is the ensemble of such rules for the manipulation of data which Leibniz named the algorithm of the calculus. As Niccolò Guicciardini has noted, due to the secrecy surrounding the Newtonian fluxional calculus, "the published sources for the early British 'fluxionists' were the *Acta Eruditorum* [where Leibniz's 'Nova Methodus' was published] and, from 1696, L'Hospital's *Analyse des Inifiniments Petits*."[78] The earliest expositions of infinitesimal limits in English thus followed Leibnizian rather than Newtonian principles, simply replacing Leibniz's d-notation (e.g. dx, dy) with Newton's dot-notation (e.g., $\dot{x}$, $\dot{y}$). Texts like Harris's *Algebra* introduce the "algorithm" to its expanded sense (i.e., beyond the Hindu-Arabic algorism) via Leibniz's calculus.

An association between the algorithm concept and *calculi* extended beyond Leibniz's time. Later treatments of the differential and integral calculus proceeded "algorithmically" as well. It is telling that in his elaboration of the theory of analytic functions, *Théorie des fonctions analytiques* (1797), Joseph-Louis Lagrange wrote of "the manner of *employing* the algorithm of functions,"

---

[77] Leibniz, "A New Method for Maxima and Minima," p. 272.

[78] Guicciardini, *The development of Newtonian calculus in Britain, 1700-1800*, p. 12.

not *implementing*, *executing*, or even *performing* those functions—that is, not depicting the algorithm as a routine yielded automatically.[79] As something to instead be *used*, his algorithms must be wielded like any other tool, requiring an active subject inculcated in its techniques and skills. This nuance from current orthodoxy will undoubtedly be familiar to anyone who has completed (or, better still, failed to complete) a mathematics examination.

However closely these may seem to resemble today's algorithmic sequencing, they should thus not be mistaken as embracing similar premises. The form adopted is crucial here: not steps to be followed but a prescribed law underwriting the notation system. In the former, emphasis is placed on the mutability of process, i.e., the difference between one ordering of steps, and another by which the same result may be attained. This concern is not so much incompatible with the latter, as illegible within its discursive conditions. An algorithm in the Leibnizian tradition declares the rules of its semiotic system without spelling out the exact steps of how they should be followed. While it may not be *incorrect* to think of the eighteenth century's method of fluxions or arithmetic as executable operations, it would be *inappropriate* to do so. These algorithms connote an originary investment rather than recipes. When definitions refer to it as the set of "fundamental" or "principal" rules, this seems less in the sense of *most important* (are there non-fundamental or less important rules which do not have to be followed?) than *primary* or *first*. Particularly in connection with *calculi*, it establishes a constitutive act of founding which carries a transformative power, creating meaningful accounts from meaningless placeholders—it processes sense from nonsense, formulating a semantic regime from the raw matter of mere pebbles, the Symbolic from the Real.

---

[79] Joseph-Louis Lagrange, *Théorie des fonctions analytiques* (Paris, 1797), p. 80; my emphasis.

The strong materialist sensibility staked in stressing this coupling of the algorithm concept with *calculi* will likely be disorienting to readers more accustomed to characterizing algorithms in terms of imperceptible abstraction. However, much of today's concerns over algorithmic technologies in fact rehearse arguments elaborated during the eighteenth century in response to the deployment of calculi: Berkeley's accusations regarding an unthinking operation of method may be readily transposed into a context supposedly distinguished by the novelty of advanced machinery because they are premised on conceptions of agency still held in high regard, rooted in the exceptionalism of the human subject and wary of the introjection of technics. This attitude seems to me both unfounded and inadequate. Attending to orthographic factors introduces the possibility of another approach, redirecting theorization away from essentialist ontologies offering a false dichotomy between subjective reason and technical procedure. It instead invites consideration of algorithms in relation to the media effects of cultural techniques, asking: What sort of subject is assembled through algorithmic mediation? Adopting such a tack is particularly well-suited to engaging with the movements of the algorithm concept as it ventures beyond the differential and integral calculus. Later treatments of algorithmic inscription assume a more ambiguous posture towards the ease of use that Berkeley found objectionable; in these spheres, the omissions afforded by a summary abridged of detail were not invariably deemed illegitimate.

A somewhat obscure undercurrent of the algorithm concept follows the import of calculi into studies of logic. Leibniz himself had attempted such a "universal calculus," but such logical formalisms are more familiar to us today through the influence of efforts from the nineteenth century.[80] Augustus De Morgan's *Formal Logic* (1847) sought to extricate logical relations from

---

[80] See Gottfried Wilhelm Leibniz, "Two Studies in the Logical Calculus, 1679," in *Philosophical Papers and Letters*, 2 vols., trans. and ed. Leroy E. Loemker (Dordrecht, Netherlands: Kluwer Academic Publishers, 1989), 2:235–47.

their particular instances through the use of symbols for "abstracting what is necessary to an examination of the laws of inference."[81] His book's subtitle thus referred to a *"Calculus of Inference,"* highlighting that his project of creating a symbolic system was based on the traces of graphic inscription. Likewise, George Boole described a "Calculus of Deductive Reasoning" in *The Mathematical Analysis of Logic* (1847) and wrote in *An Investigation of the Laws of Thought* (1854) of his intention "to give expression in this treatise to the fundamental laws of reasoning in the symbolical language of a Calculus," repeatedly referring to a "Calculus of Logic."[82]

In line with these attempts, the Belgian philosopher and psychologist Joseph Delboeuf presented his article on deductive logic by means of a conventional system of signs as an exposition of algorithmic logic, "Logique algorithmique: Exposé de la logique deductive au moyen d'un système conventionnel de signes" (1876):

> Not all sciences are imparted (*enseigne*) in the same manner. There are some for which an algorithm has been invented, that is to say a system of signs which, at the very least, facilitates exposition. These are arithmetic, algebra, analytic geometry, mechanics, certain parts of physics, or, in a word, mathematics. There are some, especially the biological sciences, whose nature seems incompatible with the application of symbols. Other sciences, finally, for example, chemistry, crystallography, use signs and characters, but their equations only imperfectly represent the facts, and are only a conventional way of shortening the description of phenomena. In certain regards, logic, at least at the moment, falls into this last category of human knowledge.[83]

---

[81] Augustus De Morgan, *Formal Logic: or, The Calculus of Inference, Necessary and Probable* (London: Taylor and Walton, 1847), p. 47.

[82] George Boole, *The Mathematical Analysis of Logic: Being an Essay Towards a Calculus of Deductive Reasoning* (Cambridge: Macmillian, Barclay, & Macmillian, 1847); and, *An Investigation of the Laws of Thought, on Which are Founded the Mathematical Theories of Logic and Probabilities* (London: Walton and Maberly, 1854), p. 5.

[83] Joseph Delboeuf, "Logique algorithmique: Exposé de la logique deductive au moyen d'un système conventionnel de signes," *Revue Philosophique de la France et de l'Étranger* 2 (July-December 1876): "On n'enseigne pas toutes les sciences de la même manière. Il en est pour lesquelles on a inventé une algorithmie, c'est-à-dire un système de signes qui, tout au moins, en facilite l'exposition. Telles sont l'arithmétique, l'algèbre, la géométrie analytique, la mécanique, certaines parties de la physique, ou, pour n'employer qu'un mot, les mathématiques. Il en est, notamment les sciences biologiques, dont la nature semble incompatible avec l'application de symboles. D'autres sciences enfin,

Delboeuf's use of the verb *enseigne* presents some difficulties in translation but touches on many of the stakes involved in his account. The standard rendering of *enseigner* (to teach) is of little direct relevance in this context. Its deployment is perhaps more legible when read in conjunction with *enseigne* as a noun (sign-board or shop display), an association bearing connotations of the sign systems Delboeuf addresses here. From the latter, we etymologically get *ensign* and *insignia*, hinting at a semiotic culture in which expressive manifestation is connected with the intrinsic qualities of what is symbolized—emphasized when Delboeuf claims the incompatibility of biology with an algorithm. Thus, not only does Delboeuf preserve the algorithm concept's mercantile roots as a commercial arithmetic, but he also seems to convey sympathy for cultures in which syntax and orthography are tightly entwined.

What is an algorithm here? "A system of signs," Delboeuf clearly states. Sociological factors are central to his epistemological concerns. Techniques of signification spearhead the transmission of scientific knowledge and hence can be appropriately situated in relation to matters of pedagogy. Algorithms provide a basis for instruction (*enseigne*), shaping the institution of acculturation through inscription as a process of mediation.

Delboeuf's terminological intervention appears to have had limited success: an article by J. Homans on "La logique algorithmique" (1902) defines it as the science of reasoning with the aid of algebraic symbols;[84] Louis Couturat, who also published a key study on Leibniz's logic, examined algorithmic logic and the calculus of probabilities, "La logique algorithmique et le calcul

---

par exemple, la chimie, la cristallographie, se servent de signes et de caractères, mais leurs équations ne représentent qu'imparfaitement les faits, et ne sont qu'une façon conventionnelle d'abréger la description des phénomènes. A certains égards, la logique, actuellement du moins, se range dans cette dernière catégorie des connaissances humain" (p. 225).

[84] J. Homans, "La logique algorithmique," *Revue néo-scolastique* 9, no. 35 (1902): 343-364.

des probabilités" (1917).[85] Despite its lack of success as a heading, however, this sense that an algorithm "facilitates exposition" continued to linger around the development of logical calculi. In Edmund Husserl's *Logical Investigations* (1900), the algorithm concept makes a brief cameo in a discussion of "abbreviations," emphasizing this characterization as a semiotic aid. Husserl's primary example of this operation are "the extraordinarily fruitful algorithmic methods, whose peculiar function is to save us as much genuine deductive mental work as possible by artificially arranged mechanical operations on sensible signs." He goes on to include, as further examples,

> what are literally mechanical methods—one may think of the apparatus for mechanical integration, calculating machines, etc.—as well as the methodical procedures for establishing objectively valid empirical judgements, such as the various methods of determining the position of a star, electrical resistance, inert mass, refractive index, the gravitational constant, etc. Each such method represents a set of provisions whose choice and arrangement is fixed by a validatory context, which shows, in general, that such a procedure, even when blindly performed, must necessarily lead to an objectively valid individual judgement.[86]

Thus, for Husserl, although "algorithmic methods" are linked to exact "methodical procedures" and even "calculating machines," they refer to something else—namely, as in Delboeuf, the system of "sensible signs" such as the logical calculi of de Morgan and Boole. His portrayal uncannily echoes Berkeley's concerns that proponents deploy the fluxional algorithm "to save themselves the trouble of thinking," but stripped of pejorative overtones. In Husserl's vocabulary, algorithms are not depicted in opposition to subjective reason, but as a sympathetic partner that, aids these faculties. They refer to systems of shorthand that condense procedures of calculation, effectively standing in for them; as a form of abbreviation, an algorithm's effects could be compared to the

---

[85] Louis Couturat, "La logique algorithmique et le calcul des probabilités," *Revue de Métaphysique et de Morale* 24, no. 3 (May 1917): 291-313.

[86] Edmund Husserl, *Logical Investigations,* trans. J. N. Findlay, 2 vols. (New York: Routledge, 2001), 1:24.

transformations between *Jan.* and *January*, or *Dr.* and *Doctor*, providing an expression *already* equivalent to its result, articulated with brevity for the sake of descriptive ease.

Particularly in English, the school of inquiry Delboeuf advocates is instead more likely to be referred to as de Morgan did ("formal logic"), or through a title introduced in John Venn's *Symbolic Logic* (1881). Venn is perhaps most widely remembered today for his diagrammatic representations of these logical relations, i.e., Venn diagrams. Discussing his choice of the word, "symbolic," Venn made note of Delboeuf's slightly earlier contribution "on the same kind of subject." "It is," he elaborated, "to this generalized symbolic language, much as we are here employing it, that some writers have applied, by a revival of an old word, the term *Algorithm*." Venn clarified that he had "no objection whatever to the word," simply maintaining a preference for the former due to its relative familiarity, putting an end to any possible uncertainty between the two by judging them compatible: "'symbolic' as I understand it, being almost exactly the equivalent of 'algorithmic.'"[87]

Lacan would surely approve. His deployment of the algorithm concept is fully in tune with its heritage of symbolization. Few, however, could share this understanding today. Who would find the words *algorithmic* and *symbolic* interchangeable now? Without reference to an alien past, it would be unfathomable to discern their link, much less their equivalence. Such usage of the algorithm concept, despite bearing a rather sturdy provenance from Leibniz's *calculi*, is exceedingly rare in contemporary discourse, likely to the point of illegibility.[88]

---

[87] John Venn, *Symbolic Logic* (London: Macmillan and Co., 1881), p. 98.

[88] A case in point here is the following passage from Giorgio Agamben, *The Signature of All Things: On Method*, trans. Luca D'Isanto with Kevin Attell (Cambridge, MA: MIT Press, 2009): "The consistency of the 'fringe of ultra-history' that the historian attempts to reach here is therefore intimately tied to the existence of the Indo-European language and of the people who spoke it. It exists in the same sense and in the same measure in which an Indo-European form exists (for example, *deiwos or *med, forms that are usually preceded by an asterisk so that they can

The extent of this discursive break may be demonstrated by reading Lacan against one of his contemporaries for whom the pairing did not suggest an affinity but a discrepancy posing an insurmountable obstacle. In *The Raw and the Cooked* (1964), Claude Lévi-Strauss targeted this connection, specifically urging clarification of the functions performed by abbreviated shorthand:

> I shall deal much more rapidly with another feature of my book: the occasional use of apparently logico-mathematical symbols, which should not be taken too seriously. There is only a superficial resemblance between my formulas and the equations of the mathematician, because the former are not applications of algorithms which, if rigorously employed, allow demonstrations to be chained or condensed. Their purpose is quite different. Certain analyses of myths are so long and detailed that it would be impossible to carry them through to the end, if one did not have at one's disposal some abbreviated form of writing—a kind of shorthand which allows one to indicate rapidly the intellectual course to be pursued; it can be grasped intuitively in broad outline, but one cannot follow it with the certainty of not going astray, unless it has been reconnoitered piecemeal.[89]

Just seven years separate the instances of the algorithm in Lacan and Lévi-Strauss, who both took great interest in the emerging technologies of information and computing.[90] But the intervening period between 1957 and 1964 is a crucial point of inflection. It included the initial proposals for what Louis Fein in 1959 dubbed the "computer sciences" and, more importantly, the consolidation

---

be distinguished from the words belonging to the historical languages). However, rigorously speaking, each of these forms is nothing but an algorithm that expresses a system of correspondences between existing forms in the historical languages, and, in Antoine Meillet's words, what we call Indo-European is nothing but 'a system of correspondences ... that presupposes a language x spoken by people x at place x and at time x,' where x merely stands for 'unknown'" (pp. 91-92). Agamben's usage of the algorithm concept seems to have more resonance with Husserl's abbreviations than contemporary usage, and he elsewhere deploys it—like Lacan—in conjunction with "the [Saussurian] algorithm S/s" (*Stanzas: Word and Phantasm in Western Culture*, trans. Ronald L. Martinez [Minneapolis; London: University of Minnesota Press, 1993], p. 156). I must admit, however, that I find it harder to understand what sense he intends than what he does *not*—that is to say, although these expressions remain somewhat perplexing to me, it is quite clear that they are *not* references to sequential operation.

[89] Claude Lévi-Strauss, *The Raw and the Cooked*, trans. John and Doreen Weightman (New York: Harper & Row, 1969), p. 30; trans. mod.

[90] See Lydia H. Liu, "The Cybernetic Unconscious: Rethinking Lacan, Poe, and French Theory," *Critical Inquiry* 36, issue 2 (Winter 2010): 288–320; and Bernard Dionysius Geoghegan, "From Information Theory to French Theory: Jakobson, Lévi-Strauss, and the Cybernetic Apparatus," *Critical Inquiry* 38, issue 1 (Autumn 2011): 96–126.

of this new field's operative terminology.[91] Lévi-Strauss adopts a decidedly computer-scientific understanding of what an algorithm is, forwarding an early indication of the place it has come to occupy in today's conceptual milieu. Beyond these critical years, the gap between an abbreviation and its fully processed result yields an increasing density, and the algorithm concept's resonance with orthographic factors fades correspondingly.

Knuth notes that "by 1950, the word algorithm was most frequently associated with Euclid's algorithm, a process for finding the greatest common divisor of two numbers" (*FA*, p. 2). Such usage, common in introductory texts on number theory, is quite compatible with current sensibilities. In a demonstration of "Euclid's Algorithm" in their *Elementary Number Theory* (1939), J. V. Uspensky and M. A. Heaslet provide a definition: "at present it applies to any formalized procedure whereby requested mathematical objects are found by a definite chain of operations."[92] Similarly, Oystein Ore's *Number Theory and Its History* (1948) offered "Euclid's Algorism" as an example, explaining that "a repeated calculating process is called an algorism."[93]

By then, the algorithm concept had been adopted in discussions at the intersection of symbolic logic and mathematics around the problem of what Alan Turing termed "computable numbers."[94] While Turing himself did not use the word, it featured prominently in the writings of Alonzo Church, who noted the equivalence of Turing's independently developed project with his own contemporaneously articulated concept of "effective calculability," discussing both in terms

---

[91] Louis Fein, "The Role of the University in Computers, Data Processing, and Related Fields," *Communications of the ACM* 2, issue 9 (September 1959): 123.

[92] J. V. Uspensky and M. A. Heaslet, *Elementary Number Theory* (New York, 1939), p. 26.

[93] Oystein Ore, *Number Theory and Its History* (New York, 1948), p. 20.

[94] See A. M. Turing, "On Computable Numbers, with an Application to the Entscheidungsproblem," *Proceedings of the London Mathematical Society* 42, n.s. (November 1937): 230–65.

of "the existence of an algorithm."[95] Although indeed foundational to subsequent work in computer science, this discourse in fact remained coherent with the conception of algorithmic methods found in Delboeuf and Husserl, as a form of abbreviation that "facilitates exposition." For instance, when W. V. Quine extolled the "algorithmic facility" of his proposed method in *Mathematical Logic* (1940), this was in reference to its "manipulative convenience" and strength as a "smooth-running technique."[96]

I suspect that the centrality of this intellectual tradition for disciplinary self-understanding has occluded the difficulties in collapsing two distinct kinds of work expected from the algorithm. The general tendency to locate the origins of computer science in the work of Church and Turing (i.e., in the Church-Turing thesis) has implied a search for precedents, favoring historiography that charts how earlier work (from mathematical logic) anticipates later developments (in computer science). In a way, however, the logico-mathematical algorithm connotes the exact opposite of the computer-scientific one: for the former, including the work of Church and Quine, procedural effects are predetermined and thus can be safely ignored; from the viewpoint of computer science, exemplified by Knuth's approach, procedures also imply predetermined effects but, for that same reason, must be thoroughly interrogated.

Not only do they express different goals (whereas the logician seeks correctness, the computer scientist is further concerned with efficiency; whereas the mathematician examines computability, the computer scientist further addresses computational tractability) but they

---

[95] See Alonzo Church, "An Unsolvable Problem of Elementary Number Theory," *American Journal of Mathematics* 58 (Apr. 1936): 345–63. See also Church, review of "On Computable Numbers, with an Application to the Entscheidungsproblem" by A. M. Turing, *Journal of Symbolic Logic* 2 (March 1937): 42–43.

[96] Willard Van Orman Quine, *Mathematical Logic* (New York: W. W. Norton, 1940), p. vii and p. 166.

encapsulate distinct models of agency and dispositions of knowledge. Encyclopedic projects like Knuth's tackle the variety of distinctions that are elaborated in the new discourse of computing, formulating taxonomies and establishing criteria for analysis. For such a science, intervening steps can no longer be the mere means of those initiated into the workings of algorithmic rules but become legible as an object of knowledge in their own right, liable to specification within a regime of classification. The waning fortunes of an orthographic subject are thus directly entwined with a shift in emphasis towards sequential operation. An account of algorithms from this juncture, such as A. A. Markov's *Theory of Algorithms* (1954), would have determined that even notions like "generally comprehensible prescription" lacked sufficient precision, requiring "some regulation of the prescription," such that "applying the algorithm will then consist of separate elementary steps."[97] Markov's appraisal of a link associating the "generally comprehensible" with "elementary steps" suggests the arrival of a competing idiom to that drawing on a calculus of graphical inscriptions and its equivalence between the algorithmic and the symbolic—as Turing infamously claimed, "intelligence" (general comprehension) was instead to be defined in terms of "computing machinery" (step-based operation).[98]

Two episodes at the end of the 1950s are especially noteworthy in the rather abrupt shift that has set the course of the algorithm concept up to today. First, beginning in February 1960, a new section of the *Communications of the ACM*, a professional journal of the Association for Computing Machinery, was established. Published under the title, "Algorithms," this editorial department collected "algorithms consisting of 'procedures' and programs in the ALGOL

---

[97] A. A. Markov, *Theory of Algorithms*, trans. Jacques J. Schorr-Kon et al. (Jerusalem, 1961), p. 59 and p. 63.

[98] See A. M. Turing, "Computing Machinery and Intelligence," *Mind* 49, no. 236 (October 1950): 433–60.

language."[99] Contributions of this sort had been regularly submitted and requested prior to this but not necessarily named as such—only following its institution did the algorithm concept become the definitive term of choice.[100]

A second transformation is related. Between 1958 and 1959, what had initially been called the International Algebraic Language (IAL) was renamed ALGOL, short for *ALGO*rithmic *Language*. The language specification was a joint project between the ACM and their German counterparts, the GaMM (Gesellschaft für Angewandte Mathematik und Mechanik, or Association for Applied Mathematics and Mechanics). From the early 1950s, Heinz Rutishauser had worked on "automatic programming" systems based on Konrad Zuse's *Plankalkül*—an early schema for programming, translatable as "plan" calculus, but also quite literally "plane" calculus in reference to the two-dimensionality of Zuse's notation system which took advantage of the spatial properties of the surface of inscription.[101] Inspired by Rutishauser's proposal for a "unified algorithmic notation," Hermann Bottenbruch suggested the expression, "algorithmic language." This was quickly adopted by his European colleagues and subsequently accepted as the project's new title.[102]

---

[99] "Algorithms: Announcement," *Communications of the ACM* 3, issue 2 (February 1960): 73.

[100] For an example of one such conspicuous absence of the word *algorithm*, see D. L. Shell, "A High-Speed Sorting Procedure," *Communications of the ACM* 2 (July 1959): 30–32.

[101] See Heinz Rutishauser, "Automatische Rechenplanfertigung bei programmgesteuerten Rechenmaschinen," *Zeitschrift für angewandte Mathematik und Physik ZAMP* 3, issue 4 (July 1952): 312-313. On Zuse, see Wolfgang K. Giloi, "Konrad Zuse's Plankalkül: The First High-Level, 'non von Neumann' Programming Language," *IEEE Annals of the History of Computing* 19, no. 2 (April-June 1997): 17-24.

[102] See Helena Durnová and Gerard Alberts, "Was Algol 60 the First Algorithmic Language?" *IEEE Annals of the History of Computing* 36 (Oct.–Dec. 2014): 102.

In these works, the algorithm concept seems to be situated at a threshold between its current sense and a now-defunct understanding. It might refer to *an* algorithm (such as Euclid's), i.e., the objects represented by the language. However, it also retains associations with the calculus of expression, referring to the language or notation system itself. Rutishauser emphasized this latter sense in an article from this period, suggesting the scriptural inflection that the word *algorithm* could express in 1955: "The customer [user of the computer] has to write down the formulas of his problem in a special but quite natural manner, which we call the *algorithmic writing* of the problem."[103] It seems to me quite plausible that even as late as the mid-1950s, on the cusp of the formation of computer science, Venn's evaluation that *symbolic* and *algorithmic* were equivalent might still have been legible. ALGOL was an algorithmic language in the same way that Delboeuf's logic was an algorithmic logic—these both present a "system of signs."

One can speculate as to why this potential ambiguity did not survive its transatlantic passage. Perhaps the German *algorithmische* (found in Husserl) presented nuances that strained the English *algorithmic* (rejected by Venn). Perhaps Germanic intellectual traditions on programming (most notably Zuse's *Plankalkül*) encouraged dispositions more in tune with Leibnizian associations between algorithms and their calculi largely absent in Anglophone studies (stemming principally from Herman Goldstine and John von Neumann's deployment of step-based flow diagrams).

But my motivation in historicizing the algorithm concept is not the establishment of an explanatory hagiography; instead, I mean to highlight the concept's contingency and how it might otherwise be understood. While it may sound fanciful to suggest envisioning a form of algorithmic

---

[103] Heinz Rutishauser, "Some Programming Techniques for the ERMETH," *Journal of the ACM* 2, issue 1 (January 1955): 2.

processing not rooted in sequential or step-based operations, this was in fact until recently not only possible but primary. Like in the late-seventeenth and early-eighteenth centuries, the algorithm concept in the years (or maybe decades) leading up to 1958 was situated at a threshold between ascendant and soon-to-be-illegible senses. If a restricted conception has since prevailed, this reorientation was not the inevitable culmination of a grand intellectual trajectory but the byproduct of mundane and inconspicuous administrative resolutions regarding nomenclature. Historically sensitive accounts of today's so-called algorithmic culture might begin from this point, recognizing that current ordinary usage is nothing other than a hangover from that moment. Tarrying with the algorithm concept's deep history shifts the focus from that concept's fixation on automation to an assessment of the conditions which lead it to be framed in that way. More importantly, it also provides an opening for the expanded critical imaginaries for what else an algorithm could be; the following section explores one such possibility.

§1.4: Red-Black Trees: or, What Does Color Want?

In the Anglophone world, rather than Konrad Zuse's calculus, the exemplary point of reference for computer programming was Herman H. Goldstine and John von Neumann's 1947 report on the "Planning and Coding of Problems for an Electronic Computing Instrument." Their approach emphasized the control flow of logical procedures, arguing: "Since coding is not a static process of translation, but rather the technique of providing a dynamic background to control the automatic evolution of a meaning, it has to be viewed as a logical problem and one that represents a new branch of formal logics."[104] The assertion that logic "has to be viewed" must have been meant idiomatically but could also be read quite literally. To depict computational processes, Goldstine and von Neumann adopted the visual idiom of the flowchart, a schematic of the possible courses that may be taken through a coded instruction sequence. Such techniques were an established mode of representation in manufacturing and engineering, where it had been used to chart complex "material flows" since the 1920s.[105] The visual logic of flowcharting figures an industrialized condition. It maintains a clear hierarchy separating planning and coding, operating the distinction between a synoptic overview of the system as a whole and the granular perspective of movement through code—that is, between design (quite precisely as *disegno*) and execution. As a type of paper tool, it alleviates the demand to incorporate procedure, leaving the possibility of a managerial outlook aloof from the trenches of code. Under this image of programming, even those mathematically inclined would have been predisposed to associate the logical dimension of algorithms with the "planning" of control flow over the "plane" of symbolic calculi that had populated the intersection of mathematics and logic.

If, as Knuth claims, "an algorithm must be seen to be believed," the specific belief system espoused in his conception of algorithmic analysis was supported through such flowcharts. As opposed, for instance, to John Venn's diagrams—which present the static symbolism of "algorithmic logic" through their shaded territories—flowcharts are instead the spatialization of vectors. Another kind of seeing comes to the fore here in support of other cultures of beliefs;

---

[104] Herman H. Goldstine and John von Neumann, "Planning and Coding of Problems for an Electronic Computing Instrument: Report on the Mathematical and Logical Aspects of an Electronic Computing Instrument: Part II, Volume 1," (Princeton, NJ: Institute for Advanced Study, 1947), p. 2.

[105] S. J. Morris and O. C. Z. Gotel, "Flow Diagrams: Rise and Fall of the First Software Engineering Notation," in *Diagrammatic Representation and Inference: 4th International Conference, Diagrams 2006*, eds. Dave Barker-Plummer, Richard Cox, and Nik Swoboda (Berlin: Springer-Verlag, 2006), pp. 130-144.

diagrams do not just represent content, but also reify values. Whereas the former leaves the procedures of computation invisible, only concerned with the resolved outcomes, the latter renders "step-based" operation legible.

However, as historian of computing Nathan Ensmenger has observed, flowcharts would also generate a great deal of ire, as much due to the incapacity of idealized depictions to usefully and accurately express complex procedures as to the hierarchical model of work it emblematized.[106] Ensmenger points to a four-page supplement to the September 1963 issue of the data-processing journal *Datamation*, "The Programmer's Primer and Coloring Book," where the heading of one cartoon reads: "Here is a Flowchart. It is usually wrong." Beneath a collection of scribbles, a final instruction commands: "Fill in the missing lines."

The problem, in short, was that while flowcharts were conceived of and promoted as *paper tools*, they would instead be deployed as *data visualizations*. As envisioned by Goldstine and von Neumann, these diagrams were intended as a part of the construction process: it would precede the detailing of coded instructions, serving as a blueprint or design outline to be followed by subordinates. Instead, flowcharts more often functioned as "*ex post facto* justification," documenting already written code. The need for regular maintenance of code, however, meant that these diagrams were also often outdated due to the frequent changes that had to be added. Ironically then a visual apparatus geared towards the dynamics of process would act as a monument to inertia. Frederick Hosch explained the problem in 1977:

> While the program is modified and corrected, the flowchart is usually ignored, so that even if a beautifully drawn flowchart originally existed, it almost certainly bears no relationship to the program by the time it is needed. If a project manager

---

[106] See Nathan Ensmenger, "The Multiple Meanings of a Flowchart," *Information & Culture: A Journal of History* 51, no. 3 (2016): 321-351.

does succeed in having a flowchart kept up to date, after a few modifications it will be no easier to read than the associated code (although it will undoubtedly be more colorful). The end result is that it is ultimately easier to go directly to the appropriate code than to bother with the flowchart.[107]

Hosch adds a rather fitting twist to *Datamation*'s coloring book in describing the "colorful" results of repeated amendments: what Ensmenger calls the "multiple meanings" of the flowchart—an interpretive flexibility that affords a range of constituents' varied modes of grasping it—condenses a constellation of forces that surrounded computing, attesting to conflict between programmers and managerial control, as well as preserving the scars of the fraught terrain of visuality around algorithmic media.

Hosch's verbal happenstance ("colorful") calls attention to the fact that amidst the humor suggested in "The Programmer's Primer and Coloring Book," a curious discrepancy lurks: If this is a *coloring* book, why do its directions instruct the filling in of *lines*? What would a scopic regime of programming as an activity of coloring look like? Can color be anything other than an ornamental supplement to the primary task of an essential out*line*? When thinking along such lines, so to speak, color is envisioned as decorative rather than structural.[108]

1963 was a crucial year for the techniques and technologies of color—and, not just on account of *Datamation*'s coloring book. Two contrasting approaches are epitomized by, respectively, the publication of Josef Albers's book on the *Interaction of Color* and the codification of Pantone's color system. Albers's approach to color sought to develop nuances of sensitivity in students, staging a process of inculcation through which the slightest chromatic distinctions would

---

[107] Quoted in Ensmenger, "The Multiple Meanings of a Flowchart," p. 337.

[108] The prevalence of this conception in Western culture has been widely addressed. See, for example, David Batchelor, *Chromophobia* (London: Reaktion Books, 2000); Michael Taussig, *What Color Is the Sacred?* (Chicago; London: University of Chicago Press, 2009).

become apparent to the discerning eye.[109] His bearing on the problem bore only a superficial resemblance with the protocol of Pantone's notation, which instead tamed the unruly deviations within industrialized production through a color matching system. The standards set by Pantone followed decades of efforts at "color management" that attempted to establish regularity over inconsistent interpretations by quashing rather than refining the subtleties of subjective perception.[110] A designer's "red" might differ from that of a factory's, but mediated by a (proprietary) Pantone color swatch, the specific dimensions would be articulated and engineered with precision, e.g., "PMS 1795 C."

Challenges of this sort were especially severe in the chromatization of electronic imagery. Over the 1960s, as color television was normalized as a consumer standard in the United States, the recalcitrance of individual sets to perfect calibration threatened to plunge its vivid imagery into an uncanny valley: "what both sponsors and colors experts understood was that if color harmony and calibration were not practiced carefully, colors could appear 'off' and thereby disrupt the selling process."[111] This could hardly be resolved with a color swatch: the problem was not for an absence of precise notation, but arose due to the obstinacy of material substrates in agreeing to submit to disciplinary specifications. Further complicating the transition to color, the continued service of monochrome models had to be accounted for. When NTSC standards for color television were set in the 1950s, they were designed to be backward compatible with then-working standards (which, in any case, had only recently been agreed upon). The additive combination of red, green,

---

[109] Josef Albers, *Interaction of Color* (New Haven, CT: Yale University Press, 1963).

[110] On color management and the cultural history of the industrialization of color more generally, see Regina Lee Blaszczyk, *The Color Revolution* (Cambridge, MA: MIT Pres, 2012).

[111] Susan Murray, *Bright Signals: A History of Color Television* (Durham, NC; London: Duke University Press, 2018), p. 99.

and blue (RGB) electric signals was thus instead expressed through a *luminance* (or, brightness) component as the main signal, and a *chrominance* subcarrier providing "additional 'coloring' information ... transmitted simultaneously in the form of two independent signals."[112] While color receivers would take advantage of both, monochrome receivers could process the same broadcast by ignoring or filtering the chrominance, working as if only the luminance signal were transmitted. Thus, in the encoding of electronic imagery, color is treated as an appendage to form (chrominance affixed to or subtracted from luminance), rather than as an intrinsic element of it (an aggregate of red, green, and blue). This conception occurs in spite of the technical structure of cathode-ray tubes (CRTs), rather than because of it.

In search of "a more natural way to select a palette of colors" when working with early computer graphics, Alvy Ray Smith took advantage of research that had already been conducted for television. The program that he worked with when based at Xerox's Palo Alto Research Center (PARC), Dick Shoup's SuperPaint, "used the same electronic technology [as television], that of broadcast video." For Smith, however, the impetus for an alternate notation system to the RGB fed into CRT monitors was legacy cultural paradigms rather than legacy hardware: "RGB space controls are the natural ones for computer graphics and video, but I had trouble mixing, say, pink or brown with them." Smith instead preferred "the more intuitive hue-based world that [he] knew from painting: Mix a color by choosing a base with the desired hue; add white or black paint to lighten or darken it. So pink and brown are just red lightened with white and darkened with black, respectively."[113]

---

[112] See W. R. G. Baker, "The Future of Color Television," *Proceedings of the IRE* 42 (January 1954): 5-7, here p. 5. See also, Murray, *Bright Signals*, pp. 86-126.

[113] Alvy Ray Smith, "Digital Paint Systems: An Anecdotal and Historical Overview," *IEEE Annals of the History of Computing* 23, issue 2 (April-June 2001): 12.

Thus, the prevalence of "paint" as a metaphor in computer graphics is not merely a sentimental anachronism, but quite deeply inscribed within its technical standards. In his 1978 article presenting the technical details of his "alternate models of the RGB monitor gamut" for the "digital control of color television monitors," Smith offered two systems: one based on hue, saturation, and value (HSV); the other based on hue, saturation, and brightness (HSL; *L* referring to *luminance*). The first two dimensions, *H* and *S*, were shared across both models: "hue is the dimension with points on it normally called red, yellow, blue-green, etc. Saturation measures the departure of a hue from achromatic, i.e., from white or gray." Only the third, V or L, diverged. The rationale behind their difference derived from their intended applications:

> The distinction between value and brightness is important. It is illustrated by this example: Red, white, and yellow all have the same value (no blackness), but red has one third the brightness of white (using definition L_U [defined earlier as: $L_U = (R + G + B)/3$, i.e. luminance = the aggregate of red, green, and blue normalized over the appropriate range]), and one half the brightness of yellow. The principal distinction between the two is the manner in which the pure (fully saturated) hues are treated. There is a plane containing all pure hues in HSV space, but not in HSL space. Hence V would be used where the pure hues are to be given equal weight—e.g., in a painting program. L would be used where colors must be distinguished by their brightness—e.g., in choosing colors for an animated cartoon such that the colors are distinguishable even on a black-and-white television receiver.[114]

Smith's tenure at Xerox PARC was brief. When Xerox's personnel office initially refused to sanction his hire, he was requisitioned through less official channels as a purchase order, effectively resulting in an employment status equivalent to that of a piece of furniture. Several months later, amidst departmental strife, his purchase order was cancelled.

---

[114] Alvy Ray Smith, "Color Gamut Transform Pairs," *ACM SIGGRAPH Computer Graphics* 12, issue 3 (August 1978): p. 12 and p. 13.

In his account of the PARC's so-called Golden Age, Michael Hiltzik describes Smith and Shoup's attempt to develop digital video in the 1970s as "the only invention too farsighted even for PARC's Computer Science Lab ... all because it thought in color." Management, Hiltzik argues, was "constitutionally unable to imagine color contributing anything other than window-dressing," an attitude keeping with prevailing cultural perspectives that consider color to be a merely epiphenomenal effect.[115] Reflecting on his rejection decades later in 2001, Smith still conveyed a sense of dismay, describing the preference for black-and-white as "flabbergasting":

> Bad timing. Xerox chose then to pull the rug out—deciding not to do color! I was dumbfounded. This was like a major film studio deciding, in the 1930s, not to do sound. I was convinced that color was the future of computer pictures, that Xerox had the lead on the world. I tried to argue this vision to my managers, Jerome Elkind and Bob Taylor, but they informed me that it was a "corporate decision" to go with black and white—silent movies were good enough.[116]

Failure to recognize the potential in color is yet another contribution to the mythology of PARC, a site canonized as much for its seminal contributions to personal computing, as for Xerox's inability to capitalize on innovations developed there. Smith's condemnation was a history of victors, benefitting from the security of retrospective assessment: not only had it become clear that monochromatic graphics was not "good enough," Smith had by then himself become the founder of a "major film studio," Pixar.

Color had in fact been a marginal but steady concern at Xerox since its earliest ventures into photocopying. Chester Carlson had included a brief claim describing the possible applicability of his invention in "Color Photography" as part of his initial 1939 patent for "Electrophotography,"

---

[115] Michael Hiltzik, *Dealers of Lightning: Xerox PARC and the Dawn of the Computer Age* (New York: HarperCollins, 1999), p. 229 and p. 238; see also, on Shoup, Smith, and SuperPaint, pp. 229-241.

[116] Smith, "Digital Paint Systems," p. 10.

the process which Xerox would market as Xerography (competitors making use of the same techniques would, however, continue to refer to electrophotography in their own patent applications to downplay the claims Xerox maintained over the process):

> It has already been mentioned that colored powders may be used in developing the image. It is thereby possible to produce a copy in any color, either the same as or different from that of the original.
>
> The process can also be used for multi-color photography by exposing a plate first to the original through light filters which enable one color to be recorded, and then developing with colored powder to produce a copy of that color, then repeating for each other color and superimposing the dust images on the same copy sheet.[117]

Decades later, researchers at PARC extended Carlson's ideas in the development of laser printing, a technology involving comparable principles to xerography. If color is emblematic of Xerox "fumbling the future," as the title of one book puts it, the monochromatic laser printer seems to represent the opposite: a commercial success, indicating the possibility that PARC's research endeavors could be translated into viable products.[118] After nearly a decade stalled in product development, a commercial black-and-white model, the Xerox 9700, was presented to company executives in 1977 at a corporate demo in Boca Raton dubbed, "Futures Day."

Alongside it, a color prototype named the Pimlico made its debut as well. Alas, unlike its monochromatic counterpart, the Pimlico's "futures" did not extend far beyond the confines of PARC's laboratories—at least not as a working product. Color laser printing would not reach

---

[117] Chester Carlson, Electrophotography, US Patent 2,297,691, filed 4 April 1939, and issued 6 October 1942, https://patents.google.com/patent/US2297691A/en, p. 6.

[118] See Douglas K. Smith and Robert C. Alexander, *Fumbling the Future: How Xerox Invented, then Ignored, the First Personal Computer* (San Jose; New York; Lincoln; Shanghai: toExcel, 1999).

commercial production until the mid-1990s, by which time Xerox had long since lost its eminence as perhaps *the* premier site for cutting-edge technological innovation.

As the Pimlico was quietly retired from public view, two researchers visiting PARC for the academic year would open another episode of chromatism. Their work would find more success. The "red-black trees" that computer scientists Leo J. Guibas and Robert Sedgewick proposed in their 1978 paper, "A Dichromatic Framework for Balanced Trees," have since become a standard—indeed, perhaps the *de facto*—means of implementing balanced binary trees, adopted in standard libraries of popular programming languages like Java and C++.[119] According to Guibas, the name, red-black tree, owes its rather vivid styling to quotidian origins: they "had red and black pens for drawing the trees."[120]

In this regard, they might be considered a descendent of Maxwell's "apparatus of pen, ink, and paper." However, this version of events is complicated by a competing account from the paper's other author. In Sedgewick's recollection, PARC's mythic reputation features more prominently. Aware of a project on color laser printing their colleagues had developed, he and Guibas were eager to sample its goods—amongst the available colors, red printed the best.[121]

The latter's anecdote would, surely, have been a reference to the model presented at Futures Day just a year before the publication of Guibas and Sedgewick's paper. Media archaeologists delight in excavating the dead-ends of artifacts like the Pimlico. However, the idiosyncrasies

---

[119] Leo J. Guibas and Robert Sedgewick, "A Dichromatic Framework for Balanced Trees," *19th Annual Symposium on Foundations of Computer Science* (1978): 8-21.

[120] "Where does the term 'Red/Black Tree' come from?" Stack Exchange, https://softwareengineering.stackexchange.com/questions/116614/where-does-the-term-red-black-tree-come-from.

[121] "Red-Black BSTs," lecture presented as part of the course, Algorithms, Part I | Coursera, https://www.coursera.org/lecture/algorithms-part1/red-black-bsts-GZe13.

around color laser printing at Xerox warn of the hazards that might be encountered in any attempts at reanimation. Even as one imagines the lonely prototype impounded on a corporate campus—a ruin from "futures" that never would be—declarations of extinction were perhaps premature. It was neither quite *dead* nor can it really be said to have suffered an *end*. Sedgewick's tale suggests something of an artifactual afterlife, in which a media technical phantom seems to have embarked on the perilous voyage from one realm to another.

In computer science, *trees* are a fundamental data structure for a range of operations, including search, insertion, deletion, merging, and splitting. *Balanced* trees establish a limit on the asymptotic runtime of key operations like search and insertion, allowing them to be completed in logarithmic time. That is, they ensure that the maximum amount of computation which has to be performed to complete the operation grows at a much slower rate than the size of the dataset: in an unbalanced tree of a billion elements, it might take as many as a billion comparisons to search or insert an element (it grows linearly, at the same rate as the input); in a balanced tree, however, it would take only around thirty comparisons (it grows logarithmically). It is easy to see why these concerns over algorithmic efficiency, exemplary of what Knuth called the "analysis of algorithms," are of interest to computer scientists: they may result in a decisive difference between a program that is feasible and one that is not.

Guibas and Sedgewick's project might be thought of (to use Aho, Hopcroft, and Ullman's supplement) as a practice of "design"—but perhaps not one expressed as *disegno*. They introduce their own approach with reference to an existing self-balancing search tree, the "2-3 tree," a type of tree comprising of 2-nodes and 3-nodes. The novelty offered in their paper was "to represent a 2-3 tree as a binary tree" by coloring its nodes: external (or, "explicit") links in the 2-3 tree are designated *black*, and 3-nodes are "binarized" as a series of 2-nodes with a connection indicated by a *red* link. "Within this framework," Guibas and Sedgewick note, "we were able to develop new algorithms which perform as well but are significantly simpler than the classical algorithms."[122]

What was at stake in this reformulation? If algorithmic analysis is central to computer science, what kind of work is expected from the computer scientist? What is the nature of the scholarly intervention that Guibas and Sedgewick are performing? Above all, what is the significance in their move from a property nearly synonymous with the digital—i.e., *number* ("2-3")—to one that seems incompatible with such logic—i.e., *color* ("red-black")?

Their contribution, clearly, was not speed; that is, it was not the standard basis by which algorithms are analyzed and measured. It may seem self-evident that a simpler implementation is preferable to the more convoluted, but contextualization with contemporaneous work on algorithms shows the irregularity of foregrounding such concerns. On this matter, the direction conventionally taken by computer scientists is echoed in reflections by cultural theorists on automation, where the critical imaginary commonly describes the algorithm as a "black box," another chromatic—or, more precisely, *a*chromatic—model.[123] The black box is an abstraction that reduces a system to its input and output by occluding its inner workings. By contrast, a "dichromatic framework" promises a visualization and conceptualization of computational procedures. In other words, whereas the former is primarily concerned with effects resulting from the *technology* of computers, the latter displaces focus onto the *techniques* of computing. To borrow terminology from their colleagues at PARC, it might be said that Guibas and Sedgewick

---

[122] Guibas and Sedgewick, "A Dichromatic Framework for Balanced Trees," p. 20.

[123] See, for example, Pasquale, *The Black Box Society*.

introduce the problem of usability into the design of algorithms: their red-black tree offers a more user-friendly experience—"significantly simpler," as they put it.

Perhaps red-black trees are best thought of as *second-order algorithms*—a sort of algorithm about algorithms; or, the reflexive interrogation and reconfiguration of what an algorithm is and does through the medium of an algorithm itself.[124] They do not merely function as the logical substrate to other media like films or novels—in this capacity, red-black trees would function no differently from 2-3 trees—but are themselves symbolic material, an immanent expression of their cultural conditions.

Color makes a deliberate appeal to the human sensorium, addressing the algorithm as an engine for envisioning. In its medial capacity, algorithmic visuality participates in a revaluation of sense, working in the gap distinguishing varied modalities of code. When presented as an *algorithm* rather than as a *program*, code becomes an example, and functions according to such a logic; it *can* work, but it *does* not. It is printed in journal articles and textbooks, not compiled or interpreted as software; it is read by humans, not machines. Samples of algorithms are not intended to be blindly copied wholesale into working programs—i.e., not intended as a black box—but function as part of a pedagogical apparatus that targets capacities for reasoning.

Yet, the sensuality of chromatism should not be mistaken as an appeal to ahistorical biologism. The red-black tree becomes possible as a form of algorithmic media only under conditions of advanced machinery and institutional alienation, when procedures have been

---

[124] In speaking of the reflexive examination of the algorithmic through algorithms, I have in mind media theoretical work that defines cultural techniques as "second-order techniques." See Thomas Macho, "Second-Order Animals: Cultural Techniques of Identity and Identification," trans. Michael Wutz, *Theory, Culture & Society* 30, no. 6 (November 2013): 44-45; and Bernhard Siegert, *Cultural Techniques: Grids, Filters, Doors, and Other Articulations of the Real*, trans. Geoffrey Winthrop-Young (New York: Fordham University Press, 2015), p. 11.

externalized and demand coordination between distinct actors, rather than smoothly incorporated and inhabited with immediacy. Color, in this context, teases the promise of sensorial engagement with the technical apparatus, raising the hope that through the "computer sciences," an epistemic culture headed towards "opacity" and "impenetrability" might be made meaningful, perhaps even a habitable milieu.

The best indication of the vicissitudes encountered by color in its flirtations with algorithmic visuality may be found in the raw traces of Guibas and Sedgewick's published text, including their diagrams of supposedly "red-black" trees—printed, however, entirely in black-and-white. Pens and printers may have haunted its inscription, but they would leave no stain on paper. If color, in 1978, signified a certain potential, it was to remain precisely just that: something yet to be realized.

Chapter 2: Turology, An Imaginary History of Computer Programming

§2.1: Decorative Programming Languages

A defining trait of cognitive science is its recourse to a computer metaphor of mind. Its interdisciplinary program of research is premised on the claim that the mind is a computer, or at any rate that mental activity can be studied in computational terms—"the faith," as Howard Gardner put it, "that central to any understanding of the human mind is the electronic computer."[1] Given this tight coupling, it would not be entirely inaccurate to consider the emergence of cognitivist accounts in the late 1950s a historical development inextricable from the contemporaneous maturation of modern computing technologies. Yet, such a description is also somewhat misleading in that it frames the association between these two spheres in terms of a relation between a solid referent and its analogical reflection, as if computing provided a stable and immutable ground from which psychology was remodeled, the latter supposedly rooted in or drawing on the former. Rather, they might better be understood as having developed in tandem; the reformulation of mind also involved a redefinition of the computer. Indeed, whereas the key developments that propelled the coagulation of cognitivism took place in 1956—notably, the presentations of Noam Chomsky's "Three Models of Language," Allen Newell and Herbert Simon's "Logic Theory Machine," and George A. Miller's "The Magical Number Seven," all introduced publicly on the same day at a symposium held at MIT in September that year[2]—the

---

[1] Howard Gardner, *The Mind's New Science: A History of the Cognitive Revolution* (New York: Basic Books, 1985), p. 6). Likewise, Margaret Boden defines cognitive science as "the interdisciplinary study of mind, informed by theoretical concepts drawn from computer science and control theory" (*Mind as Machine: A History of Cognitive Science* [Oxford; New York: Oxford University Press, 2006], p. 12).

[2] For Miller's reflections on the development of the cognitive revolution, see George A. Miller, "The Cognitive Revolution: A Historical Perspective," *TRENDS in Cognitive Sciences* 7, no. 3 (March 2003): 141-144. On broader developments in the social sciences in that moment, see Hunter Heyck, *Age of System: Understanding the Development of Modern Social Science* (Baltimore: Johns Hopkins Press, 2015), esp. "Chapter 3: The Magical Year 1956, Plus or Minus One," pp. 81-125.

earliest known published use of the word, *software*, in today's familiar sense dates to 1958, two years after the so-called "cognitive revolution" had been launched and more than a decade after the production of the first electronic digital computers.

It was specifically the traits foregrounded in an idiom of software that were appealing for cognitivist theories. These posed a figure through which a putative mind of the computer could be decoupled from its material body. Alongside affiliated regimes like the linguistic conception of programming and the acceptance of algorithmic abstraction as the normative unit of computer scientific analysis (both also initiated in 1958), software afforded a basis for conceiving of the computer as "an infinitely protean machine," capable of being addressed independently from its underlying machinery—that is, removed from the electronics of its *hardware*.[3] As historians of computing have pointed out, however, it was in fact the latter that had received priority in the modern computer's earliest years. The task of designing architectures for electronic machinery was deemed the proper vocation of scientists and engineers. By contrast, the coding of instructions was seen primarily as a matter of translation, and hence associated with the manual and menial clerical labor of transcription practices—a chore best left to the scribes.[4]

---

[3] David Nofre, Mark Priestley, and Gerard Alberts, "When Technology Became Language: The Origins of the Linguistic Conception of Computer Programming, 1950-1960," *Technology and Culture* 55, no. 1 (January 2014): 44.

[4] See Nathan Ensmenger, *The Computer Boys Take Over: Computers, Programmers, and the Politics of Technical Expertise* (Cambridge, MA: MIT Press, 2010): "Of all the unanticipated consequences of the invention of the electronic computer in the mid-1940s, the most surprising was the sudden rise to prominence of the computer programmer. While the computer revolution itself might not have been unforeseen, the role of the computer programmer in bringing about that revolution certainly was. In all of the pioneering computer projects of this period, for example, programming was considered, at best, an afterthought. It was generally assumed that coding the computer would be a relatively simple process of translation that could be assigned to low-level clerical personnel. … Computer programming began as little more than an afterthought in most of the pioneering wartime electronic computing projects, an offhand postscript to what was universally regarded as the much more pressing challenge of hardware development" (p. 29 and p. 34).

For personnel in this nascent industry, the difficult process of revaluation through which the occupation of computer programming would achieve respectability was wrought with anxieties over professional identity. It was, above all, imperative that social distinction be maintained. A letter addressed to the *Communications of the ACM*, a forum of members from the Association for Computing Machinery, lamented how poor branding had hamstrung the legibility of this role within the popular imaginary. "What," that correspondent had wondered, "is your reply when someone asks your profession?"[5] Options available in April 1958 were methodically listed, but solely for rhetorical effect, as if merely spelling them out sufficed as evidence of their inadequacy; they were clearly regarded as unsatisfying:

> Computing Engineer? Numerical Analyst? Data Processing Specialist? To say "Computer" sounds like a machine, and "Programmer" has been confused with "Coder" in the public mind (if your particular segment of the public knows what you are talking about at all!). It would help our profession to be widely recognized if it had a brief, definitive, and distinctive name.

Envious glances were cast towards more established peers who, it was believed, had secured a rank befitting their standing. And why shouldn't those working *with* computers—not *as* computers!—be allowed this courtesy? "Consider the solid professional sound of such terms as 'Petroleum Engineer' or 'Nuclear Physicist.' What can we use that will be equally clear-cut—and at least half as impressive? So far our ideas have been supremely uninspired. Any suggestions?"

Serious resolution would have to wait—it would only be in 1965 that the title of "software engineer" was introduced. In the meantime, the editor of the *Communications* compiled a "facetious" shortlist of candidates, none of which could have been mistaken as in any way viable:

---

[5] "Letters to the Editor," *Communications of the ACM* 1, issue 4 (April 1958): all quotes from p. 6.

"Turingineer, Turologist, Flow-Chartsman, Applied Meta-Mathematician and Applied Epistomologist [sic]."

This chapter expands on that editorial jest. It could, perhaps, be read as a history of Turology. My selection of topic undoubtedly appears lacking in promise, not least due to the limited reach the proposal achieved; the above quote is to my knowledge the sole reference to this imaginary discipline. Yet, perhaps precisely due to its abbreviated existence, the term also affords some leverage into a crucial moment in the history of modern computing, pointing at a juncture of multiple incongruent trajectories as they were condensed within a single entity. It catches a chronological interstice, a moment when the figure of the software engineer was no longer completely unthinkable but yet also not quite inevitable. As such, pursuing this heading might also be considered an antidote to analytic formations such as software studies, which are founded on the assumption of software's prevalence rather than an interrogation of the circumstances conditioning its very possibility. Instead, Turology avails a means to broach the shifting epistemological and ontological regimes implicated within the cultural politics of labor in the era of modern computing, charting a genealogy of disembodiment in which cognition came to be affixed to computing and dematerialization considered a corollary symptom of digitization.

The swift deification of Turing as the supposed inventor of the computer following his death in 1954 is perhaps symptomatic of the triumph of a certain conception of the computer above others, suggesting the ascendence of the universal *Turing* machine (software) as paradigmatic, as opposed for instance to the *von Neumann* architecture (hardware) implemented as standard in modern computing machinery. Nevertheless, Turing's adoption as mascot for the white-collar computing practitioner remains especially ironic given that his reputation was founded precisely on a recalcitrance towards professionalization. In this regard, the institutionally savvy polymath,

John von Neumann (who died soon after Turing in 1957 from cancer, possibly a result of his work on nuclear weaponry), should surely have been the more likely candidate for martyrdom as model worker. Fluent across the entirety of mathematics, von Neumann was, more importantly, also capable of overseeing its application in large-scale projects. Despite this, not only was the possibility of Neumannnomics overlooked, in subsequent decades the gulf in cultural iconicity has widened to such an extent that a recent popular history focusing on von Neumann's contributions to modern computing's early years even perversely bears the title, *Turing's Cathedral*.[6]

On the other hand, anecdotes of "Prof.," as Turing was honorarily nicknamed—even receiving priority to the title over actual university professors—invariably depict him floating on a plane of abstraction, seemingly insulated from the affairs of mere mortals.[7] Exemplary in this regard was his feud with J. R. Womersley, his supervisor in the immediate postwar years. Hierarchy counted for little to the former, who quickly and quite plainly made his lack of regard for management known. As Superintendent of the Mathematics Division at the National Physical Laboratory (NPL), Womersley was a channel through the intricacies of governmental offices, mediating between sources of funding and the workers assembled to construct an early digital computer, the Automatic Computing Engine (ACE). Although fluent in the techniques of bureaucracy—his skills included: "a mastery of name-dropping, a genial enthusiasm, a pleasant office manner to important visitors, a diplomatic sense of what to report"[8]—Womersley's aptitude

---

[6] George Dyson, *Turing's Cathedral: The Origins of the Digital Universe* (Pantheon Books: New York, 2012).

[7] "Another exception to the general use of Christian names was Turing, but this was not because of any need of formality with the head of Hut 8: he was widely known by his nickname, Prof., even during the short time when an actual university professor was working with us." See Joan Murray (née Clarke), "Hut 8 and naval Enigma, Part I," in *Codebreakers: The Inside Story of Bletchley Park*, eds. F. H. Hinsley and Alan Stripp (Oxford; New York: Oxford University Press, 1993), p. 114.

[8] Andrew Hodges, *Alan Turing: The Enigma* (Princeton, NJ; Oxford: Princeton University Press, 2014), p. 398, hereafter abbreviated *AT*.

at mathematics was no match, to say the least, for his subordinate's. Turing's biographer, Andrew Hodges, recounts a bet amongst Division staff challenging any to accomplish the feat of extracting an equation from their boss: "it was abandoned and conceded, Alan reported, 'for lack of entries'" (*AT*, p. 398).

A disagreeable atmosphere thus prevailed at the NPL. Would Womersley meekly retreat in shame? Should he concede Turing's superiority and thereby restore a fragile peace? Surely not! He had, after all, talents of his own—and could stand his ground on *those* terms: "Conversely, Womersley would show visitors round Cromer House, pointing at the Turing office from afar with exaggerated awe, and saying 'Ah, that's Turing, we mustn't disturb *him*,' as of some rare zoological exhibit" (*AT*, p. 398).

Hodges attributes an inability to appreciate institutional finesse to rigorous belief in and commitment to "rational argument"; Turing, he claims, "was still the least political person" (*AT*, p. 398). This line of rhetoric leaves me perplexed. Juvenile stunts of the sort Turing and his colleagues indulged in seem to me precisely the stock of office *politics*, in the most pejorative sense that Hodges intends.

It is, for this reason, particularly difficult to assess Turing's place as a character in such historical narratives as their depictions suggest a recursive application. That is, if the *standards* of what Hodges calls "rational argument" are accepted, the biographical *scope* of the narrative he wrote should be dismissed as irrelevant, mere gossip; the dichotomy thematized between rationality and sociality maps back onto the criteria through which the story should be evaluated, and, as Wolfgang Ernst points out, the inevitable conclusion is that the life of Turing should itself be processed in the machinic terms of signals processing, "archaeographically" not "historio- or biographically":

As expressed in Andrew Hodges' Turing 'bio'-graphy, *Enigma*, instead of narrativizing Turing with its 'life' effects, his existence should be approached in discrete states, as expressed by the collection of his papers at the Archives of King's College, Cambridge. Man, when operating symbol manipulation on squared paper with a pencil and eraser, is in a non-affective 'paper machine' state, as Turing's text 'Computing Machinery and Intelligence' from 1951 explicitly self-expresses. What humans, when reading his papers in the archives, anthropomorphize as 'Turing' should be read and written rather archaeographically than historio- or biographically—as Turing-machine not 'him-', but 'it'-self.[9]

Historiography, following Ernst, splinters into the genres of the technical manual and the gossip column. Although Hodges projects belief in the possibility and authority of an asocial form of technical expertise, the account he writes to express this compulsively gravitates towards nothing other than the elaboration of trivia, i.e., precisely the social circumstances that Turing found himself in. There is a mismatch between ideological ambition and inherited formal means: an aspiration to expel egocentric ideals resorts to rehearsing a mode of expression dedicated to cults of personality.

These contradictions particular to the recollection of Turing's life and achievements hint at a more general set of difficulties involved in coming to terms with cultural memory as it contends with technicity. Insofar as cultural histories of computing dissect (or celebrate) its myths, they demonstrate how technology does not reside in a vacuum but is in fact laden with values and beliefs. Yet, displacing the scope of critical reflection to supposedly extra-technical domains alone merely inverts the dichotomy that Hodges delineates between sociality and technicity, shifting weight from one aspect to the other. Such a discursive style, in other words, specifies the obverse to Hodges's biographical valorization, performing the very arrangement that it seeks to dispute. Insofar as such analyses of culture shy away from addressing the dynamics of technological

---

[9] Wolfgang Ernst, "Existing in Discrete States: On the Techno-Aesthetics of Algorithmic Being-in-Time," *Theory, Culture & Society* 38, no. 7-8 (November 2020): 23.

assemblages, rather than engaging the ways they are irreducibly permeated, this withdrawal reinforces a schism between culture and technology; attempts at showing a cultural dimension to technology perpetuate their division into two mutually exclusive spheres.

Two responses to this exceptionalism of technicity as a cultural factor highlight the complications in its study but do so in subtly distinct ways. In his study of armaments in the French Revolution, historian Ken Alder points out the absurdity of neglecting the practical performance of artifacts: "Guns *kill*," he reminds us, collateralizing the meaning of material production with the potency of brute force.[10] A somewhat different sensibility is developed in media theoretical accounts that challenge the sharp delineation between "first-order techniques" (that act upon things) and "second-order techniques" (that thematize meaning symbolically). Exemplary in this regard, Bernhard Siegert has suggested a counterintuitive direction towards the cultural-technical properties of weaponry that in effect inverts the eminently sensible line of reasoning charted by Alder: "What if the arrow can be used only after it has been 'decorated'? What if said 'decoration' is part of the arrow's technical make-up?"[11] The point for both Alder and Siegert is neither to restore the primacy of functionality over symbolism nor iconography over efficacy but to trouble their clean distinction. Yet, whereas the former may stake its claim through an appeal to common sense, the latter's provocation stems from the ancillary status that (cultural) signification maintains relative to the pragmatics of (technical) operation. While there can hardly be any more obvious

---

[10] Ken Alder, *Engineering the Revolution: Arms & Enlightenment in France, 1763-1815* (Chicago: University of Chicago Press, 2010): "Guns, like all artifacts, participate in a material culture which imbues objects with meaning. But guns cannot be understood solely as cultural signifiers. As Mao and the other masters of police and armies have all too well understood, power flows out of the barrel of a gun. Guns *kill*" (p. xiii).

[11] Bernhard Siegert, *Cultural Techniques: Grids, Filters, Doors, and Other Articulations of the Real*, trans. Geoffrey Winthrop-Young (New York: Fordham University Press, 2015), p. 13.

claim that guns "prove themselves"[12] through their work in battle and acquire their value as symbols in relation to this, it is by contrast difficult to understand how decorative elements should have any impact whatsoever on the execution of combat. Siegert's approach to cultural techniques differs from scholarship on material culture in that it hinges on this asymmetry between a dominant factor and its supplement, displacing the division to instead emphasize the processing of thresholds between "first" and "second" order techniques, two apparently incommensurable domains.

My history of programming as a cultural technique follows this seemingly bizarre line of questioning, reading its role in the development of computing as an apparatus not merely encased in but thoroughly permeated with its cultural situation. Paraphrasing Siegert, I ask: *What if a programming language can be used only after it has been "decorated"? What if said "decoration" is part of the programming language's technical make-up?* These concerns animate the stakes in the brief efflorescence of the Turologist.

"Turing," B. Jack Copeland echoes in a more recent biography, "was a loner, not a team player."[13] This trait was not confined to Turing's quirks of personality alone but imbued in the character of the projects he developed. At Manchester, where he settled after moving on from the NPL, Turing's contributions to their computing machine, the Mark II, took the form of a notoriously arcane programming system which confounded basic standards of legibility. For Turing, digital computers were symbolic processors, and the sign systems they operated were a

---

[12] See again, for example, Alder, *Engineering the Revolution*: "That is because guns—unlike more purely iconographic objects—also must prove themselves in practice. A cockade may not be revolutionary unless it is red, and breeches may be reactionary if they are worn in 1794, but the color red is not inherently revolutionary, and breeches are not inherently reactionary, apart from what human memory assigns them. Whatever symbolic significance the Revolutionaries attached to the gun, they had also, presumably, to take cognizance of the performance of guns in battle.... [T]here is undoubtedly some sense in which guns (in tandem with a vast military organization) must prove themselves on the field of battle" (p. 17).

[13] B. Jack Copeland, *Turing: Pioneer of the Information Age* (Oxford: Oxford University Press, 2012), p. 139.

matter of mere convention. As noted in the *Programmers' Handbook* he wrote as a guide, any symbol was potentially replaceable with another, their meaning deriving from structural relations rather than an intrinsic association to a referent:

> There may in fact be anything from 10 to 100 different symbols used, and there is no particular need to decide in advance how many different symbols will be concerned. With an electronic computer however such a decision has to be made; the number of symbols chosen is ruled very largely by engineering considerations, and with the vast majority of machines the number is two. Machines (e.g. ENIAC) have however been made with 10 different symbols. ... There is an infinity of alternative possible conventions. However we are not obliged to choose any one of them.[14]

"It is not difficult," Turing would claim, "to see that information expressed with one set of symbols can be translated into information expressed with another set by some suitable conventions, e.g. to convert sequences of decimal digits into sequences of 0's and 1's we could replace 0 by 0000, 1 by 1000, 2 by 0100, 3 by 1100, 4 by 0010, 5 by 1010, 6 by 0110, 7 by 1110, 8 by 0001, and 9 by 1001" (*PH*, p. 2).

Quite to the contrary, however, it appears that what he considered intuitive was decidedly less apparent to everyone else. Especially for those with a technical background in engineering, rather than Turing's high scholarship of pure mathematics and formal logic, binary notation would have at the time been a novelty, an initiation into the possibility of alternatives to the default decimal numeral system.

Indeed, little concession was made to existing cultural convention. Despite admitting that "although the scale of two is appropriate for use within an electronic computer it is not suitable for work on paper, and it is not possible to avoid paper work altogether" (*PH*, p. 2), Turing proceeded

---

[14] Alan Turing, *Programmers' Handbook for Manchester Electronic Computer Mark II*, pp. 1-2, hereafter abbreviated *PH*.

from the assumption that such paper-based scribal activity was a transcription from machine-formatted output rather than an adaptation of standard mathematical notation. Most frustratingly, the place-value system implemented in the Mark II echoed the computer's electronic output, scaling incrementally from left to right rather than right to left (i.e., the number, "one," was transcribed 1000 rather than 0001; "two" as 0100 rather than 0010; etc.).

It may truly be, as Turing argued, "not difficult" to see that standard orientation may be reversed without disturbing logical coherence. Even in the more common decimal format, it is easily demonstrated that any given number can be expressed according to other conventions: "one thousand two hundred thirty-four," for instance, not written as 1234 but 4321. To insist on one over the other would surely be to ascribe a crucial place to merely decorative effects, i.e., outward manifestations which may be replaced without disrupting an underlying logic. Yet, this blatant disregard for even the most elementary habits of orthography is revealing of the attitude assumed in the construction of the Mark II's coding apparatus. Turing's symbolically inclined take on the computer led to a conception that was both highly abstract, as well as rigorously material. As Hodges points out, while "one might regard pulses as representing number, or as representing instructions," computing machinery "in fact operated not on numbers nor on instructions, but on electronic pulses" (*AT*, p. 410). This unadorned truth—that "there were no 'numbers' inside the machine, only pulses" (*AT*, p. 411)—was taken earnestly in Turing's approach. His system assumed the perspective of an individual in direct communion with a machine, not the sociotechnical space of programmers working within institutions; one could say, following Copeland, it was designed towards the disposition of "a loner, not a team player."

Regarding Turing's time at Manchester, Hodges laments in particular a missed opportunity to make good on his potential:

> The development that could have absorbed both his liberated understanding of symbolism, and his willingness to do the donkey work when necessary, was that of designing programming languages, the development he described as 'obvious' in 1947. But this was precisely what he did not do; and thus he failed to exploit the advantage that a grasp of abstract mathematics gave him. (*AT*, p. 504)

This uncharacteristic shift in Hodges's account into speculative commentary regarding what might have been rather than strict adherence to the recital of actual occurrences presents a rare instance of narrating the history of computing in a register of failure; it locates a point of entry into a historical impasse. In spite of ostensibly serendipitous circumstances, Turing's work set out in a direction that would not achieve significant traction, quickly becoming the sort of regrettable anomaly that had to be explained away as an idiosyncrasy of genius.

In 1958, a spurt of new formulations attempted to make sense of the activity of programming, indicating this moment as a critical junction in its development: the "Turingineer" and "Turologist" were accompanied by the introduction of "software" and "programming language," terminology which has proven somewhat more resilient and indeed remain familiar today. The latter is distinguished by a concern for what Turing had dismissed as "paper work." In sharp contrast to Turing's specification for the Manchester Mark II, the linguistic conception of programming outlined in the International Algebraic Language (IAL; later renamed ALGOL) took great care to accommodate existing practices of reading and writing. A transcontinental collaboration including both professional and academic institutions, it was unusual for its time in omitting reference to any particular hardware configuration, instead seeking to provide "a natural and simple medium for the expression of a large class of algorithms."[15]

---

[15] A. J. Perlis and K. Samelson, "Preliminary Report—International Algebraic Language," *Communications of the ACM* 1, issue 12 (December 1958): 8.

As such a "medium," a primary objective in its proposal held that "the new language should be as close as possible to standard mathematical notation and be readable with little further explanation," affording the possibility "to use it for the description of computing processes in publications."[16] To this end, three levels of language were defined: (1) a *Reference Language*; (2) a *Publication Language*; and (3) *Hardware Representations*. Although the reference language would be considered definitive, it was emphasized that this styling would "*not normally be used* [for] *stating problems*."[17] Rather, the task of communication was fulfilled through the use of publication languages which expressed "permissible variations of the reference language (e.g., subscripts, spaces, exponents, Greek letters) according to usage of printing and handwriting."[18] This allowed for adaptation to discrepancies across sociocultural context, sensitive to the detail that "the characters to be used may be different in different countries."[19]

Decoration was indispensable to this new linguistic conception. It was precisely the addition of ornamental embellishment that distinguishes programming languages from earlier coding systems. Whereas Turing had responded to the mutability of notation conventions by collapsing the divide between programmer and machine, the specification of IAL and ALGOL confined this to a separate level of hardware representations based on "the limited number of characters on standard input equipment." Given the need to accommodate variation across machinery, an indefinite number of such representations could be defined per "the character set of a particular computer," each "accompanied by a special set of rules for transliterating from

---

[16] Ibid., p. 9.

[17] Ibid., p. 10.

[18] Ibid.

[19] Ibid.

Publication language."[20] Thus, regardless of Turing's competencies and interests, it should be unsurprising that his work did not presage the development of programming languages. His efforts at coding on the Manchester Mark II were situated in a distinct milieu: someone working with a single machine as a frame of reference could hardly have addressed the problem of achieving compatibility across multiple devices, precisely the problem which linguistic models had been introduced to address. Programming *languages* indicate a disposition stemming from the corporate environment of team players, not loners.

The introduction of linguistic models was a landmark in the transformation of programming from notations derived from hardware to the machine-independent abstractions of software. As historians of computing have noted:

> The emergence of programming languages entailed not only a transformation in the understanding of the activity of programming, but also in the way we think of the electronic digital computer. By abstracting away from the machine, programming languages and, more generally, software came to mediate our understanding of what a computer is, leading eventually to the conceptualization of the computer as an infinitely protean machine.[21]

My interest here builds on these histories but focuses instead on specters and hesitations. The predilection towards symbolic abstraction identified in such accounts was indicative of a preference towards higher-level languages that would allow programming to be conducted in the *declarative* style of classical mathematics ("as close as possible to standard mathematical notation") rather than the *imperative* style of primitive coding systems: in the terms an influential

---

[20] Ibid.

[21] Nofre, Priestley, and Alberts, "When Technology Became Language," p. 44. See also, David Nofre, "Unraveling Algol: US, Europe, and the Creation of a Programming Language," *IEEE Annals of the History of Computing* 32, no. 2 (April-June 2010): 58-68; Mark Priestley, *A Science of Operations: Machines, Logic and the Invention of Programming* (London: Springer, 2011).

computer science textbook would later articulate, it sought to establish the scope of an idiom based on "what is" rather than the specification of "how to."[22] Yet, at the core of this push towards mathematical formalism, attention was in fact directed towards typography and chirography—the conventions of "printing and handwriting" that comprise the "paper work" Turing had been quite keen on ignoring. These specifics in the mediation of programmability preserve the troublesome status of orthographic inscription, indicating a persistence of its materialities as an irreducible problem subtending the fantasy named software. Although aspiring to the abstraction of a logical system, the concrete implementation of programming languages was unlike the purely formal grammars of Noam Chomsky which inspired them in that, as Hodges would note, computing machinery dealt neither with numbers nor even with symbols but rather with actual pulses. The extensive listing of calculi—"e.g., subscripts, spaces, exponents, Greek letters"—allude to the histories of not just a declarative style of programming but also of a decorative style of programming.

"When meanings shrink down to sentences, sentences to words, and words to letters, then no software exists either," Friedrich Kittler would assess at precisely the moment of software's apparent supremacy. I take his polemic—that "There Is No Software"—not as a denial of the plain facticity of software (*qua* industrial complex) but as rejecting the illusion of molar consistency it promulgates against the intransigence of an unruly molecular substrate—that is, the senseless operation of machinic procedures. Software's claim that it simulates a rarefied realm of purely symbolic meaning can, according to Kittler, remain compelling only until its capacities are "demonstrated in combat, when computers made it perfectly clear that they were hardware for

---

[22] Harold Abelson and Gerald Jay Sussman, with Julie Sussman, *Structure and Interpretation of Computer Programs* (Cambridge, MA: MIT Press, 1985), p. xvi; hereafter abbreviated *SICP*.

destroying enemy hardware."[23] To paraphrase Alder's truism: (programmed) missiles *kill*. But—*what if a missile can be used only after it has been "decorated"? What if said "decoration" is part of the missile's technical make-up?* As Kittler acknowledged, "compelling economic reasons have fundamentally done away with the modesty of an Alan Turing—who, during the Stone Age of the Technical Era, preferred reading machine output in binary numbers to decimal computations." Such an approach has, indeed, since become a curiosity forgotten by all except scholars of media history. In its place, Kittler continues, the tendency towards higher-level programming languages has been characterized by "hiding hardware behind software, and electronic signifiers behind human/machine interfaces."[24] This is not untrue. Yet, it is *also* only after meanings have been deflated to sentences and words and letters—and an extended set of "subscripts, spaces, exponents, Greek letters"—that software may proceed: software's overt disavowal of its material underpinnings operates in step with a furtive embrace of decorative "paper work."

Defined as the other half of a dichotomy against hardware, software presents, in Hodges's terms, an idealization of number without pulse. Lingering on the cultural-technical function of orthographic operations, however, suggests a different range of coordinates against which practices of computing may be oriented, neither hardware nor software but the medial operations that process the possibility of their distinction. The techniques deployed towards a *screening* of number from pulse will be discussed more thoroughly in Chapter 3. First, the remainder of this chapter will elaborate on the broader intellectual regimes that software participates in. Its

---

[23] Friedrich Kittler, "Protected Mode," in *The Truth of the Technological World: Essays on the Genealogy of Presence*, trans. Erik Butler (Stanford, CA: Stanford University Press, 2013), p. 209.

[24] Friedrich Kittler, "There Is No Software," in *The Truth of the Technological World*, p. 223.

conceptual apparatus is conveniently encapsulated in a description by Ted Nelson, cited by curator Jack Burnham in his catalog essay for the landmark 1970 exhibition, *Software*:

> Plans and procedures for action, as distinct from the equipment that carries the action out. Thus in a transportation system the hardware consists of cars, highways, traffic lights and policemen, while the software consists of rules, such as drive on the right, stop on a red light, etc. Another example: subway cars and tracks are hardware, routes A, E, and BB are software. Finally: our bodies are hardware, our behavior software.[25]

Where specifically did Nelson decouple software from hardware? Insofar as "bodies" were to be disregarded, this possibility is implicated within the long histories of the fraught concept, "behavior" (**§2.2**). As opposed to mere "equipment," esteem was credited to "plans" (**§2.3** and **2.4**) and "procedures" (**§2.5**).

Nelson's contribution to the exhibition proper was a "hypertext" project he had developed in collaboration with Ned Woodman, *Labyrinth: An Interactive Catalogue* (1970). It presented an "interactive text retrieval system" that demonstrated a means of engaging with texts beyond their conventional linear structure. In addition to reading text from any given section of the catalogue, a "user" of *Labyrinth* could also access related topics by typing in the relevant code. This aspiring Theseus could then claim as reward a relic that preserved a record of their adventure: "Before leaving the show, the museum goer may obtain a printout of what he himself has selected to read in the interactive catalogue by giving his name to an attendant at the line printer by the main exit."[26]

The resulting trail—exemplary of the sort of "routes" that Nelson associated with software by way of contrast to the vehicles and infrastructure of hardware—was undoubtedly the crux of

---

[25] Theodore H. Nelson cited in Jack Burnham, "Notes on art and information processing," in *Software: Information Technology: Its Meaning for Art* (New York: Jewish Museum, 1970), p. 12.

[26] Ned Woodman and Theodor H. Nelson, "Labyrinth: An Interactive Catalogue," in *Software*, p. 18.

the project, to the effect that *Labyrinth* might have more accurately been titled, *Thread* (as has in fact become idiomatic in the vernacular of hypertext networks today). There was, of course, no possibility of getting lost in the catalog, no threat of even a symbolic Minotaur to swallow unsuspecting visitors. As such, given that one could neither in any meaningful way escape nor succumb to the contraption, it can hardly be compared to a maze; the upshot here was precisely the multiple equally legitimate paths that could be traversed through the thicket of information, not the identification of a solution to be untangled.

In this regard, Nelson's vision appears somewhat tame, especially when set in contrast to another exhibit on display at *Software*. *Seek* (1969-1970), an installation by MIT's Architectural Machine Group, involved a comparatively messier predicament:

> *Seek* is a sensing/effecting device controlled by a small general purpose computer. In contrast to an input/output peripheral, *Seek* is a mechanism that senses the physical environment, affects that environment, and in turn attempts to handle local unexpected events within the environment. *Seek* deals with toy blocks which it can stack, align and sort. At the same time, these blocks form the built environment for a small colony of gerbils which live within *Seek*'s three-dimensional world.
>
> Unbeknownst to *Seek*, the little animals are bumping into blocks, disrupting constructions, and toppling towers. The result is a substantial mismatch between the three-dimensional reality and the computed remembrances which reside in the memory of *Seek*'s computer. *Seek*'s role is to deal with these inconsistencies. In the process, *Seek* exhibits inklings of a responsive behavior inasmuch as the actions of the gerbils are not predictable and the reactions of *Seek* purposefully correct or amplify gerbil-provoked dislocations.[27]

Here, agency has been displaced from the liberal fantasy of interactive users. In its place, a feral colony. "Routes"? "Plans"? "Rules"? If these are the dynamics that for Nelson constitute software, gerbils must indisputably be hardware. Resemblance to a maze is equally absent here. Indeed, the

---

[27] The Architecture Machine Group, M.I.T., "Seek," in *Software*, p. 23.

constant disturbances—*bumping, disrupting, toppling*—seems to defy the possibility of formal specification altogether. Any "routes" are liable to be blocked, the best laid "plans" left a shambles; gerbils do not play by the "rules."

Yet, I believe that a comparison with the maze has the potential to be quite suggestive in this instance, as the arrangement staged evokes the long shadows cast by an entrenched laboratory apparatus whilst enacting its schema in a markedly singular configuration. *Seek* affords its gerbils a scene unlike any prior, and consequently extends them an opportunity never availed their predecessors. No longer compelled to stand in as experimental psychology's surrogate for Ariadne, they inflicted upon the computing mechanism a fate that might have driven even Sisyphus past the point of despair. Software had inherited the cybernetic function of control engineering, responsible for the interminable task of imposing intelligence on a world of errant things. *Stack, align, sort*— order must be restored.

But, block by block, the gerbils would take their revenge.

§2.2: "Rat Theory" (I): Complications in the Behavior Concept

The "cognitive revolution" had to contend with rats. The *Rattus norvegicus domestica*, to be precise: domesticated lab rats. Less liable than their wild counterparts to protest their subjection to an endless cycle of frustrations (i.e., less likely to bite their handlers en route to experimental setups), these creatures had been the material substrate of behaviorist theory. John Broadus Watson, the founder of behaviorism, had praised the "exceedingly tame" participants of his experimental study on *Animal Education* (1903), noting that unlike the "timid and flighty" rats of other experimenters, his laboratory-raised subjects "were not disturbed by handling and at once investigated all new objects in their neighborhood."[28] Insofar as psychology would be reconceptualized over the 1950s from "the science of behavior" into "the science of mental life," this resuscitation of factors involving the mind was less a contest of ideas than the pursuit to secure a sustained partnership with rats.[29] After all, without their enthusiastic exertions, what hope would there have been of accumulating the "observable reactions" needed to construct the stimulus-response models that behaviorist psychology's rigidly empirical approach was built on?

Watson was not alone in championing this apparatus of research, nor did his rats achieve a full monopoly over psychological experimentation. Just a few years later, for instance, Robert M. Yerkes explained his preference for their cousins, *The Dancing Mouse* (1907), detailing a list of vital attributes they fulfilled:

> It is small, easily cared for, readily tamed, harmless, incessantly active, and it lends itself satisfactorily to a large number of experimental situations. For laboratory courses in Comparative Psychology or Comparative Physiology it well might hold the place which the frog now holds in courses in Comparative Anatomy.[30]

With the cooperation of tame rats and dancing mice, scientists seeking insight into *human* psychology could devote their attention to observing *animals* instead. Although, as historian Rebecca Lemov has noted, "in 1908 working with animals was generally a guaranteed ticket to

---

[28] John Broadus Watson, *Animal Education: An Experimental Study on the Psychical Development of the White Rat, Correlated with the Growth of its Nervous System* (Chicago: University of Chicago Press, 1903), p. 9.

[29] Standard histories of the cognitive sciences tend to focus on the development of ideas, directing little attention to the material apparatus of experimental techniques that underwrite its claims. See, for example, Gardner, *The Mind's New Science* and Boden, *Mind as Machine*.

I take the sharp—and highly illuminating—contrast between two definitions of psychology, "the science of behavior" and "the science of mental life" (both by George A. Miller), from Hunter Crowther-Heyck, "George A. Miller, Language, and the Computer Metaphor of Mind," *History of Psychology* 2, no. 1 (1999): 37-64.

[30] Robert M. Yerkes, *The Dancing Mouse: A Study in Animal Behavior* (New York: Macmillan, 1907), p. viii.

obscurity within the field of psychology," a swift change in fate would soon follow, and "within a decade animal experimentation would become the cutting edge."[31]

A potential defection was thus no small matter. For cognitivists seeking the reintroduction of concepts dismissed as unobservable by behaviorists, such as "cognition" and "purpose," forging an alliance of their own with rats would have been quite the coup.[32] The intellectual histories of the cybernetic twentieth century have thus been plagued by a rodent infestation, symptomatic of the disjointed lines on which this conflict was waged. Aside from those clearly committed to one side or the other—*either* behaviorist *or* cognitivist—others pursued a more ambivalent mix. Edward Chace Tolman's conceptualization of "cognitive maps" was one instance of this, especially notable given the interest it would attract from domains well beyond the behavioral sciences.[33]

Tolman had introduced his concept in a 1948 article on "Cognitive Maps in Rats and Men."[34] There, he discussed the results of several studies which in his assessment demonstrated complications unexplainable in terms of straightforward stimulus-response connections. Citing an experiment initially conducted by H. C. Blodgett, Tolman noted that its findings implied a degree

---

[31] Rebecca Lemov, *World as Laboratory: Experiments with Mice, Mazes, and Men* (New York: Hill and Wang, 2005), p. 33.

[32] In speaking of defections and alliances (and protests!), I am echoing scholars like Michel Callon, whose "actor-network theory" extends sociality across human and non-human actors. Much as Callon would argue that gaining the agreement of non-humans like scallops is an "obligatory passage point" when marine biologists seek to establish scientific knowledge, here too a "domestication" of rodents is indispensable to the consistency of intellectual formations in psychology. See Michel Callon, "Some elements of a sociology of translation: domestication of the scallops and the fishermen of St Brieuc Bay," *Sociological Review* 32, issue 1 (May 1984): 196-233.

[33] On "mental mapping" in urban planning, see Kevin Lynch, *The Image of the City* (Cambridge, MA: MIT Press, 1960); and, on "cognitive mapping" in critical theory, see Fredric Jameson, "Cognitive Mapping," in *Marxism and the Interpretation of Culture*, eds. Cary Nelson and Lawrence Grossberg (Urbana; Chicago: University of Illinois Press, 1988), pp. 347-357.

[34] Edward C. Tolman, "Cognitive Maps in Rats and Men," *Psychological Review* 55, no. 4 (July 1948): 189-208.

of plasticity in rat behavior exceeding direct correspondence between incentive and conditioned response. A first group of rats that Blodgett ran as the experiment's control displayed a gradual decrease in times taken to reach the goal-box, where they expected to find food. This indicated an increasing familiarity with their surroundings, as researchers had anticipated: these rats were, so to speak, *learning* the maze. Their counterparts, on the other hand, were obliged to complete the maze as well, but were only fed in their home cages two hours after their trials. Lacking an association linking reward with destination, they showed little improvement—again, this behavior occurred as expected. However, once a bait was added, the performance of this second group in subsequent iterations revealed a sharp drop in their error curve, quickly achieving times comparable to those of their previously swifter peers in the control group. From this, Blodgett concluded that his second group of rats had also been *learning* but had simply had no interest in *demonstrating* their acquired competency. He termed this "latent learning,"[35] reflecting the function of a dimension beyond the immediately observable; Tolman's discussion would expand upon the philosophical import of this finding. Standard behaviorist reasoning had explained change in the control scenario as stemming from the strengthening of behavioral patterns, the optimal route hard-wired through repetition. But this could not account for—indeed, was contradicted by—the abrupt acceleration observed in the second test group. There was no room for latent capacities in theories based solely on physiological reflex.

Following these results, Tolman argued that the rats "had been building up a 'map,' and could utilize the latter as soon as they were motivated to do so."[36] He consolidated this claim with

---

[35] Hugh Carlton Blodgett, "The Effect of the Introduction of Reward and of Complex Incentives on Maze Performance," *University of California Publications in Psychology* 4, no. 8 (1929): 113-134.

[36] Tolman, "Cognitive Maps in Rats and Men," p. 195.

reference to a range of other experimental typologies, demonstrating through these varied tests that associations were formed beyond simple connections. This led him to conclude that "the central office is far more like a map control room than it is like an old-fashioned telephone exchange. The stimuli, which are allowed in, are not connected by just simple one-to-one switches to the outgoing responses. Rather, the incoming impulses are usually worked over and elaborated in the central control room of a tentative, cognitive-like map of the environment."[37]

The rhetorical restraint here—"cognitive-*like*," not cognitive—is crucial. Despite his rejection of the extreme reductivism dominant in psychology at the time, Tolman considered himself a behaviorist, espousing a seemingly contradictory brand of "purposive behaviorism." Earlier in his career, he had pursued this tension by coining a distinction between "molar" and "molecular" scales. These concepts were useful both in clarifying the differences in his approach from standard treatments of behavior, such as Watson's, as well as in distinguishing the scope of psychology as an autonomous discipline from other sciences that might have claimed it as a subfield belonging to their own domain, such as biology and physiology. In *Purposive Behavior in Animals and Men* (1932), Tolman defined the relation linking behavior to physical and physiological processes through an analogy with the relation between a beaker of water and the individual water molecules contained within it: observation of "molecular" detail, he argued, was an inadequate indicator for properties of aggregative or "molar" wholes. Whereas the model of a "telephone exchange" espoused by radical behaviorists like Watson had grounded psychological theories in terms of "strict underlying physical and physiological details, i.e., in terms of receptor-process, conductor-process, and effector-process per se" (that is, *molecular*), his alternative

---

[37] Ibid., p. 192.

considered "behavior-acts" to be "an 'emergent' phenomenon that has descriptive and defining properties of its own" (that is, *molar*).

> Behavior as such cannot, at any rate at present, be deduced from a mere enumeration of the muscle twitches, the mere motions *qua* motions, which make it up. It must as yet be studied first hand and for its own sake.
>
> An act *qua* "behavior" has distinctive properties of its own. These are to be identified and described irrespective of whatever muscular, glandular, or neural processes underlie them. These new properties, thus distinctive of molar behavior, are presumably strictly correlated with, and, if you will, dependent upon, physiological motions. But descriptively and per se they are other than those motions.
>
> A rat running a maze; a cat getting out of a puzzle box; a man driving home to dinner; a child hiding from a stranger; a woman doing her washing or gossiping over the telephone; a pupil marking a mental-test sheet; a psychologist reciting a list of nonsense syllables; my friend and I telling one another our thoughts and feelings—*these are behaviors* (qua *molar*). And it must be noted that in mentioning no one of them have we referred to, or, we blush to confess it, for the most part even known, what were the exact muscles and glands, sensory nerves, and motor nerves involved. For these responses somehow had other sufficiently identifying properties of their own.[38]

This new frame of reference was adopted with great "eagerness" amongst psychologists, to the extent that the molar-molecular distinction came to subsume an exceedingly broad array of meanings by the late-1940s, prompting some to suggest "that the terms be abandoned, for it does not seem possible to purge them of their confusing connotations."[39] Tolman counted amongst these mutineers, encouraging the substitution of the terms he had himself introduced earlier. His later effort, the "cognitive map," was precisely such a sharpened conceptual tool that could occupy the

---

[38] Edward C. Tolman, *Purposive Behavior in Animals and Men* (New York; London: The Century Co., 1932), p. 7 and p. 8.

[39] See Richard A. Littman and Ephraim Rosen, "Molar and Molecular," *Psychological Review* 57, no. 1 (January 1950): p. 58 and p. 65. Littman and Rosen add, in a footnote, that "Dr. Tolman has indicated that he shares this opinion as to the future role of molar and molecular (personal communication)" (p. 65f). Of course, by that time, Tolman had already introduced his substitute, the "cognitive map."

role once fulfilled through the calibration provided by a "molar" scale: it injected an intermediary space between input and output. This medial function was a key preoccupation in Tolman's theorization.

Tolman's fidelity to the behaviorist project took precedence over the mentalistic idiom he deployed. In fact, his book was prefaced with a disclaimer of his "distaste for most of the terms and neologisms [he had] introduced": "I especially dislike the terms *purpose* and *cognition* and the title *Purposive Behavior*. I have, I believe, a strong anti-theological and anti-introspectionistic bias; and yet here my words and my title seem to be lending support to some sort of an ultimately teleological and ultimately mentalistic interpretation of animal and human behavior."[40] As early as 1922, Tolman had staked the direction he intended to pursue as "A New Formula for Behaviorism," defining his strict adherence to outward (i.e., observable) behavior in terms of an objection to claims regarding inner (i.e., unobservable) states of consciousness. "Ever since the days of [Hermann] Ebbinghaus's experiments on memory," his article began, "the inadequacy of the introspective method as such has been becoming more and more obvious. And the recent work in mental tests and animal psychology has strengthened this conviction." "Consciousness," he continued, "is assumed by [introspective psychology] to be something private to each individual which he alone can analyze and report upon. And the introspective account purports to be such an analysis and report. ... Our behaviorism will reply that whether or not there is such a private something or other present in the conscious behavior situation and lacking in the unconscious one, this private something never 'gets across,' as such, from one individual to another. All the things

---

[40] Tolman, *Purposive Behavior in Animals and Men*, p. xi-xii.

that do 'get across' are merely *behavior* phenomena or the objective possibilities of such phenomena."[41]

Tolman's wariness may be most readily understood by foregrounding the dichotomy between phenomenal and noumenal dimensions. The challenge for psychologists, in particular, lay in examining attributes beyond those immediately manifest, such as the "mapping" even unmotivated rats performed in mazes. Experimentation afforded a behavioral (*qua* phenomenal) basis for making latent factors apparent, i.e., ensuring that they "get across"—it established the possibility of transmission. Given this emphasis on a communicative function, Tolman's "purposive behaviorism" might be more accurately described as a kind of media behaviorism. In his experimental apparatus, the maze was a cultural technique which processed fundamental ontological distinctions, redefining the thresholds at which the phenomenal was distinguished from the noumenal. Viewed through its lens, what was once ineffable could become sensible. Whereas those less circumspect might have taken such findings as evidence of a "cognitive" or "mental" faculty, Tolman's reluctance to adopt regular vocabulary—finding these symptoms merely "cognitive-like"—seems to stem from his resolution to decline metaphysical speculation (*qua* noumenal). Insofar as his concerns expressed a scope which was primarily negative (i.e., geared towards *dis*proving the claims of reductive behaviorism rather than constructing a system of its own), the concepts derived from it occupied a strange epistemic status, as if they were mere placeholders standing in for a hollow core. Devoid of aspirations towards solidity and permanence, the "molar" concept could thus be easily replaced by "cognitive mapping" in Tolman's vocabulary without too much trouble; his investments lay elsewhere.

---

[41] Edward C. Tolman, "A New Formula for Behaviorism," *Psychological Review* 29, no. 1 (January 1922): p. 44 and p. 47.

The determination of Tolman's dichotomy hinged, above all, on method. Unlike the experimental procedures of mentalism, animal psychology did not rely on any examination of "inner" conscious contents. Whatever their other virtues, rats and mice could hardly be counted on to observe, verbalize, and report on their thoughts and feelings. For Tolman, this scored in their favor. These targets of introspection, he had reasoned, "by very definition are said to be private and non-communicable."[42] Indeed, the tensions inciting his dilemma might be traced yet earlier still to the years he had spent as a graduate student working on an Ebbinghaus-style study of memory under the supervision of Hugo Münsterberg. Münsterberg's efforts at instituting laboratory work as standard practice in American psychological research had included advocacy for introspective self-observation, a direction Tolman had little appreciation for. Even as a student, he was already instead more attracted to the style of comparative psychology Yerkes had recently begun pursuing as a young lecturer in his department.[43] (In fact, despite their divergent methodological commitments, Yerkes had himself been a student of Münsterberg's as well, completing his dissertation on *The Dancing Mouse* under the latter's direction.[44])

---

[42] Ibid., p. 44.

[43] On Tolman's early studies, see David W. Carroll, *Purpose and Cognition: Edward Tolman and the Transformation of American Psychology* (Cambridge: Cambridge University Press, 2017), pp. 24-48. Carroll suggests that although introspection occupied a central place in Münsterberg's methodological repertoire according to Tolman's recollection, this might not quite be doing the latter full justice, noting: "It is difficult to fully reconcile Tolman's account with Münsterberg's published views on introspection, which were somewhat complex and perhaps more nuanced than Tolman acknowledged" (p. 38). It is thus perhaps appropriately ironic that the nuances in Tolman's approach would, in turn, be eroded as well in its later reception by cognitive psychologists.

[44] After achieving great success in his work on psychobiology, Yerkes would reflect fondly on his personal relation with his former advisor, but his comments on Münsterberg's methods were less favorable: "From the beginning of our acquaintance, Hugo Münsterberg, with almost paternal interest and solicitude, and with rare generosity, aided me both professionally and personally, and, although I never was able to admire him as scientist, I learned to prize highly his friendship, enthusiasm for research, and scholarship." Robert M. Yerkes, "Robert Mearns Yerkes," in *A History of Psychology in Autobiography, Volume II*, ed. Carl Murchison (Worcester, MA: Clark University Press, 1932), p. 389.
Yerkes's interests in the then-unfashionable domain of animal psychology had an adverse impact on his career prospects: "For a time it seemed that the dream [of an institute of comparative psychobiology] might speedily come true in Harvard, but President Eliot, wise and far-sighted promoter of productive scholarship and of medical

It is peculiar, however, that Tolman should have persisted in delineating his objections along these lines, especially so as debates over mentalism that he had encountered as a student would have faded by the 1930s when he coined the molar-molecular distinction. By then, animal experimentation was no longer an emerging insurgency but a firmly established approach. This commitment presented a challenging hurdle, even to sympathetic readers. One such potential supporter was the Gestalt psychologist Kurt Koffka, with whom Tolman had worked during short stints at Giessen early in his career and maintained in contact with for decades after. In a review of *Purposive Behavior*, Koffka would temper admiration for the experimental skills Tolman demonstrated with reservations over the interpretations forwarded: "I believe that many readers will feel as I do that this whole difficulty is created by Tolman's wish to be a behaviorist as well as a purposive one. He is so much afraid of falling into the snares of mentalistic theories that he sacrifices the concreteness of his own theory without being able to escape 'mentalism,' and at the risk of inconsistencies."[45] Behavior *or* purpose? Koffka's own commitments were firmly with the latter; and, he believed, the psychologist had to choose between the two, one *or* the other. Soon, the possibility of collapsing this dichotomy would prompt the articulation of the new science of cybernetics to pursue precisely the teleological implications that psychologists had disavowed.

Regardless, Tolman seems to have adopted other criteria having little to do with this discursive terrain, and if psychological schools figured in any way at all in his assessments it was

---

education and research, retired from his responsibilities just too soon. Instead of receiving encouragement in such seemingly impractical planning as I had been indulging in, I was gently and tactfully advised by the new administration that educational psychology offered a broader and more direct path to a professorship and to increased academic usefulness than did my special field of comparative psychology, and that I might well consider effecting a change" (pp. 390-391).

[45] Kurt Koffka, review of *Purposive Behavior in Animals and Men*, by Edward C. Tolman, *Psychological Bulletin* 30, no. 6 (June 1933): 442.

but as a more respectable front for his main patrons. That, at least, is the impression one gets from his declaration of indebtedness to "M. N. A.," to whom his book was dedicated. Perhaps it would come at the cost of "the concreteness of his own theory," as Koffka accused, but there was no doubt that *Purposive Behavior* was entirely contingent on the collaboration of the *Mus norvegicus albinus*.

§2.3: "Rat Theory" (II): The Cultural Techniques of Cognitivism

None of Tolman's philosophical apprehension would be retained in the turn towards cognitivism proper. Others, less sensitive to the epistemological vicissitudes of experimental research, did not share his devotion to the albino mouse. One particularly sardonic account drew attention to the undercurrents of absurdity inherent in its promotion to axiomatic status:

> For reasons that are not entirely clear, the battle between these two schools of thought [theories based, alternately, on conditioned reflexes or a cognitive faculty] has generally been waged at the level of animal behavior. Edward Tolman, for example, has based his defense of cognitive organization almost entirely on his studies of the behavior of rats—surely one of the least promising areas in which to investigate intellectual accomplishments. Perhaps he felt that if he could win the argument with the simpler animal, he would win it by default for the more complicated ones.[46]

Its authors—a trio of psychologists: George A. Miller, Eugene Galanter, and Karl H. Pribram—had little patience for Tolman's vacillation between this dichotomy, simply grouping him amongst the cognitive theorists. (Tolman would surely have objected.) This younger generation of researchers did not share a distaste for expressions like "purpose" and "cognition." Their focus in

---

[46] George A. Miller, Eugene Galanter, and Karl H. Pribram, *Plans and the Structure of Behavior* (London: Holt, Rinehart and Winston, 1960), p. 8.

writing *Plans and the Structure of Behavior* was firmly centered on outlining a positive conception of mental activity.

Plans would be a key anchor, perhaps even the founding landmark, in the establishment of the cognitive sciences. Its accomplishments in this regard required forgetting the ghosts of introspective mentalism that had constrained earlier investigations of a cognitive faculty. To this end, another approach to the practice of mapping was needed. Here, the writings of economist Kenneth Boulding were useful as a convenient proxy from which the venture of cognitivism could be launched.

Written following a stint at the Center for Advanced Study in the Behavioral Sciences at Stanford, Boulding's short tract on *The Image* was perhaps less a scholarly survey than a manifesto. Its proposal of "eiconics" as a new transdisciplinary science rooted in imaging did not so much seek to chart a rigorously argued set of claims than outline a suggestive proposal of how topics *could be* understood if posed in certain terms. Other scholars-in-residence that academic year, 1954-1955, included the systems biologist Ludwig von Bertalanffy, with whom Boulding had already been in correspondence with and was keen to engage further. The interlude appears to have provided a congenial research environment; Boulding even found it necessary to preface his book by apologizing for "a certain atmosphere of intellectual exaltation which inevitably pervades it and which no sober editing can quite remove." Right from the outset, his tract reads as a blend of genres, routing motifs broached in Edmund Husserl's phenomenology via Walter Lippmann towards a distinctly Californian vibe more likely to be taken as a cosmic meditation anticipating Charles and Ray Eames's film, *Powers of Ten* (1977):

> As I sit at my desk, I know where I am. I see before me a window; beyond that some trees; beyond that the red roofs of Stanford University; beyond them the trees and the roof tops which mark the town of Palo Alto; beyond them the bare golden

hills of the Hamilton Range. I know, however, more than I see. Behind me, although I am not looking in that direction, I know there is a window, and beyond that the little campus of Center for the Advanced Study in the Behavioral Sciences; beyond that the Coast Range; beyond that the Pacific Ocean. ... I know, furthermore, that if I go far enough I will come back to where I am now. In other words, I have a picture of the earth as round. I visualize it as a globe.[47]

Eiconics was presented as "a new science" oriented around this function of picturing. Although Boulding respectfully adhered to vocabulary from information theory, it is unclear how deeply he adhered to its principles. Instead, he seems more invested with reconciling information with a hermeneutic sensibility: "We must distinguish carefully between the image and the messages that reach it. The messages consist of *information* in the sense that they are structured experience. *The meaning of a message is the change which it produces in the image.*"[48]

Miller and his colleagues might perhaps have appreciated Boulding's approving reference to Gestalt psychology; they undoubtedly would have celebrated the categorical rejection of behaviorist doctrine he forwarded in *The Image*. "The attempt to interpret the organism as a stimulus-response slot machine was terribly good for the rat business," Boulding had determined,

---

[47] Kenneth E. Boulding, *The Image* (Ann Arbor: University of Michigan Press, 1956), p. 3.
It is difficult to avoid a comparison of this passage with Husserl's writings, which narrated an account of consciousness according to an analogous structure: "I am conscious of a world endlessly spread out in space, endlessly becoming and having endlessly become in time. I am conscious of it: that signifies, above all, that intuitively I find it immediately, that I experience it. By my seeing, touching, hearing, and so forth, and in the different modes of sensuous perception, corporeal physical things with some spatial distribution or other are *simply there for me, 'on hand'* in the literal or the figurative sense, whether or not I am particularly heedful of them and busied with them in my considering, thinking, feeling, or willing. ... But it is not necessary that they, and likewise that other objects, be found directly in my *field of perception*. Along with the ones now perceived, other actual objects are there for me as determinate, as more or less well known, without being themselves perceived or, indeed, present in any other mode of intuition. I can let my attention wander away from the writing table which was just now seen and noticed, out through the unseen parts of the room which are behind my back, to the verandah, into the garden, to the children in the arbor, etc., to all the Objects I directly 'know of' as being there and here in the surroundings of which there is also consciousness – a 'knowing of them' which involves no conceptual thinking and which changes into a clear intuiting only with the advertence of attention, and even then only partially and for the most part very imperfectly" (Edmund Husserl, *Ideas Pertaining to a Pure Phenomenology and to a Phenomenological Philosophy—First Book: General Introduction to a Pure Phenomenology*, trans. F. Kersten [The Hague: Martinus Nijhoff Publishers, 1983], pp. 51-52).

[48] Boulding, *The Image*, p. 7.

"but it certainly was not eiconics."⁴⁹ I suspect, however, that even if Boulding had neglected to mention theories of psychology altogether, his sketch would have fulfilled their needs just fine. As an interlocutor from a foreign discipline, Boulding offered the benefits not only of an expansive outlook that encompassed a variety of fields (touching on biology, sociology, politics, history, philosophy, as well as psychology and economics), but also of a liberated attitude towards the intricacies of scholarly tradition. That is to say, whereas Tolman saw himself (and his mice) as participating in a conversation with peers and predecessors, Boulding was not bound by—or, perhaps, was simply not aware of—the feuds which had been waged over generations.⁵⁰ As Hunter Crowther-Heyck has noted, Miller's professionalization as a scientist had been shaped by his formative wartime experience as a military research worker, and the attitude he assumed would be especially influenced by organizational formations which had little investment in disciplines and their autonomy: "The military, though very concerned with discipline, was not interested in disciplines. The military approach to a research problem was to assemble an interdisciplinary team of experts oriented around the task at hand. For example, in his communications research, Miller, a psychologist, worked with engineers, physicists, mathematicians, and linguists."⁵¹ A willingness to accommodate Boulding's musings was perhaps one result of this inclination towards scientific interdisciplinarity. Another perhaps more significant consequence was the abstraction of theories from the contexts in which they were formed and the questions that had prompted them: *what* had

---

⁴⁹ Ibid., p. 151.

⁵⁰ Boulding later expressed his surprise at the significant role his "little book" had played in the burgeoning literature on cognitive mapping, and that he had not even encountered Miller, Galanter, and Pribram's seminal book "until long after it was published": "as far as I knew," he confessed, "it had never penetrated the boundary of the behavioral sciences, for whose benefit it was ostensibly written." See Kenneth E. Boulding, "Foreword," in *Image and Environment: Cognitive Mapping and Spatial Behavior*, eds. Roger M. Downs and David Stea (Chicago: Aldine Publishing, 1973), pp. vii-xi.

⁵¹ See Crowther-Heyck, "George A. Miller, Language, and the Computer Metaphor of Mind," p. 43.

been written would be detached from *why*; Tolman's introduction of "cognitive-like" mapping would be decoupled from his residual attachment to behavior and skepticism towards the cognition concept.

In this regard, Boulding's articulation of an "Image" was useful primarily insofar as it provided a foil in the development of an alternative. This alternative was the eponymous Plan. As Miller *et al.* defined it, a Plan "*is any hierarchical process in the organism that can control the order in which a sequence of operations is to be performed*" (*PSB*, p. 16).

Their amendment from Image to Plan was, however, but one part of the thesis developed. More startlingly, *Plans* advanced an analogy that linked the processes of planning with the subroutines of computers, and thereby humans with machines: "A Plan is, for an organism, essentially the same as a program for a computer" (*PSB*, p. 16). The most immediate spur to this provocation was the success that Allen Newell and Herbert Simon had recently achieved in their "Logic Theory Machine" (1956), a system "capable of discovering proofs for theorems in elementary symbolic logic."[52] Just as Pierre Menard had accomplished the heroic feat of rewriting *Don Quixote*, the so-called "Logic Theorist" would—if given the axioms of Alfred North Whitehead and Bertrand Russell—tirelessly attempt to re-"discover" the canonical theorems of *Principia Mathematica*. (Indeed, the resemblance is uncanny: like Menard, the Logic Theorist only managed to fulfill its commission partially, completing 38 of the 52 theorems Whitehead and Russell worked out in Chapter 2 of *Principia*.)

---

[52] Allen Newell and Herbert Simon, "The Logic Theorist Machine: A Complex Information Processing System," *IRE Transactions on Information Theory* 2, no. 3 (September 1956): 61.

An evocation of personhood—not just a "Theory *Machine*" but a "Theor*ist*"—was no accident. In a follow-up study Newell and Simon completed with J. C. Shaw, the authors argued that "the behavior of this program, when the stimulus consists of the instruction that it prove a particular theorem, can be used to predict the behavior of (certain) humans when they are faced with the same problem in symbolic logic."[53] The project was, to be sure, not simply an instrumental exercise in solving problems, nor should its products be mistaken for a mere facsimile of logical proof; no more, at any rate, than Pierre Menard may be insulted as derivative with respect to Cervantes. "Those who have insinuated that Menard devoted his life to writing a contemporary *Quixote* besmirch his illustrious memory. Pierre Menard did not want to compose *another* Quixote, which surely is easy enough—he wanted to compose *the* Quixote. Nor, surely, need one be obliged to note that his goal was never a mechanical transcription of the original; he had no intention of *copying* it. His admirable ambition was to produce a number of pages which coincided—word for word and line for line—with those of Miguel de Cervantes."[54] Hence, too, the ambition of the Logic Theorist in the realm of human problem solving, tasked as it was with "discovering proofs for theorems" that had already been discovered; much to the dismay of its guardians, some would find little to admire in such a pursuit.

When informed of his digital doppelgänger, Russell acknowledged the news with affirmation: "I am delighted to know that *Principia Mathematica* can now be done by machinery. I wish Whitehead and I had known of this possibility before we wasted ten years doing it by

---

[53] Allen Newell, J. C. Shaw, and Herbert A. Simon, "Elements of a Theory of Human Problem Solving," *Psychological Review* 65, no. 3 (1958): 153-154. Note that the article was published in a psychology journal, as opposed for instance to a journal specializing in logic or computing. This perhaps accounts for the deployment of jargon ("behavior," "stimulus") otherwise absent their discussions of the Logic Theorist.

[54] Jorge Luis Borges, "Pierre Menard, Author of the *Quixote*," in *Collected Fictions: Jorge Luis Borges*, trans. Andrew Hurley (New York: Penguin Books, 1999), p. 91.

hand."[55] My own impression is that this correspondence suggests a tone of professional courtesy rather than keen interest, and that Simon may rather have overestimated Russell's appreciation—there was, for instance, no enthusiasm for further details nor any request to be kept abreast of new developments. (Simon obliged anyway.) Above all, Russell seems to have construed the achievement in terms of *automation* of proof rather than the *simulation* of reasoning, contrasting work "done by machinery" with the tedious effort completed "by hand." In any case, others were far more blunt in their dismissal. The editor of the *Journal of Symbolic Logic*, Stephen Kleene, declined to publish a paper "co-authored" by the Logic Theorist on the grounds that it did not advance research into the field: in Simon's recollection, "[s]ince the methods of *Principia Mathematica*, [Kleene] said, were now outmoded, it was no accomplishment to prove a theorem using that system."[56]

Simon felt especially aggrieved by the rejection as he believed that the objectives of the Logic Theorist had been misunderstood. He regretted, in particular, the unfavorable comparison of his approach against alternate solutions that had achieved greater computational efficiency (i.e., could be processed faster on actual machines) and a more complete scope (i.e., could prove a larger range of theorems); Hao Wang, a logician who successfully pursued such strategies, delivered a brutal assessment of Simon's work with Newell and Shaw: "There is no need to kill a chicken with a butcher's knife. Yet the net impression is that Newell-Shaw-Simon failed even to kill the chicken with their butcher's knife."[57] For Simon, however, it was not out of a lack of awareness that the

---

[55] Bertrand Russell, cited in Herbert Simon, *Models of My Life* (Cambridge, MA: MIT Press, 1996), p. 208.

[56] Simon, *Models of My Life*, p. 209.

[57] Hao Wang, "Towards Mechanical Mathematics," *IBM Journal of Research and Development* 4, issue 1 (January 1960): 4.

implementation of the Logic Theorist followed its design. Rather, he would later again emphasize in his memoirs, his research was prompted by an interest in "simulating *human problem solving*, and not simply in demonstrating how computers could solve hard problems."[58]

To this end, a distinction between the "*algorithmic*" and the "*heuristic*" was delineated.[59] By the former, Newell-Shaw-Simon referred to the "systematic computational processes" which they wished to differentiate from "complex information processing" proper. Their predilections were categorically inclined towards the latter. Whereas a systematic algorithm might identify a proof by exhaustively enumerating all possible combinations of axioms and rules, heuristic methods relied on a hierarchy of subroutines that provided cues intended to limit the range of its search. The point was not just *that* heuristics pruned a search space that quickly grew intractably large; even what were referred to as algorithmic methods had to engage optimization techniques for any but the most trivial of problems. Rather, the authors were concerned with *how* this pruning was discharged. It was specifically the hierarchical format that they considered comparable with human approaches to problem solving. This nuance prompted them to add a qualification to their analogy between computational information processing and human behavior: "This assertion [that the Logic Theorist simulates human problem solving] has nothing to do—directly—with computers. Such programs could be written (now that we have discovered how to do it) if computers had never existed."[60]

---

[58] Simon, *Models of My Life*, p. 209.

[59] See Newell and Simon, "The Logic Theory Machine," 61.

[60] Newell, Shaw, Simon, "Elements of a Theory of Human Problem Solving," p. 153.

Whereas Russell had assumed a dichotomy between execution "by machinery" and "by hand," it was repeatedly stressed (with a parenthetical qualification) that the operations completed electronically "could be written" (in principle, if not in fact; if its findings were already known; if one just had enough time; etc.). Indeed, even in Newell and Simon's earliest sketch, the Logic Theorist had been characterized specifically as a system "not so large that it can be hand simulated (barely)."[61] Inscription was essential to the project (albeit in a somewhat disavowed, parenthesized way) as it stood in as a proxy for thinking. Absent the availability to inspection of mental processes themselves, observation had to be redirected to manual behavior instead. Annotation transformed the system into a psychological experiment of sorts, conducted however with computer programs rather than rodents. Thus, analogies to human problem solving would be supported with the quasi-empirical evidence of paperwork:

> We can learn more about LT's approximation to human problem solving by instructing it to print out some of its intermediate results—to work its problems on paper, so to speak. The data thus obtained can be compared with data obtained from a human subject who is asked to use scratch paper as he works a problem, or to think aloud.[62]

Perhaps some of the difficulties the Logic Theorist encountered may have arisen from this unorthodox deployment of the medium of "scratch paper." In discussing the "economy of the scribble" that characterizes the interstitial awkwardness of such notetaking, Hans-Jörg Rheinberger has pointed out that these drafts "lie *between* the materialities of experimental systems and the conceptual constructs that leave the immediate laboratory context behind in the guise of sanctioned research reports": "They are not yet of the order of printed communications addressed

---

[61] Newell and Simon, "The Logic Theory Machine," p. 61.

[62] Newell, Shaw, Simon, "Elements of a Theory of Human Problem Solving," p. 156.

to the scientific community; they are still of the order of the experimental engagement and entanglement."[63] Rheinberger, in short, highlights how the scribble recedes from publicity, refusing the economy of communication proper: it is not a product of research but a byproduct. The Logic Theorist, however, seems to have embraced these "intermediate results" with a view specifically towards the communicative function of transmission—in the context of quasi-behaviorist experimentation, "scratch paper" was the means by which an ineffable process could, in Edward Tolman's words, "get across."

As Stephanie Dick has observed, work on the Logic Theorist took advantage of a division of labor that was reflected in the material competencies each researcher favored: whereas Newell pointed out that Shaw was "the one guy who understood what computers are all about," Simon dwelled on his "pen-and-pencil work" and "hand simulations."[64] Although Dick may be correct in her assessment that, for Simon, "the material substrata in which the problem-solving behavior was implemented was always secondary to the model," his lack of interest in circuitry should not detract from the displacements that he instigated *between* software and hardware. That is to say, his abstention should not be understood through a dichotomy that privileges form over matter but as indicating the work of mediation that occludes itself to preserve a smooth translation from one to the other. (In a way, then, "pen-and-pencil work" might be said to act quite precisely in a parenthetical register, staging an interjection that makes a corollary dimension manifest whilst retaining the impression that it has left the principal argumentative thread undisturbed.) Insofar as the Logic Theorist could make a plausible claim to offer insights into human problem solving, this

---

[63] Hans-Jörg Rheinberger, *An Epistemology of the Concrete: Twentieth-Century Histories of Life* (Durham: Duke University Press, 2010), p. 245.

[64] Stephanie Dick, "Of Models and Machines: Implementing Bounded Rationality," *Isis* 106, no. 3 (September 2015): 629.

was less due to any evident affinity with mental activity than through its simulation of a manual apparatus, and one is thus almost tempted to suggest that the cognitive sciences may "(barely)" be conceived of as the chirographic sciences—a science not of the mind, but of scribbles.

It was, after all, precisely its mimetic inclinations that accounted both for the Logic Theorist's illegibility within the disciplinary specificity of symbolic logic, *as well as* its appeal for an interdisciplinary approach to cognition. From the perspective of researchers solely invested in proving logical theorems, a pursuit of anthropomorphism was not only farfetched but an unnecessarily elaborate complication ("a butcher's knife"), especially if it imposed limitations on the method's problem-solving efficacy ("failed even to kill the chicken"). Considered according to such terms, any merit to the use of electronic machinery stemmed specifically from its affordance of computational power orders of magnitude beyond handwriting, and the anachronism of scribal computation was not just counterproductive but outright perverse: it would deny specifically the traits that lent the computer its attractiveness.

Miller, on the other hand, provided another frame of reference that was more germane to the Logic Theorist's heuristic constitution, and specifically to its hierarchical disposition. He had taken great interest in developments from cybernetics and information theory, and his work with Galanter and Pribam would reflect this pedigree. The computer in this context was mobilized less as an instrument whose utility resulted from executional performance, than as a figure that prompted a basis to rethink existing conceptual frameworks. As opposed to the frame of reference oriented around the reflex arc typical in experimental psychology, *Plans* sought to account for the role of "feedback" in behavioral sequences, coining the Test-Operate-Test-Exit (TOTE) loop as its elementary unit of analysis. The TOTE loop structured stimulus and response "as phases of the organized, coordinated act," treating them not in terms of a strictly unidirectional vector of causality but as "correlative and contemporaneous": "the stimulus processes must be thought of not as preceding the response but rather as guiding it to a successful elimination of the incongruity" (*PSB*, p. 30). As such, it suggested a recursive format comprising of processes regulated hierarchically:

> the operational components of TOTE units may themselves be TOTE units. That is to say, the TOTE pattern describes both strategic and tactical units of behavior. Thus the operational phase of a higher-order TOTE might itself consist of a string of other TOTE units, and each of these, in turn, may contain still other strings of TOTEs, and so on. (*PSB*, p. 32)

In this schema, complex sequences of operation were not conceived of in terms of cause inducing effect (i.e., stimulus preceding response), but according to a coordinated hierarchy of instructions (i.e., a recursive feedback loop)—that is, not as a reflex arc but as a Plan.

This prevalence of a hierarchical format extended the trajectory of Miller's intellectual outlook, which shifted from his early behaviorist commitments towards a computationally inflected cognitivism over the 1950s. In "The Magical Number Seven, Plus or Minus Two" (1956), he had articulated the psychological subject through the informatic terms formulated in Claude Shannon's mathematical theory of communication, depicting it as a "communication channel."[65] His findings suggested a surprising finitude in human channel capacity when dealing with "absolute judgment" in one-dimension: just around three bits—that is, "seven, plus or minus two." One type of experiment cited by Miller to substantiate this claim involved a setup of flashing random patterns of dots on a screen. Participants were tasked with reporting on the number of dots, which ranged between one to more than 200. Their accuracy in this endeavor was marked by a sharp threshold: "on patterns containing up to five or six dots the subjects simply did not make

---

[65] George Miller, "The Magical Number Seven, Plus or Minus Two: Some Limits on our Capacity for Processing Information," *Psychological Review* 63, no. 2 (March 1956): 82.

errors. The performance on these small numbers of dots was so different from the performance with more dots that it was given a special name. Below seven the subjects were said to *subitize*; above seven they were said to *estimate*."[66]

The distinctiveness to Miller's study derived perhaps not so much from positing or even quantifying limitations to judgment, a line of research that had been explored by Hermann Ebbinghaus even in the earliest experimental studies of psychology. A further novelty followed from how he sought to resolve the apparent contradiction between this evid*ence* of a diminished bandwidth found in human cognition (*qua* communications channel) and the rather evid*ent* fact that human memory was capable of dealing with stimuli at rates well beyond those limits. Even at a glance, it was noted, a single face could be identified from hundreds; a single word distinguished from thousands; etc.: how was this achieved with such a poor resolution? Drawing from the vocabulary of engineers, Miller repurposed the concept of "chunking" that had been used in the technical context of communications engineering to refer to the process of "recoding" bits of information into larger groups.

> A man just beginning to learn radio-telegraphic code hears each *dit* and *dah* as a separate chunk. Soon he is able to organize these sounds into letters and then he can deal with the letters as chunks. Then the letters organize themselves as words, which are still larger chunks, and he begins to hear whole phrases. ... [T]he dits and dahs are organized by learning into patterns and ... as these larger chunks emerge the amount of message that the operator can remember increases correspondingly. In the terms I am proposing to use, the operator learns to increase the bits per chunk.
>
> In the jargon of communication theory, this process would be called *recoding*. The input is given in a code that contains many chunks with few bits per

---

[66] Ibid., p. 90.

chunk. The operator recodes the input into another code that contains fewer chunks with more bits per chunk.[67]

Miller posited that memory span was not defined by a fixed number of *bits* but rather by a fixed number of *chunks*. Increasing the throughput of bits processed by human memory, consequently, did not require an increase in the number of items processed but was simply a matter of mnemonic techniques for recoding bits into chunks of a larger size.

Appropriated for psychology, procedures of signals processing provided the terminology for a description of mental activity; the telegraphic operator would become a model subject for the workings of human cognition: "Since the memory span is a fixed number of chunks, we can increase the number of bits of information that it contains simply by building larger and larger chunks, each chunk containing more information than before."[68] Unsurprisingly, Miller found strong resonance with Newell and Simon's Logic Theorist, a project that was publicly introduced at the same symposium he first presented "The Magical Number Seven." The reliance of the latter's heuristic approach on nested subroutines echoed the hierarchical schema of subsuming smaller chunks within informatically-richer chunks, and would suggest the recursive structure of TOTE loops containing TOTE loops later elaborated in *Plans*.

Reflecting on the limited attention afforded to such hierarchical processes in psychological studies, Miller pointed to methodological habits as the root of this deficit in research, suggesting that "probably because recoding is less accessible to experimental manipulation than nonsense syllables [studied by Ebbinghaus; see further **§3.1**] or T mazes [preferred by Edward Tolman; see further **§2.2**], the traditional experimental psychologist has contributed little or nothing to their

---

[67] Ibid., p. 93.

[68] Ibid.

analysis."[69] He, presumably, saw his own turn to a computational idiom as a corrective in this regard. And, surely, he could count on the support of allies like Shannon and Simon on this quest? Yet, any pretensions that formal mathematics sufficed to extricate the human psyche from the scurrying of its creaturely counterparts would be proven sorely mistaken; any anticipation of solidarity from his colleagues was deeply misplaced.

Shannon, for his part, was well attuned to the plight of rats. At the 1951 edition of the Macy Conferences, he had staged a "Presentation of a Maze-Solving Machine."[70] The setup comprised of a 5x5 grid within which a "sensing finger" driven by motors attempted to reach the position on the grid designated as the "goal." Given the absence of organic appetites, a simple pin sufficed as symbolic substitute for cheese. The machine's strategy of maze-solving consisted of two phases. In the first, the finger deployed an "exploration strategy," exhaustively testing possible routes until the goal was reached. Having achieved this, it followed a "goal strategy" when returned to its starting point, heading directly to the goal without excursions. If, instead, repositioned to an unexplored region of the maze, the machine could engage in exploration until it reached familiar territory, at that point switching to its second strategy.

Discussion at the conference sought elaboration on edge cases. Responding to Heinz von Foerster's query on arrangements in which a goal was not defined, Shannon explained:

> If there is no goal, the machine establishes a periodic path, searching for the goal; that is, it gradually works out a path which goes through every square and tries every barrier, and if it doesn't find the goal, the path is repeated again and again.

---

[69] Ibid., p. 96.

[70] Claude Shannon, "Presentation of a Maze-Solving Machine," in *Cybernetics: The Macy Conferences, 1946-1953—The Complete Transactions*, ed. Claus Pias (Zurich; Berlin: Diaphanes, 2003/2016), pp. 474-479.

The machine just continues looking for the goal throughout every square, making sure that it looks at every square.

"It is all too human," conference organizer Lawrence Frank drolly remarked in turn.

Goal-seeking behavior had been a defining staple of cybernetics since its formation as a science cast from the operations of control engineering. The pursuit of a target was precisely what had prompted its emblematic study, mathematician Norbert Wiener's wartime efforts with electrical engineer Julian Bigelow on antiaircraft systems.[71] In collaboration with cardiologist Arturo Rosenblueth, Wiener and Bigelow would theorize the more general stakes involved in the project beyond the specifics of ballistics by outlining a classification of "purposeful behavior" in their seminal paper, "Behavior, Purpose and Teleology" (1943).[72] This articulation of a cybernetically-inflected telos functions as a historical joint, marking the seam at which the sciences of behavior would be folded into technologies of computation. As media historian Claus Pias has observed, "'non-deterministic teleology' became a magic expression that led some to believe that they could define goals, introduce a system, and then walk away from it all with the expectation that their desired results would necessarily come to be."[73] In subsequent decades, computer scientists would retain such aspirations albeit through an updated lexicon, instead speaking in terms of a declarative style when referring to the ability to prescribe *what is* without the need for

---

[71] See Peter Galison, "The Ontology of the Enemy: Norbert Wiener and the Cybernetic Vision," *Critical Inquiry* 21, no. 1 (Autumn 1994): 228-266.

[72] See Arturo Rosenblueth, Norbert Wiener, and Julian Bigelow, "Behavior, Purpose and Teleology," *Philosophy of Science* 10 (January 1943): 18-24.

[73] Claus Pias, "The Age of Cybernetics," in *Cybernetics: The Macy Conferences, 1946-1953—The Complete Transactions*, p. 21.

specifying *how to*; Pias's observation remains perfectly valid if taken instead as a description of the ambitions of declarative programming languages.

Despite their clear resonance—and, indeed, shared concerns regarding the extraction of (inner) "purpose" from (outward) manifestations of "behavior"—there are nevertheless acute discrepancies between the cybernetic invocation of "purposeful behavior" and the tensions embedded in the earlier psychological turn towards "purposive behaviorism." Whereas behaviorists had approached metaphysical vocabulary with suspicion—recall Tolman's disdain for his own terminology: "I especially dislike the terms *purpose* and *cognition* and the title *Purposive Behavior*"—cyberneticians like Wiener had no such qualms. Indeed, they seemed to formulate their conceptual idiom in a deliberate attempt at stretching conventional sense, reveling in the challenge that these provocations posed. For them, even inanimate ballistics could be said to "behave" with reference to a "purpose" (i.e., to seek enemy aircraft) and robots not just capable of the mechanistic execution of logic but also fallible in ways that were "all too human."

Shannon's eccentric undertakings might have been received with less enthusiasm had this general ambience of irreverence not been prevalent. One feature of the maze-solver that he was especially keen to highlight was an "antineurotic circuit" that lent the system robustness when confronted with changes to the maze configuration. A freshly placed obstacle along the established path, for instance, might result in a "vicious circle" wherein the now-obsolete solution led the machine into a repetitive loop. In anticipation of this contingency, the descent into madness was forestalled by resetting the solver after a given number of cycles, thereby interrupting its unhealthy habit, allowing it to proceed unencumbered by its previous beliefs.

These peculiarities in Shannon's mechanism derived from the unique architecture through which its search function had been implemented, namely, a "field vector" comprising of a linked collection of directions that funneled towards the goal. Given the limitations of available hardware, the maze-solver's design was constrained by a need to ration stored information. A solution of exaggerated elegance followed: simply repeat the direction taken when last at those coordinates. This strategy sufficed to trim any excursions leading to dead ends, although likely not to find the quickest path. The apparatus made no effort at charting landmarks and their consequence on its situation, instead pursuing a mode of orientation ignorant to the broader range of possibilities, more reflective of a minimal rather than the optimal basis for articulating a viable route. It did not, in other words, *map* where obstacles were, only how it should *behave* at any previously encountered position; maze and solution were strangely disconnected, as if the objective facts of terrain were irrelevant in the exercise of navigation. Thus, if a distinguishing trait in the machine was its ability to withstand disruptions, any potential resilience it achieved in fact ensued from an indifference to actual layout; it was capable of overcoming alterations to its environment as it was simply oblivious of those circumstances to begin with.

One result of this informatic parsimony was an asymmetry of directionality, wherein a path leading inwards to the target could not be reversed to trace outwards back to its point of origin. At a recognized position, the "goal-strategy" would point the machine to the next step, heading closer to its target. Yet, since this step might have been sourced from any one of a number of surrounding points, the topology of Shannon's field vector implied the formation of bottlenecks, making retreat impossible: the machine would not know from which amongst these alternatives its current state had been derived. As statistician L. J. Savage pointed out, "it is not organized around any particular initial point"; conference chair Warren McCulloch claimed the last word of the proceedings with a more flamboyant anthropomorphism: "Like a man who knows the town, so he can go from any place to any other place, but doesn't always remember how he went."[74]

Another consequence of the strategic architecture Shannon deployed was, however, left unmentioned at the time. Its significance is perhaps clearer in retrospect, especially if read in light of the claims forwarded in the cognitive turn. Insofar as the maze-solver eschews ambitions of a complete overview (or, indeed, any interest whatsoever in establishing an account of its world), Shannon might even be said to have offered a more radical instantiation of the tenets that would link the mental capacity for planning to a computer's execution of its programs. "Unless you can use your Image to do something," Miller *et al.* argued, "you are like a man who collects maps but never makes a trip" (*PSB*, p. 2). These objections to existing theories of cognition could almost be read as a rejoinder to McCulloch's conclusion: absent the ability to "go from any place to any other place," can one really be said to know the town? The pragmatics of operation elaborated in *Plans* argued for this *necessity* of control over representation; Shannon, however, went further in demonstrating its *sufficiency*. Hence, perhaps, the stakes involved in the rigorous questioning of technical minutiae at the conference: these practical techniques of maneuvering implied an entire mode of existence in concentrate. Shannon's machine was not modelled on an Image of a world, as Boulding had proposed; it did not require a cognitive map of its spatial condition, just a Plan to be followed.

---

[74] Topological formatting "not organized around any particular point" (i.e., without a center) resonated with contemporaneous paradigms in urban planning, which sought to mitigate threats to the smooth functioning of thoroughfares. See Peter Galison, "War Against the Center," *Grey Room*, no. 4 (Summer 2001): 5-33. The currency of these concerns has hardly receded with time, but only gained in prominence as a mode of reasoning. For a theorization of the ideology of "hope" in the historical legacies of this rhetoric of resilience (especially as it pertains to contemporary discourse), see further Orit Halpern, "Hopeful Resilience," *e-flux Architecture* (April 2017): https://www.e-flux.com/architecture/accumulation/96421/hopeful-resilience/.

Already in Shannon's early schema, then, we should discern hints of a thematic concern that von Foerster would go on to develop as "second-order cybernetics," namely, the impossibility of an external viewpoint for observation. If part of the appeal in the maze-solving machine was its ability to generate a solution without instructions specific to its configuration (i.e., its capacity for "non-deterministic teleology," or autonomous problem-solving intelligence), another equally important facet was a complete immersion within the maze, never attempting a transcendent position. The premise of von Foerster's inflection to the cybernetic project would be explained by the sociologist Niklas Luhmann in these terms: "The theorist of cognition himself becomes a rat in the labyrinth and must consider from which position he observes other rats."[75] "There are," Luhmann argued, "only rats in the labyrinth that observe each other and that can thus perhaps arrive at system structures, but can never reach consensus. There is no labyrinth-free, no context-free observation. And a theory that describes this is, of course, a rat theory."[76]

But "rat theory" amounts, quite evidently, to nothing more than an ironic contradiction. Etymologically, *theoria* carries the promise of a scopic regime based precisely on an overview—and who else is this "rat" but that figure denied such a distanced perspective, that creature whose capacity for sight has so rudely been impeded? Rats herald the closing of an epoch of theory.

---

[75] Niklas Luhmann, *Erkenntnis als Konstruktion* (Bern, 1988), p. 24. Cited in translation, Eva M. Knodt, Foreword to *Social Systems*, by Niklas Luhmann, trans. John Bednarz, Jr., with Dirk Baecker (Stanford, CA: Stanford University Press, 1995), p. xxxvi. On rat mazes and their significance in von Foerster, Luhmann, and Shannon, see also Maren Lehmann, "Ratten Im Labyrinth, Oder: Lernen Mit Theseus," *The Design Journal* 8, issue 3 (2005): 13-24.

[76] Niklas Luhmann, *Soziologische Aufklärung 4: Beiträge zur funktionalen Differenzierung der Gesellschaft* (Opladen: Westdeutscher Verlag, 1987): "Es gibt nur Ratten im Labyrinth, die einander beobachten und eben deshalb wohl zu Systemstrukturen, nie aber zu Konsens kommen können. Es gibt kein labyrinthfreies, kein kontextfreies Beobachten. Und selbstverständlich ist eine Theorie, die dies beschreibt, eine Rattentheorie" (p. 6).

§2.4: "Rat Theory" (III): Crustacean Theologies and an Expanded Bestiary of Animacy

Although historical reflection tends to emphasize how the cybernetic project established transitivity between human and machine, contextualizing this with a deep history of the "behavior" concept and the vicissitudes that inflected its entanglements with "purpose" nuances the supposition of a sharp ontological break: humans had long since been entangled with surrogate actors, i.e., rats and mice. Their footsteps would not so easily be forgotten—an expanded bestiary of animacies would continue to haunt the fantasies of post-cybernetic theorization.

In the assessment of Miller and his colleagues, rat behavior was disparaged as "surely one of the least promising areas in which to investigate intellectual accomplishments" (*PSB*, p. 8). Yet, the somewhat snarky gibe should not be mistaken as straightforward dismissal. Much of their thesis in fact hinged on the unassuming suggestion that followed, added almost as if its reasoning was an afterthought: "Perhaps [Edward Tolman] felt that if he could win the argument with the simpler animal, he would win it by default for the more complicated ones" (*PSB*, p. 8). The so-called cognitive revolution, and in particular its recourse to computation, was driven by such a hierarchy of animacy that led from "simpler" to "more complicated": "If the description of a rodent's cognitive structure is necessary in order to understand its behavior, then it is just that much more important for understanding the behavior of a dog, or an ape, or a man" (*PSB*, p. 8)—and, we may infer, if the description of a *computer*'s cognitive structure is necessary to understand its behavior, then it must be even more important in the study of the *human* psyche. Computing machinery offered the perfect specimen as a model of mind not *in spite* of its relative obtuseness but precisely *because* of this.

Behind this comparative scale was a strongly normative dimension that channeled the ambitions of distinguishing human rationality from the instinctive compulsions of base animality. As Miller *et al.* argued:

> In lower animals it appears that the pattern of their behavior is normally constructed more or less fortuitously by the environment—only man cherishes the illusion of being master of his fate. That is to say, the environment provides stimuli that 'release' the next stage of the animal's activity. ... As we ascend the evolutionary scale we find in mammals an increasing complexity in the kind of tests the animals can perform. In man we have a unique capacity for creating and manipulating symbols. (*PSB*, 38)

The importance that cognitivists attributed to the abstraction of symbolic activity derived from its distance to and insulation from the exigencies of immediate circumstance. Self-determination (i.e., "the illusion of being master of his fate") was coupled with a capacity for handling complexity, both traits characterized by the construction of behavioral patterns shaped by motives that transcended the deterministic trajectory of a stimulus-response arc—in other words, characterized by the rational activity of Planning.

In this regard, cognitivism followed rather than broke with orthodoxy in established psychological doctrine. Tolman, for instance, had been quite explicit when framing the stakes of cognitive mapping in terms of capacities for rationality. To this end, he had distinguished "narrow strip-maps" from "broad comprehensive maps."[77] The occluded condition of the former resulted in pathologies such as "regression," "fixation," and the "displacement of aggression onto outgroups."

By introducing a spectrum of breadth, Tolman was able to circumvent a difficulty that his proscription of mentalism entailed, namely: if discussion of minds was prohibited, where should

---

[77] See Tolman, "Cognitive Maps in Rats and Men," esp. pp. 207-208.

rationality be located? Insofar as an account of reason had to be articulated solely through behavioral (*qua* observable) effects, it would not be identified as the property of an inscrutable faculty but rather through displayed competencies in the practice of cognitive mapping; reason was presented as functionally equivalent to an ability to plot broad maps, to the effect that these terms should be deployed synonymously:

> Over and over again men are blinded by too violent motivations and too intense frustration into blind and unintelligent and in the end desperately dangerous hates of outsiders. And the expression of these their displaced hates ranges all the way from discrimination against minorities to world conflagrations.
>
> What in the name of Heaven and Psychology can we do about it? My only answer is to preach again the virtues of reason—of, that is, broad cognitive maps. And to suggest that the child-trainers and the world-planners of the future can only, if at all, bring about the presence of the required rationality (*i.e.*, comprehensive maps) if they see to it that nobody's children are too over-motivated or too frustrated. Only then can these children learn to look before and after, learn to see that there are often round-about and safer paths to their quite proper goals. ...
>
> We dare not let ourselves or others become so over-emotional, so hungry, so ill-clad, so over-motivated that only narrow strip-maps will be developed. ...
>
> We must, in short, subject our children and ourselves (as the kindly experimenter would his rats) to the optimal conditions of moderate motivation and of an absence of unnecessary frustrations, whenever we put them and ourselves before that great God-given maze which is our human world.[78]

Drawing on the psychoanalytic vocabulary of Sigmund Freud, Tolman warned against the dangers of indulging in the immediate gratifications of the Pleasure Principle (that is, the narrow mapping of stimulus to response), arguing that its temptations could only be inhibited through adherence to the Reality Principle (that is, comprehensive maps that indicated the available range of incentives).

---

[78] Ibid., p. 208.

This predisposition followed principles from Gestalt psychology in that it privileged what Wolfgang Köhler had called "the product of a complete survey of the whole situation." As Köhler elaborated:

> We can, in our own experience, distinguish sharply between the kind of behaviour which from the very beginning arises out of a consideration of the structure of the situation, and one that does not. Only in the former case do we speak of insight, and only that behavior of animals definitely appears to us intelligent which takes account from the beginning of the lay of the land, and proceeds to deal with it in a single, continuous, and definite course. Hence follows this criterion of insight: *the appearance of a complete solution with reference to the whole lay-out of the field.*[79]

His treatment of "insight" would be influential in the development of comparative psychobiology.[80] Following an encounter with Köhler's *The Mentality of Apes* (1925), Robert Yerkes's earlier endorsement of dancing mice would be supplanted by an enthusiasm for primates. The relative ease of observation offered by the former proved an insufficient bait for his loyalties against the scope for research opened by the latter. Donna Haraway has detailed how, in the psychological doctrine Yerkes espoused, primatology contributed to "a teleology of mind" that placed the capacity for "insight" at its apex: for Yerkes, "the mind was divided into faculties, which in turn were arranged into a scale of increasing powers from sensation to insight. The three principal levels of function were called 'monkeying' (fooling with things, getting useful

---

[79] Wolfgang Köhler, *The Mentality of Apes*, trans. Ella Winter (New York: Harcourt, Brace & Company, 1925), p. 198.

[80] The concept of *"Einsicht"* (translated as "insight") was introduced to psychological vocabulary by Köhler in *The Mentality of Apes*, and would be adopted in debates over behaviorism—including several rat experiments which sought to demonstrate their capacity for such a function: first, in a study by Hsiao Hung Hsiao; and, subsequently, Tolman addressed this concept as well in a paper co-written with C. H. Honzik. See Hsiao Hung Hsiao, "An Experimental Study of the Rat's 'Insight' Within A Spatial Complex," *University of California Publications in Psychology* 4, no. 4 (1929): 57-70; Edward C. Tolman and C. H. Honzik, "'Insight' in Rats," *University of California Publications in Psychology* 4, no. 14 (1930): 215-232.

experience by accident); 'aping' (imitating another organism, goal direction unclear); and 'thinking' (solving problems by insight or foresight)."[81]

Nor was such a normative order limited to the behavioral sciences. A distinction echoing Köhler's association of intelligence with "a single, continuous, and definite course" formed the basis of architect Le Corbusier's affirmation of goal-driven behavior.

> Man walks in a straight line because he has a goal and knows where he is going; he has made up his mind to reach some particular place and he goes straight to it.
>
> The pack-donkey meanders along, meditates a little in his scatter-brained and distracted fashion, he zigzags in order to avoid the larger stones, or to ease the climb, or to gain a little shade; he takes the line of least resistance.
>
> But man governs his feelings by his reason; he keeps his feelings and his instincts in check, subordinating them to the aim he has in view.

When Corbusier bemoaned the deficiencies of narrow cognitive mapping (i.e., "takes the line of least resistance"), he portrayed this failure as an inability to abide by the Reality Principle (i.e., "keeps his feelings and his instincts in check, subordinating them to the aim he has in view"). "The pack-donkey," he emphasized, "thinks of nothing at all, except what will save himself trouble."[82] Corbusier's rationalist approach to (urban) planning instead drew from the insight of a comprehensive overview.

Here, I must admit that my own sympathies have little in common with Corbusier's. Convinced by an expanded bestiary, I have come to embrace rather than fault the meandering

---

[81] Donna J. Haraway, *Primate Visions: Gender, Race, and Nature in the World of Modern Sciences* (New York; London: Routledge, 1989), p. 74.

[82] Le Corbusier [Charles-Édouard Jeanneret], *The City of To-morrow and its Planning*, trans. Frederick Etchells (London: The Architectural Press, 1947), pp. 23-24.

itinerary of the pack-donkey. Indeed, even in the Anglophone philosophical tradition, where cognitivism's computational slant exerted its strongest attractions, the legitimacy of charting cognition according to an evolutionary hierarchy would swiftly become questionable. When Thomas Nagel questioned, "What Is It Like to Be a Bat?" (1974), his response was outlined not in terms of a scale of increasing rationality but through the density of radical alterity. As Nagel argued, any attempt to imagine an answer in terms of "our own experience" only clarifies "what it would be like for *me* to behave as a bat behaves."[83] Instead, he insisted, an adequate response would necessarily engage with "what it is like for a *bat* to be a bat," an endeavor in which mere descriptions or even imitations of behavior carried no weight. Considered this way, there was no basis to privilege capacities for symbolic manipulation over other modalities of experience such as the mimetic practices of *monkey*-ing and *ape*-ing—or, for that matter, *donkey*-ing and even *bat*-ing, whatever these could possibly mean;[84] each, in Nagel's ethics, were simply incommensurable, incapable of fully coinciding with any other.

It is somewhat more difficult to pin down the implications of alternate forms of worlding in Jakob von Uexküll's theorization. Uexküll's tract, "A Stroll Through the Worlds of Animals and Men," is a particularly noteworthy document in the post-cybernetic legacies of comparative biology as the latency between its original publication in German (1934) and its translation into English as the anchor for a collection of theses on the topic of *Instinctive Behavior* (1957) spans precisely the crises under discussion here, corresponding at one end to concerns over the legibility

---

[83] Thomas Nagel, "What Is It Like to Be a Bat?" *Philosophical Review* 83, no. 4 (October 1974): 439.

[84] *Donkey*-ing, according to Le Corbusier at any rate, seems to bear a great deal of resemblance to *horse*-ing around.

of purposiveness in psychology and on the other with the emergence of cognitivism.[85] This displacement perhaps accounts for the unsettled character of its legacy that Geoffrey Winthrop-Young has (generously) explained by suggesting that Uexküll is "a highly detachable theorist. It is easy to dip into his writings and extract certain portions."[86] Focusing rigorously on the initial context Uexküll worked in, however, Gottfried Schnödl and Florian Sprenger have drawn attention to the resonance of his theories with totalitarian ideologies, pointing out the tendency of his worldview towards "holism." Schnödl and Sprenger emphasize the importance of *Planmäßigkeit* (or, "conformity with a plan") in Uexküll's framework, indicating "a purposiveness, systematicity, or planned quality given by nature." Insofar as each organism's distinct *Umwelt* is said to maintain a unique surrounding-world, for Uexküll this results from a fixed and unchanging order, expressing "an identitarian logic where everything has its place according to a plan and whatever is wrongly placed is to be excluded."[87] As he conceived it, the difference arising from multiperspectivalism entailed a condition of separation across which transmission cannot occur. Uexküll, in other words, deployed the concept of the *Umwelt* as a barrier that ensures mutual unintelligibility. (In this regard, one might contrast Uexküll's *Umwelt* against Edward Tolman's deployment of an experimental apparatus, in that the latter seeks precisely to bridge a chasm at the point that the former locates inaccessibility; for Uexküll, it is impossible for any sense to "get across."[88])

---

[85] Jakob von Uexküll, "A Stroll Through the Worlds of Animals and Men," in *Instinctive Behavior: The Development of a Modern Concept*, ed. Claire H. Schiller (New York: International Universities Press, 1957), pp. 5-80, hereafter abbreviated "S."

[86] Geoffrey Winthrop-Young, "Afterword: Bubbles and Webs: A Backdoor Stroll Through the Readings of Uexküll," in *A Foray into the Worlds of Animals and Humans: With a Theory of Meaning*, by Jakob von Uexküll, trans. Joseph D. O'Neil (Minneapolis: University of Minnesota Press, 2010), p. 243.

[87] Gottfried Schnödl and Florian Sprenger, *Uexküll's Surroundings: Umwelt Theory and Right-Wing Thought*, trans. Michael Thomas Taylor and Wayne Yung (Lüneburg: Meson Press, 2021), p. 24 and pp. 13-14.

[88] Or, put another way, Uexküll's ontology was founded on denying the function of cultural techniques.

Thus, although "Stroll" appears at first glance to offer a celebration of the diversity of experience, parsing the stakes behind its insistence on the irreducible subjectivity of worlding accentuates the nuances to its claims. Uexküll is perhaps most pointed in flattening ontological hierarchies when vividly rendering the *Umwelten* of scientific research. His account begins with the (only apparently) broadest of maps: the astronomer as surveyor of the universe.

> High on his tower, as far as possible from the earth, sits a human being. He has so transformed his eyes, with the aid of gigantic optical instruments, that they have become fit to penetrate the universe up to its most distant stars. In his *Umwelt*, suns and planets circle in festive procession. Fleet-flooted light takes millions of years to travel through his *Umwelt* space.[89]

Any pretensions to a comprehensive scope, however, are quickly dispelled: "And yet this whole *Umwelt* is only a tiny sector of nature, tailored to the faculties of a human subject."[90] The cosmic grandeur of astronomy could claim no privilege within an inventory of sciences. The deep-sea researcher, the chemist, the nuclear physicist, even the behaviorist and the psychologist—each, Uexküll points out, accomplish investigations of nature on a par with the astronomer's. Most intriguingly, these *Umwelten* derive incompatible experiences from encounters with the same object. Whereas the physicist finds in an investigation of light "just waves, nothing more," the physiologist studying the senses sees colors: "Red and green fuse into white, and shadows, thrown onto a yellow surface, become blue. Processes unheard-of in waves, and yet the colors are just as real as are the ether waves."[91] Likewise, there is a chasm "between the *Umwelten* of a student of

---

[89] Uexküll, "A Stroll Through the Worlds of Animals and Men," pp. 76-77.

[90] Ibid., p. 77.

[91] Ibid., p. 78.

air waves and of a musician": "In the one there are only waves, in the other only sounds. Yet both are equally real."[92]

It is appraisals like these—that is, his refusals to deny the legitimacy of interpretative plurality—which suggest a sense of generosity in Uexküll's ontology. Upon careful reading, however, it becomes apparent that the emphasis of this schema is placed on an incapacity for communication across worlds, and the assertion of equivalence in their reality was motivated less by an egalitarian outlook than to emphasize an inescapable blindness. As Uexküll concluded, "all these diverse *Umwelten* are harbored and borne by the One that remains forever barred to all *Umwelten*": "Behind all the worlds created by Him, there lies concealed, eternally beyond the reach of knowledge, the subject—Nature."[93] His suspension of scientific mastery was rooted in monotheism not panpsychism; it was geared towards establishing the finitude of all creatures—great and small—in the face of an immeasurably higher power.

As a consequence, despite his disdain towards behaviorism, its experimental apparatus, and especially the mechanical outlook implied by stimulus-response models, Uexküll could find little relief from deterministic tendencies in the model of intelligence promoted by Gestalt theory and its allies (e.g., broad cognitive maps). Indeed, if any hierarchy was admissible in this postlapsarian condition, rather than the so-called higher animals encased in the elaborate constructions of their *Umwelt*, it was simpler organisms who ranked closer to the (unknowable) truth of "Nature": "The amoeba is less of a machine than the horse," Uexküll argued in an early text.[94] Responding to this

---

[92] Ibid., pp. 78-80.

[93] Ibid., p. 80.

[94] Jakob von Uexküll, *Innenwelt und Umwelt der Tiere* (Berlin; Heidelberg: Springer-Verlag, 1921), p. 21.

comparison, the biologist Konrad Lorenz would ascribe Uexküll's verdict to his static understanding of the conditions of possible experience that placed limits on the extent of knowledge. In such an immutable system, Lorenz noted, "this limit would be the same of man and amoeba—infinitely far from the thing-in-itself."[95]

For Lorenz, such a conception was "no longer tenable" given "the indubitable fact of evolution," a framework that Uexküll had rejected. Instead, he argued, the biological process of adaptation posed epistemological implications, such that "the boundaries of the transcendental begin to shift":

> Is not human reason with all its categories and forms of intuition something that has organically evolved in a continuous cause-effect relationship with the laws of the immediate nature, just as has the human brain? Would not the laws of reason necessary for a priori thought be entirely different if they had undergone an entirely different historical mode of origin, and if consequently we had been equipped with an entirely different kind of central nervous system? ("KD," pp. 182-183)

Lorenz speculated that "many aspects of the thing-in-itself which completely escape being experienced by our present-day apparatus of thought and perception may lie within the boundaries of possible experience in the near future, geologically speaking."[96]

The systemic conservatism of Uexküll's predetermined structures precluded any combinations or intermixing of worlds. In the harmonious order he elaborated, there was no scope for assemblages of being. One could not be both a physicist *and* a physiologist, simultaneously investigating light as waves *and* as color; or, when studying sound, consider it both as waves *and*

---

[95] Konrad Lorenz, "Kant's Doctrine of the A Priori in the Light of Contemporary Biology," in Richard I. Evans, *Konrad Lorenz: The Man and his Ideas*, trans. Charlotte Ghurye (New York; London: Harcourt Brace Jovanovich, 1975), p. 184. Lorenz is especially important as an interlocutor to Uexküll as his writings constitute the bulk of the companion pieces to the translation of *Stroll*—of the other seven texts in the collection, Lorenz was the sole author of four and co-author of another. See Claire H. Schiller (ed.), *Instinctive Behavior*, pp. 83-310.

[96] Lorenz, "Kant's Doctrine of the A Priori in the Light of Contemporary Biology," pp. 182-185.

music. And, as Schnödl and Sprenger note, assigning each individual to their proper place within the whole meant that those who failed to fit were deemed "parasites," most notably manifested through antisemitism.[97] When Lorenz sought to redress the epistemic paralysis of Uexküll's theorization, he did so in a way that extended the latter's attitude towards miscegenation. An evolutionary framework—if anything, more easily aligned with the hierarchies of social Darwinism—displaced change onto the scale of geological time, leaving no role for subjective agency in the fostering of attunements. Rather than search for the development of capacities through processes of enskilment,[98] Lorenz located the a priori of the experienceable in "organic receptacles."[99] These organs were understood as "an evolutionarily acquired 'innate working hypothesis,'" and did not refer solely to physical units.[100] The operations of reason, as well, had to be regarded "just like any organ": "just as the hoof of the horse is adapted to the ground of the steppe which it copes with, so our central nervous apparatus for organizing the image of the world is adapted to the real world with which man has to cope."[101]

In this way, Lorenz would address Uexküll's contention that the *organ*-ization of functionality into components like hooves should condemn an animal to a grade more machine-like than single-celled organisms. "The horse," he countered, "is a higher animal [than the amoeba] not despite, but, to a large extent, because of its being richer in solid differentiated structures":

---

[97] Schnödl and Sprenger, *Uexküll's Surroundings*, p. 33.

[98] The theorization of "skill" has explicitly taken this discourse of evolutionary biology as its target. See Tim Ingold, "Beyond biology and culture. The meaning of evolution in a relational world," *Social Anthropology* 12, no. 2 (2004): 209-221.

[99] Lorenz, "Kant's Doctrine of the A Priori in the Light of Contemporary Biology," p. 191.

[100] Ibid., p. 196.

[101] Ibid., p. 187.

> Organisms with as few structures as possible must remain amoebae, whether they like it or not, for without any solid structure all higher organization is inconceivable. One could symbolize organisms with a maximum of highly differentiated fixed structures as lobsters, stiffly armored creatures which could move only in certain joints with precisely allowed degrees of freedom, or as railroad cars having very few switching points.[102]

Lorenz would thus approach aspirations towards a comprehensive scope with some ambivalence. Insofar as he considered the complexity derived from structural differentiation a prerequisite of survival, it was necessary to accept the drive to ascend an evolutionary hierarchy. Yet, such a process also posed the danger of a "fettering effect": "When the human thinker, be it even the greatest, has finished his system, he has in a fundamental way taken on something of the properties of the lobster or the railroad car."[103]

The obvious conclusion to this line of thought would be recognized by Gilles Deleuze and Félix Guattari: "God is a Lobster," they pointed out.[104] Divinity (*qua* the "One" of Uexküll's "Nature") takes on a crustacean quality as its imperatives towards a fixed *Planmäßigkeit* involves "stratification" into "molar aggregates," with stultifying consequences—that is, as *encrusted*: "The strata are judgments of God; stratification in general is the entire system of the judgment of God (but the earth, or the body without organs, constantly eludes that judgment, flees and becomes destratified, decoded, deterritorialized)."[105] ("Earth," in other words, is less software-like, more gerbil-like.)

---

[102] Ibid., pp. 196-197.

[103] Ibid., p. 197.

[104] Gilles Deleuze and Félix Guattari, *A Thousand Plateaus*, trans. Brian Massumi (London; New York: Continuum, 2004), p. 45.

[105] Ibid.

As the molar-molecular distinction was inflected by Deleuze and Guattari, a molecular dimension ("earth") did not imply the simple rigors of straightforward positivism. Rather, its latent materiality fathomed an unconscious realm that receded from discernment on a molar scale. The "body without organs" of their molecular revolution might be considered in counterpoint to the psychobiological affinities of the cognitive revolution in that it confronted the molarizing tendencies in hierarchies of animacy that normatively prioritized Lorenz's "solid differentiated structures" over fluidity: "Why assume (as does Konrad Lorenz, for example) that bands and their type of companionship represent a more rudimentary evolutionary state than group societies or societies of conjugality?"[106] "We want," they answered themselves, "nothing to do with ridiculous evolutionary classifications à la Lorenz, according to which there are inferior packs and superior societies. What we are saying is that every animal is fundamentally a band, a pack. That it has pack modes, rather than characteristics, even if further distinctions within these modes are called for. It is at this point that the human being encounters the animal. We do not become animal without a fascination for the pack, for multiplicity."[107]

Deleuze and Guattari were by no means alone in their aversion to crustacean theologies; postwar French intellectual culture's response to the problem of anthropological difference was shaped by the creaturely conditions of animality, and consequently its terrain was populated with an assortment of beasts. Perhaps the most germane here are those theorists who resorted to rat techniques. Consistent with his disdain for the plan, Guy Debord took great interest in rat mazes.[108]

---

[106] Ibid., p. 38.

[107] Ibid., p. 264.

[108] On Debord and the apparatus of the rat maze, see Eric C. H. de Bruyn, "Constructed Situations, Dynamic Labyrinths, and Learning Mazes: Behavioral Topologies of the Cold War," *Grey Room* 74 (Winter 2019): 44-85.

Contra Corbusier, Debord advocated for a cartography of the pack-donkey, favoring an urbanism performed through the praxis of drifting (*dérive*). Likewise, Michel de Certeau eschewed the Icarian hubris of an elevated vista. As opposed to the strategic disposition provided by a synoptic view, his tactics of walking instead assumed the perspective of the rat in a labyrinth.[109] And, when Michel Serres wished to demonstrate the priority of noise above information, who are the parasites that we find indulging in this feast? "The city rat invites the country rat onto the Persian rug."[110]

An anecdote that summarizes the predicaments of human rationality aptly involves two of the twentieth century's most formidable exponents of the maze. Sometime in 1969 or 1970 (the record is unclear), Jorge Luis Borges found himself in a meeting with a stranger from a foreign land. The American was an expert in the science of management and had come to Buenos Aires to deliver lectures on the topic. Wishing to make the most of the long voyage, he sought out the great writer, requesting an audience. At the meeting, undoubtedly perplexed by the incongruous encounter—a fantastic pairing that would not have been out of place in his fictions—Borges asked of his guest: "But I'd like to know why you are interested in having this conversation."

Herbert Simon had long admired the stories of Borges. He explained, with reference to his own 1956 paper on "Rational Choice and the Structure of Behavior," that as a social scientist, he had developed a model of life "as a search through the corridors of a labyrinth, greatly branching and populated by a number of goals to attain."[111] Not long after, he was recommended Borges's *Ficciones*, and was especially struck by the short story, "The Library of Babel," which involved

---

[109] Michel de Certeau, *The Practice of Everyday Life*, trans. Steven Rendall (Berkeley, CA; Los Angeles; London: University of California Press, 1984).

[110] Michel Serres, *The Parasite*, trans. Lawrence R. Schehr (Baltimore; London: Johns Hopkins University Press, 1982), p. 3.

[111] Simon, *Models of My Life*, p. 176.

the traversal of a labyrinthine structure as well. Simon believed that there was an affinity between his work and that of Borges. He wanted to learn more about his counterpart's understanding of the maze: What role did it play in his thinking? How had it come to his attention?

The body of research from 1956 that Simon singled out to introduce himself to Borges had been pursued somewhat at a tangent to the other work he had initiated that same year in collaboration with Allen Newell and J. C. Shaw. Although conducted in parallel to the Logic Theorist—and, indeed, most productively considered in tandem—these theories of "rational choice" did not rely on computing machinery. They are, nevertheless, especially useful in elucidating Simon's eccentricity with respect to the mainstream of cognitivism, and in particular his incompatibility with their hierarchies of animacy. The focus in Simon's research was directed towards elaborating a model of rational behavior to rival dominant understandings of "economic man." Specifically, he contested the assumptions of complete information and perfect judgment that had underpinned the orthodoxy of economic rationality; if successful, this theory would

> replace the global rationality of economic man with a kind of rational behavior that is compatible with the access to information and the computational capacities that are actually possessed by organisms, including man, in the kinds of environments in which such organisms exist.[112]

Claude Shannon's maze solving machine was constrained by its limited memory; for Simon, this should be seen as a feature, not a bug. The "environment" Simon specified did not reflect "some physically objective world in its totality, but only those aspects of the totality that have relevance as the 'life space' of the organism considered."[113]

---

[112] Herbert A. Simon, "A Behavioral Model of Rational Choice," *The Quarterly Journal of Economics* 69, no. 1 (February 1955): 99.

[113] Herbert A. Simon, "Rational Choice and the Structure of the Environment," *Psychological Review* 63, no. 2 (1956): 130.

It was not lost on Simon that his stance threatened cherished ideals that were considered the proper dominion of a rational subject. As he acknowledged in "Rational Choice and the Structure of Behavior," the premise behind his model "is perhaps a more appropriate one for a rat than for a human."[114] In fact, the rat paradigm had already featured in his doctoral dissertation and would only be omitted from the text's published edition on the objections of a reviewer; Simon's principal reference at the time on psychological concerns were the writings of Edward Tolman, and he had appreciated that "the subjects of [Tolman's] experiments on choice were usually rats, not humans."[115] This model would remain a preoccupation throughout Simon's career. Aside from prompting the heuristic design of the Logic Theorist, the structure of a maze and the pursuit of goals within it provided the ballast for the theory he is perhaps best known for: "bounded rationality" replaced the comprehensive insight into a situation possessed by economic man with occluded views and finite processing abilities. According to Simon, rational behavior did not involve complete dedication towards finding the optimal solution; it did not seek to "maximize" the expected utility of an outcome but rather to "satisfice"—that is, to reach an acceptable compromise in terms of expenditure in obtaining a passable solution given the costs of acquiring and processing information.

Borges responded to Simon's queries with some biographical and linguistic curiosities. He recalled having seen an engraving of a labyrinth when he was a boy; he pointed to the ambiguity

---

[114] Ibid. Simon's article concludes: "The analysis set forth here casts serious doubt on the usefulness of current economic and statistical theories of rational behavior as bases for explaining the characteristics of human and other organismic rationality. It suggests an alternative approach to the description of rational behavior that is more closely related to psychological theories of perception and cognition, and that is in closer agreement with the facts of behavior as observed in laboratory and field" (p. 138).

[115] Simon, *Models of My Life*, p. 86.

in the English word, *amaze*, which simultaneously suggested both a sense of surprise (i.e., *amazement*) and embedded a reference to the labyrinth (i.e., *a maze*)—Simon was not persuaded by such factoids. He wanted to understand the reasoning that Borges followed: "What is the connection between the labyrinth of the Minotaur and your labyrinth, which calls for continual choice? Does the analogy go beyond the general concept?"

Again, Borges parried, denying that he trafficked in "abstract ideas." "When I write," he insisted, "I don't think in terms of teaching." Simon was reluctant to accept these deflections. He had, in fact, recently tried his hand at story writing (although he did not admit the novice effort to his esteemed host).[116] This literary venture—his first and last—did begin from a model: "The Apple: A Story of a Maze" was intended to convey the lessons of Simon's research into rational behavior. The same, he was confident, must have been the case for Borges. Could it be denied that "The Library of Babel" was modelled on an abstraction?

"Not true!" Borges refuted categorically. He had been working at a small library amongst a group of "disagreeable" colleagues ("ignorant people, stupid really"). Feeling that he was trapped in this library, he resolved to invent a universe that expressed its horrors—"an interminable library."

I suspect that it was not any particularities to the Borgesian fictive sensibility that the theorist of decision making had struggled with; rather, it is difficult to think of any other approach to literary production that Simon might have found resonance with. Despite his evident credentials as a rat sympathist, Simon would certainly have failed to qualify as an Oulipian, that group whom

---

[116] The full text is, however, included in his memoirs. See Simon, *Models of My Life*, pp. 180-188.

Raymond Queneau identified as "rats who build the labyrinth from which they plot an escape."[117] For Queneau, construction precedes its proposal, the dust of activity settled before any plan can be hatched; a scene has already been shaped before the prospect of conscious determination is raised. Such a twisted topology could not have even occurred to Simon, who remained a deeply committed rationalist, even if an imperfect, "bounded" one. Surely a plan must be the basis for a course of action, not its result? If one had to rely on heuristics, were these simplifications not modelled from basic reason? What good was any Image, if the imagination was not grounded in solid Understanding?

And thus, with some admirable honesty and more than a hint of disappointment, Simon had to concede: "So Borges denied that there was an abstract model underlying 'The Library of Babel' or 'The Garden of Paths that Fork.' He wrote stories; he did not instantiate models. He was a teller of tales."[118]

§2.5: The Cultural Politics of Skill: Computer Science as "Procedural Epistemology"

When Alan Turing specified his programming system for the Manchester Mark II, he took a moment to offer some words on the craft of its application. First and foremost amongst the principles he discussed was a deceptively simple piece of common sense: "Make a plan" (*PH*, p. 61). To Turing, it was clear that that such maxims bordered on the tautological and—however true they might be—could not have been particularly helpful to the eager initiate: "This rather baffling

---

[117] Raymond Queneau, *La littérature potentielle* (Paris: Éditions Gallimard, 1973): "Oulipiens: rats qui ont à construire le labyrinthe dont ils se proposent de sortir" (p. 36).

[118] Simon, *Models of My Life*, p. 179

piece of advice is often offered in identical words to the beginner in chess. Likewise the writer of a short story is advised to 'think of a plot' or an inventor to 'have an idea.' These things are not the kind that we try to make rules about" (*PH*, p. 61).

Indeed, if—as George Miller and his colleagues would soon propose—a computer program may itself be thought of as a Plan of sorts, the suggestion that programmers "make a plan" raised the threat of an infinite regress. Considered that way, preliminary work towards formulating a plan (*qua* computer program) involved outlining a plan (*qua* preparation)—and would that secondary plan not in turn require its own derivative plan? (*et cetera* ...) This potentially endless recursion could only be halted by injecting some kind of non-formalizable ingenuity from a dimension beyond the specifications of planning. Thus, although Turing persevered in the attempt to suggest a more concrete set of best practices, he was wise to have curbed his readers' expectations with the warning: "Programming is a skill best acquired by practice and example rather than from books. The remarks given here are therefore quite inadequate" (*PH*, p. 59).

An excess of subjective competency was key in the ontological and epistemological revaluations surrounding the cultural politics of planning. The "skill" referred to here is implicitly alluded to when Mark Priestley reiterates Turing's insight: "My practical experience of programming had led me to understand it as a very different type of activity from the formal manipulations of logical proof."[119] Priestley's history of the role of formalization in computing highlights the institutional work that was required to fuse these different activities into a single compound. As he argues, the connection between programming and formal logic should be understood "not as a *fact* about the two disciplines, but as something more like a *decision* made

---

[119] Priestley, *A Science of Operations*, p. v.

by identifiable historical actors as to how the new discipline of programming should be understood and structured." Towards the end of the 1950s, the priority afforded to formal expression via the linguistic conception of programming was foundational in consolidating the disciplinary hegemony of a new "computing science"; accounts such as Priestley's are indispensable in historicizing the contingency of this computer-scientific *dispositif*.

But what if the history of programming was not oriented around the legitimization of computer science but instead refracted through the specters of Turology? How should the activity of programming be rendered if not figured through a computer-scientifically trained mind but the eyes and hands of Turingineers and Turologists? The cult of genius surrounding the programmer has hardly been diminished by the drive to turn computing into a respectable science. Consequently, rather than writing Turology off as a momentary aberration, acknowledging its role as a persistent undercurrent percolating alongside the normative enterprise of computer science directs attention to the repressed contradictions of their field.

While it is unlikely that the notion of a "computer science" would appear paradoxical to anyone today, perhaps it should. This formulation expresses a project slightly distinct from a straightforward "science of computers." The two terms from which it is comprised are held together in an awkward tension in which each seems to preclude the other: any meticulous interest in computing machinery had been considered a threat to scientific propriety ("computer" = *not*-"science"), and conversely any aspirations to being scientific had entailed a disavowal of the technological substrate of computation ("science" = *not*-"computer").

In its earliest years, the credibility of this label provoked a mixture of suspicion and hostility. A common refrain at the time even held that "any science that needs the word 'science' in its name is by definition not a science."[120] John Backus's recollections of early efforts in programming depicts a culture disposed towards circumstantial fixes, appreciative as much of the ingenuity required to conjure up creative solutions (or "hacks") as of its resistance to standards of normativity. His description of the practice as "a black art, a private arcane matter" pointed to the lack of general principles and established conventions that allowed it to escape managerial discipline. "Programming in America in the 1950s," Backus wrote, "had a vital frontier enthusiasm."[121] Plagued by issues of reliability in hardware and written under pressures of limited computational resources like speed and memory, early software was characterized by the prevalence of tricks which worked only on individual machines, resulting in an artisanal (and decidedly unsystematic) mode of production. Historian of computing Nathan Ensmenger has elaborated that in order to achieve "acceptable levels of usability and performance," programmers of that era "had to cultivate a series of idiosyncratic and highly individual craft techniques designed to overcome the limitations of primitive hardware."[122] That is, a prerequisite of effective production was the acquisition of deep practical familiarity with the quirks of devices ("computer"), making the prospect of an autonomous discipline of secure knowledge appear dubious (*not*-"science").

On the other hand, those more professionally inclined sought to establish a respectable basis for their work. Backus identified the impediment to be an absence of legibility: "Existing

---

[120] See Paul Ceruzzi, "Electronics Technology and Computer Science, 1940-1975: A Coevolution," *Annals in the History of Computing* 10, no. 4 (1989): 265.

[121] John Backus, "Programming in America in the 1950s—Some Personal Impressions," in *A History of Computing in the Twentieth Century: A Collection of Essays*, eds. N. Metropolis, J. Howlett, and Gian-Carlo Rota (New York; London: Academic Press, 1980), p. 126.

[122] Ensmenger, *The Computer Boys Take Over*, p. 43.

programs for similar problems were unreadable and hence could not be adapted to new uses.... Thus each problem required a unique beginning at square one, and the success of a program depended primarily on the programmer's private techniques and invention."[123] Along similar lines, Edsger Dijkstra would question in a 1975 speech if the programmer was a "Craftsman or Scientist?"; here, as well, the challenge was treated as a problem of transmission: "To make implicit knowledge explicit and to discuss how to describe skills, so that they can be transferred, implies, if not the birth at least the conception of a new science."[124] Dijkstra would later polemically summarize the ethos he defended, comparing physical materialization of machinery to pathological infection: "I don't need to waste my time with a computer just because I am a computer scientist. (Medical researchers are not required to suffer from the diseases they investigate.)"[125] In order to acquire legitimacy as a body of knowledge ("science"), output had to be formalized in machine-independent terms (*not*-"computer").

The persistence of craftsmanship as both an unattainable ideal and looming danger against epistemic legibility plots the broader terrain in which skill was reevaluated as a mode of knowledge amidst the ascendence of modern computing. Dijkstra warned specifically against "a disastrous blending, viz. that of the technology of the craftsman with the pretence of the scientist":

> The craftsman has no conscious, formal grip on his subject matter, he just "knows" how to use his tools. If this is combined with the scientist's approach of making one's knowledge explicit, he will describe what he knows explicitly, i.e. his tools,

---

[123] Backus, "Programming in America," p. 126. Backus himself worked on technologies to formalize these processes, including the programming language Fortran and a notation for precise description of the syntax of such languages, the Backus-Naur Form. See further, for Backus's commentary on Fortran and his notation system, pp. 130-133.

[124] Edsger W. Dijkstra, "EWD480: Craftsman or Scientist?" in *Selected Writings on Computing: A Personal Perspective*, ed. David Gries (New York: Springer-Verlag, 1982), p. 105.

[125] Edsger W. Dijkstra, "EWD1305: Answers to questions from students of Software Engineering" (unpublished manuscript, 28 November 2000), http://www.cs.utexas.edu/users/EWD/transcriptions/EWD13xx/EWD1305.html.

> instead of describing how to use them! If he is a painter he will tell his pupils all he knows about all brushmakers and all he knows about the fluctuating price of canvas. If he is a professor of computing science, he will tell his students all he knows about existing programming languages, existing machines, existing operating systems, existing application packages and as many tricks as he has discovered how to program around their idiosyncrasies. And in a short while, he will not only tell what the manual says should be punched in column 17 of the first card in order to indicate your choice of priority queue, but he will also tell and explain the illegal punching in column 17 that will place your program in the highest priority queue while only charging you for the lowest priority one.[126]

This doubled affirmation ("computer" *and* "science") combined the worst attributes of craftsman and scientist, resulting in the systematic communication of trivial details. A rejection of craft did not imply the straightforward affirmation or adoption of its apparent other, science.

Dijkstra's rant suggests the impetus behind an influential textbook of computer science, *Structure and Interpretation of Computer Programs*. Determined to avoid the absurdity of rigorous instruction in contingent specifications, it prefaced its course of study with the provocation that the subject it introduced "is not a science and that its significance has little to do with computers" (*SICP*, p. xvi)—that is, *not*-"computer" but also *not*-"science." For its authors, Harold Abelson and Gerald Jay Sussman, not only did the peculiarities of machinery occlude a more philosophical interest they believed their discipline offered, so too did received patterns of thinking:

> The computer revolution is a revolution in the way we think and in the way we express what we think. The essence of this change is the emergence of what might best be called *procedural epistemology*—the study of the structure of knowledge from an imperative point of view, as opposed to the more declarative point of view taken by classical mathematical subjects. Mathematics provides a framework for dealing precisely with notions of "what is." Computation provides a framework for dealing precisely with notions of "how to" (*SICP*, p. xvi).

---

[126] Dijkstra, "Craftsman or Scientist?" p. 106.

Developed to support the entry-level course for students majoring in electrical engineering and computer science at the Massachusetts Institute of Technology (MIT) in the late 1970s, Abelson and Sussman's approach is said to have "revolutionized the landscape of the introductory computing curriculum," shifting emphasis away from the "tyranny of syntax."[127] Indeed, their choice of a less-than-popular programming language, a dialect of LISP called Scheme, as the means of instruction was motivated by its relative syntactic simplicity, with the (intended) effect that "after a short time we forget about the syntactic details of the language (because there are none) and get on with the real issues—figuring out what we want to compute, how we will decompose the problems into manageable parts, and how we will work on the parts" (*SICP*, pp. xvi and 2-4).[128]

Keen to reframe "the real issues" of computing from the day-to-day task of producing working programs, Abelson and Sussman justified their curious disregard for immediate utility (and, indeed, commercial value) by highlighting a set of alternate virtues which in effect positioned computer science within the tradition of the liberal arts. First, it was proposed that "a computer language is not just a way of getting a computer to perform operations but rather that it is a novel formal medium for expressing ideas about methodology. Thus, programs must be written for people to read, and only incidentally for machines to execute" (*SICP*, p. xv). In formulating computer science as a sort of media theoretical endeavor, importance was weighted towards the

---

[127] Matthias Felleisen, Robert Bruce Findler, Matthew Flatt, and Shriram Krishnamurthi, "The structure and interpretation of the computer science curriculum," *Journal of Functional Programming* 14, issue 4 (July 2004): 365.

[128] For an account that contests the merits of Lisp-like languages in this context, cf. Philip Wadler, "A critique of Abelson and Sussman, or, Why calculating is better than scheming," *ACM SIGPLAN Notices* 22, no. 3 (March 1987): 83-94. Wadler argues: "Some people may wish to dismiss many of the issues raised in this paper as being 'just syntax.' It is true that much debate over syntax is of little value. But it is also true that a good choice of notation can greatly aid learning and thought, and a poor choice can hinder it" (p. 85).

development of interpretative skills. Mastery entailed the introjection of a filtering operation, resulting in the cultivation of a faculty of judgment. Participants who successfully completed training were thus distinguished as much by their ability to take in arcane combinations of symbols, as by their facility at discerning what may be safely ignored and thus excluded from attention: "They should be capable of reading a 50-page-long program, if it is written in an exemplary style. They should know what not to read, and what they need not understand at any moment" (*SICP*, p. xvi).

A second point more precisely addressed the appropriate terrain for novices who "have had little or no prior formal training in computation." Priority was displaced both from the acquisition of specific empirical knowledge ("not the syntax of particular programming-language constructs, nor clever algorithms for computing particular functions efficiently"), as well as forms of abstract reasoning ("nor even the mathematical analysis of algorithms and the foundations of computing"). Instead, Abelson and Sussman considered the "essential material" for beginners to be "the techniques used to control the intellectual complexity of large software systems" (*SICP*, p. xv). Again, execution on machines, whether actual circuitry or the idealized models used in algorithmic analysis, was only of ancillary relevance. While it was common throughout the 1980s to frame the problems posed by computation in terms of (algorithmic) complexity, the focus here expressly on "*intellectual* complexity" subtly shifts the implications of the term; not only are programs primarily situated in the mind, as "techniques" they must be practiced, incorporated, and performed.[129] The precise upshot to this approach was identified succinctly by Philip Wadler— even as he took issue with details in Abelson and Sussman's textbook (such as their use of

---

[129] See Ceruzzi, "Electronics Technology and Computer Science," pp. 257-275.

Scheme), Wadler nevertheless concurred with their general outlook, stating even more explicitly that "[t]he purpose of the first course is to teach basic principles and develop good habits of thought."[130]

These values—programming as a practice of "reading" and "writing"; computer science as a pedagogy of "technique" with "basic principles" and "good habits"—are at odds with conceptions of *code* common in the critical theorization of software. The latter have tended to emphasize an operative or functional dimension, noting that code "can be rendered into machine-readable commands that are then executed," "causes things to happen," and "is the only language that is executable ... machinic first and linguistic second."[131] Self-presentation and identification by programmers like Abelson and Sussman, on the other hand, has dwelled on the exact opposite. Notably, Donald Knuth would champion the practice of "literate programming," urging that "instead of imagining that our main task is to instruct a *computer* what to do, let us concentrate rather on explaining to *human beings* what we want a computer to do."[132] Likewise, Dijkstra had characterized algorithms as a means of "executional abstraction ... to map different computations upon each other," emphasizing that "it refers to the way in which we can get a specific computation

---

[130] Wadler, "Critique of Abelson and Sussman," p. 93.

[131] Wendy Hui Kyong Chun, *Programmed Visions: Software and Memory* (Cambridge, MA: MIT Press, 2011), p. 51; N. Katherine Hayles, *My Mother Was a Computer: Digital Subjects and Literary Texts* (Chicago; London: University of Chicago Press, 2005), p. 49; Alexander R. Galloway, "Language Wants To Be Overlooked: On Software and Ideology," *Journal of Visual Culture* 5, no. 3 (December 2006): 325-326.
Chun's description of "source code as fetish" raises the point of readability: "source code must be able to function, even if it does not function – that is, even if it is never executed.... When programming, one must be able to read one's own program – to follow its logic and to predict its outcome, whether or not this outcome coincides with one's prediction" (*Programmed Visions*, p. 51).

[132] Donald Knuth, "Literate Programming," *The Computer Journal* 27, issue 2 (January 1984): 97-111.

within our intellectual grip by considering it as a member of a large class of computations"—that is, he emphasized the mental process of "abstraction" over the actual "executional" function.[133]

Such accounts prompt an understanding of the computer program as a medium of literacy. A study of computational media engaging with this terrain would takes its cue from neither hardware nor software proper, but computation's pedagogical apparatus—in other words, these concerns direct media theory towards computation's role in informing a system of inculcation and sense-making, or its operations as a cultural technique. Friedrich Kittler, who appropriated the notion of cultural techniques for a media theoretical context, also offered reflections on the concept of code more appropriate to this direction:

> The so-called "hidden layers" in today's neuronal networks present a good, if still trifling, example of how far computing procedures can stray from their design engineers, even if everything works out well in the end. Thus, either we write code that in the manner of natural constants reveals the determinations of the matter itself, but at the same time pay the price of millions of lines of code and billions of dollars for digital hardware; or else we leave the task up to machines that derive code from their own environment, although we then cannot read—that is to say: articulate—this code. Ultimately, the dilemma between code and language seems insoluble.[134]

Kittler's earlier study of German poetry circa 1800, first published in the same year as Abelson and Sussman's textbook, had turned away from interpretation of what poems mean towards an examination of the conditions through which meaning-making was instilled as a defining characteristic of subjectivity, examining the "elementary acculturation techniques" of learning to read; this initial translation of the compound word, *Kulturtechniken*, emphasizing the dynamics of "acculturation" (as opposed to a more static reference to "culture"), helpfully highlights the

---

[133] Edsger W. Dijkstra, *A Discipline of Programming* (Englewood Cliffs, NJ: Prentice-Hall, 1976), p. 1.

[134] Friedrich Kittler, "Code," in *Software Studies: A Lexicon*, ed. Matthew Fuller, trans. Tom Morrison with Florian Cramer (Cambridge, MA: MIT Press, 2008), p. 46.

processual aspects implied in the production of educated or cultured subjects.[135] His later commentary on code takes up similar concerns, situating it within histories of encoding practices such as encryption. As described and performed by Kittler (who maintained his own sort of "literate programming" practice), computing is a factor directly implicated in cultures of literacy, a matter of being able to "read" and "articulate" what is coded. Indeed, Kittler's assessment of instructional primers from the 1800s may well be applied to textbooks on computer programming from the 1970s and 80s: "The project was to replace rote learning with 'understanding.'"[136]

Addressing programming as a cultural technique recalls this early pedagogical inflection whilst also resonating with subsequent attention to threshold operations that articulate the emergence of symbolic distinction.[137] Such media theory is less concerned with the attributes of mediums *per se*, than with their bearing on conditions of legibility that establish the standards differentiating sense from nonsense, demarcating the literate from the illiterate. Following these approaches, my interest here is as well less in determining an ontology of code (the defining and definitive attributes of a medium), than in historicizing conceptions of code and placing it within

---

[135] Kittler writes: "Maternal instruction, in its positivity, was the input component of elementary acculturation techniques. Around 1800 a new type of book began to appear, one that delegated to mothers first the physical and mental education of their children, then their alphabetization. ... The titles speak for themselves. They leave little doubt about the identity of the instructor recommended; they emphasize that it is only by conferring elementary acculturation techniques on mothers that the Self of this identity has been found" (Friedrich Kittler, *Discourse Networks 1800/1900*, trans. Michael Meteer, with Chris Cullen [Stanford, CA: Stanford University Press, 1985], pp. 27-53, here pp. 27-28).
This usage puts a polemic twist on the scope of the cultured liberal arts and their disavowed relationship towards technical competency. As Bernard Dionysius Geoghegan has noted, "according to [Erhard] Schüttpelz, Kittler encountered the term as a student and instructor at the University of Freiburg in the late 1970s and early 1980s, when the term *Kulturtechniken* was resurfacing in German as a designation for competencies in reading, writing, and arithmetic. This definition recalled the 18th- and 19th-century definition of culture as liberal arts" ("After Kittler: On the Cultural Techniques of Recent German Media Theory," *Theory, Culture & Society* 30, no. 6 [2013]: 76).

[136] Kittler, *Discourse Networks*, p. 28.

[137] See Siegert, *Cultural Techniques*.

currents of knowledge practices (in what capacities, to what ends, and with what effects does a medium get treated as such).

Abelson and Sussman's thesis of (*not-*)computer (*not-*)science as "procedural epistemology" could be read as a sort of culmination to a set of contradictions latent in computer scientific discourse stemming from the vicissitudes surrounding skill. Their prioritization of a pedagogy in which students learn to "have a good feel for the elements of style and the aesthetics of programming" (*SICP*, p. xv) reiterates the sentiments of their colleague Marvin Minsky, whom they cite in an epigraph:

> A computer is like a violin. You can imagine a novice trying first a phonograph and then a violin. The latter, he says, sounds terrible. That is the argument we have heard from our humanists and most of our computer scientists. Computer programs are good, they say, for particular purposes, but they aren't flexible. Neither is a violin, or a typewriter, until you learn how to use it.[138]

Minsky's article explaining "Why Programming Is a Good Medium for Expressing Poorly-Understood and Sloppily Formulated Ideas" (1967) had disputed the notion that computing's limitations constrained its relevance to domains of "perfect precision" or "rigid rules." Initially presented at a conference on the topic of "Computers in Design and Communication," it severely departed from the discussions of possible applications of computing machinery taken up by the other papers there. Whereas, in the examples Minsky provides, the *technology* of a phonograph minimizes the impact of human factors in the operating process, comparing computers to violins implies the opposite, framing it as necessitating training in *techniques*: "To take advantage of the

---

[138] Marvin Minsky, "Why Programming Is a Good Medium for Expressing Poorly-Understood and Sloppily Formulated Ideas," in *Design and Planning II—Computers in Design and Communication*, eds. Martin Krampen and Peter Seitz (New York: Hastings House, 1967), p. 121; cited in Abelson and Sussan, *SICP*, p. xv.

unsurpassed flexibility of this medium requires tremendous skill—technical, intellectual, and esthetic."[139]

Sussman's doctoral dissertation (of which Minsky was a reader) further pursued this line of inquiry. Completed at MIT's Artificial Intelligence Laboratory, it proposed "A Computational Model of Skill Acquisition" (1973):

> An important property of skill is <u>effectiveness</u>. It wouldn't be enough to memorize all of the facts in the plumber's handbook, even if that could be done. The knowledge would not then be in an effective, usable form. One becomes skilled at plumbing by practice. Without practice it doesn't all hang together. When faced with a problem, a novice attacks it slowly and awkwardly, painfully having to reason out each step, and often making expensive and time-consuming mistakes.
>
> Thus the skill, plumbing, is more than just the information in the plumber's handbook; it is the unwritten knowledge derived from practice which ties the written knowledge together, making it usable.
>
> - Just what is this unwritten knowledge? How is a skilled person different from a knowledgeable, unskilled one?
> - What is the process by which a person develops skill through practice?
>
> The research reported in this document is an attempt to provide these questions with precise, mechanistic answers by the construction of a computational performance model, a computer program which exhibits behavior identifiable with skill acquisition.[140]

That similar concerns regarding "effectiveness" and "unwritten knowledge" had been consistently broached throughout the postwar era—for instance, in Gilbert Ryle's distinction between "knowing that" and "knowing how," as well as in Michael Polanyi's theorization of "tacit knowledge"—may have somewhat dampened the scandal of adopting plumbing as a paradigmatic

---

[139] Ibid., p. 117 and p. 121.

[140] Gerald Jay Sussman, "A Computational Model of Skill Acquisition" (PhD diss., MIT, 1973), pp. 5-6.

point of reference for advanced work in mathematics.[141] Yet, Sussman posed a somewhat more challenging proposition in his treatment of skill. Rather than contrast written knowledge with skillful practice, he sought "precise, mechanistic answers" to what would seem to be, by definition, imprecise and extra-mechanistic.

The normative priority afforded in recent critical interest to skill and craftsmanship as modes of embodied competency echoes earlier discussions that were more overtly directed against an epistemology of computing, such as Lucy Suchman's distinction between *Plans and Situated Actions* (1985):

> Skilled activities like driving proceed in a way that is only derivatively and summarily characterizable in terms of procedures or rules—and such rules as do get formulated are only used when the activity needs for some reason to be explicated, as for instruction, or at times of breakdown when otherwise transparent ways of proceeding need to be inspected or revised.[142]

Specifically, the principal target here was the computer metaphor of mind. Suchman's objections in contrasting "skilled activity" against "rules" were directed against what she referred to as the "planning model," a framework in which purposeful action was conceptualized as the implementation of an underlying design independent of the exigencies of a situation. Although the Plan had been familiar—indeed, dominant—in research on artificial intelligence and cognitive science since introduced by George Miller and his colleagues in the late 1950s, Suchman

---

[141] See Gilbert Ryle, *The Concept of Mind* (London: Routledge, 2009), pp. 14-48; and, Michael Polanyi, *Personal Knowledge: Towards a Post-Critical Philosophy* (London: Routledge, 1962), esp. "Skills," pp. 51-68.

[142] Lucy A. Suchman, *Plans and Situated Actions: The problem of human-machine communication* (Palo Alto, CA: Xerox Corporation, Palo Alto Research Centers, 1985), pp. 36-37. In an updated edition, Suchman offers reflections on the reception and readings of the original text. See Lucy A. Suchman, *Human-Machine Reconfigurations: Plans and Situated Actions, 2nd Edition* (Cambridge, UK: Cambridge University Press, 2007).
See, as examples of more recent critical reflection on skill and craftsmanship, Tim Ingold, *The Perception of the Environment: Essays on Livelihood, Dwelling and Skill* (New York; London: Routledge, 2000) and Richard Sennett, *The Craftsman* (Yale University Press, 2008).

considered this model deficient due to its neglect of the particularities of circumstance. By contrast, she championed an alternative which accounted for this "situated"-ness of actions. The influence of Martin Heidegger (via Hubert Dreyfus) was explicit, restricting the scope of planning to retrospective reflection in "times of breakdown." Understood this way, formal explication was not considered a definitive dictation of process but only resorted to as an intervention:

> The "unready-to-hand," in Heidegger's phrase, comprises occasions wherein equipment that is involved in some practical activity becomes unwieldy, temporarily broken, or unavailable. At such times, inspection and practical problem solving occurs, aimed at repairing or eliminating the disturbance in order to "get going again." In such times of disturbance, our use of equipment becomes "explicitly manifest as a goal-oriented activity," and we may then try to formulate procedures or rules....
>
> Situated action, in other words, is not made explicit by rules and procedures. Rather, when situated action becomes in some way problematic, rules and procedures are explicated for purposes of deliberation and the action, which is otherwise neither rule-based nor procedural, is then made accountable to them.[143]

For Suchman, in other words, the *mediation* of "rules" is called on to remedy a breakdown in the *immediacy* of "action."

Suchman's argument is exemplary of a tendency to narrate the historical relation between techniques and technologies as a movement from the former to the latter—that is, as reflecting a movement "to replace subject-centred skills with objective principles of mechanical functioning."[144] Skill, in other words, promised the restoration of immediacy; it contributed to a primitivist celebration of artisanal values as pre-technological or anterior to the alienating effects

---

[143] Suchman, *Plans and Situated Actions*, pp. 37-38.

[144] Ingold, *Perception of the Environment*: "the transition, in the history of human technicity, from the hand-tool to the machine, is not from the simple to the complex, but is rather tantamount to the withdrawal of the producer, in person, from the centre to the periphery of the productive process. It is a history, in other words, not of complexification but of externalization" (p. 289).

of industrial modernity. Understanding programming as a cultural technique suggests another, perhaps somewhat counterintuitive configuration of terms. It breaks apart the blunt dichotomy in which skill is set in opposition to formal explication, insisting on their coupling as a dialectically entangled pair—without one, the other would remain unthinkable.

It was only amidst the proliferation of modern computing technologies that skilled techniques became legible as a mode of knowledge; far from precipitating an eradication of technique, technology was its condition of possibility. As Bernard Stiegler has argued, "[a]t the beginning of its history, philosophy separates *tekhnē* from *epistēmē*."[145] The irony in the expression, "procedural epistemology," stems from this constitutive exclusion of the procedural from the realm of epistemology. Programming can quite appropriately be construed as "a novel formal medium" (*SICP*, p. xv) in this regard, not just as an efficient vehicle for the expression of procedures, but in redefining the thresholds of the epistemic sphere.

I find it especially compelling to elaborate on this alternative with reference to a specific historical trajectory, the development of Michael Polanyi's interest in a tacit dimension to knowledge. Stemming directly from the introduction of computing machinery, Polanyi's earliest writings addressing skill were formulated in response to "The Hypothesis of Cybernetics."[146] Published in 1952 as part of a series of articles "on the question of whether machines can be said to think," the intervention subtly reframed the provocations that his colleague at Manchester, Alan Turing, had raised less than two years earlier in suggesting the equivalence between "Computing

---

[145] Bernard Stiegler, *Technics and Time, 1: The Fault of Epimetheus*, trans. Richard Beardsworth and George Collins (Stanford, CA: Stanford University Press, 1998), p. 1.

[146] See Michael Polanyi, "The Hypothesis of Cybernetics," *The British Journal for the Philosophy of Science* 2, no. 8 (Feb 1952): 312-315.

Machinery and Intelligence" (1950).[147] Rather than directly responding to the possibility of thinking machines, Polanyi posed "the question of whether the operations of a formalised deductive system might conceivably be equivalent to the operations of the mind." His terminological shift away from what others had called "psychological" factors (i.e., thinking) to an emphasis on "unformalised" elements redirected the challenge raised by computing towards "ordinary speech," the exercise of which he considered to be grounded in the competency of "proper use":

> No undefined term can be introduced unless its use is first explained by ordinary speech or demonstrated by examples. An undefined term is a sign indicating the proper use which is to be made of it. The acceptance of an undefined term implies, therefore, that we believe that we know its proper use though this is not to be formally described. This proper use is a skill of which we declare ourselves to be possessed.

Whether or not any implementation in machinery could pass Turing's test was for him besides the point; of sole relevance was the processing of a symbolic system, and he maintained "that a formal system of symbols and operations functions as a deductive system only by virtue of unformalised supplements."

According to Andrew Hodges, these concerns had already been the focus of casual discussion between Turing and Polanyi since the late 1940s: "Alan would run over to the Polanyi home, which was not far from his lodgings at Hale. (Once Polanyi visited Alan, only to find him practising the violin in freezing cold, not bothering or not daring to ask the landlady for proper heat)" (*AT*, p. 521). Their interests would lead to a seminar on "The Mind and the Computing

---

[147] See A. M. Turing, "Computing Machinery and Intelligence," *Mind* 49, no. 236 (October 1950): 433-460.

Machine" in 1949, a year before more familiar landmarks in the history of artificial intelligence like the publication of Turing's "Computing Machinery and Intelligence."

These exchanges inflect the stakes of Turing's reference to skill in the *Programmer's Handbook* he wrote for the Manchester Mark II, and hint at what he may have had in mind when he determined: "These things are not the kind that we try to make rules about" (*PH*, p. 61). They further raise the possibility of historicizing the emergence of artificial intelligence in a way that incorporates tacit knowledge as a constitutive dimension, rather than considering it as a corrective. Although Turing is principally remembered for his speculations relating to the extreme possibilities of formal systems, his work also includes a persistent tarrying with non-formalizable virtuosity that readily lends itself to the myth of the Turologist. On this, I am especially intrigued by the bit of biographical gossip that Hodges could not resist adding as a parenthetical supplement. Hodges's intention in recalling Turing "practising the violin in freezing cold" must surely have been to underscore a sense of eccentricity by drawing attention to his disregard for conventional standards of domesticity. However, I cannot help but notice a detail that suggests another possible interpretation of this scene: when found by Polanyi, Turing was not listening to a phonograph (i.e., a deployment of technology); rather, he was engaged with the violin (i.e., an exercise of technique). Read in light of Marvin Minsky's claim that "a computer is like a violin," Hodges's quip invites a more ambiguous appreciation of practice. On the one hand, it presents the quasi-monastic indifference to bodily comfort. On the other hand, it simultaneously includes a posture of deep absorption. Both disembodiment and total sensuousness, this glimpse of Turing condenses the dilemmas of programming and the multitude of fantasies it entertained as a mode of knowledge.

Chapter 3: Sphygmography and Screening

§3.1: Screen Media: A (Non-)Philosophical History of Dots

An inquiry into "how it is possible for pure concepts of understanding to be applied to appearances as such"—into establishing any connection at all between the intellect and the senses—leads Immanuel Kant to quickly decide:

> Now clearly there must be something that is third, something that must be homogeneous with the category, on the one hand, and with the appearance, on the other hand, and that thus makes possible the application of the category to the appearance. This mediating presentation must be pure (i.e. without anything empirical), and yet must be both *intellectual*, on the one hand, and *sensible*, on the other hand. Such a presentation is the *transcendental schema*.[1]

What exactly is this mysterious *mediating third*? And what distinguishes its operations from those of an "image" (to which Kant had already assigned the seemingly similar task of synthesizing intuitions for the benefit of concepts)? Some clarification follows, but the conclusion it leads to only escalates perplexity: "This schematism of our understanding, i.e., its schematism regarding appearances and their mere form, is a secret art residing in the depths of the human soul, an art whose true stratagems we shall hardly ever divine from nature and lay bare before ourselves."[2]

Such issues are undoubtedly crucial in tackling the epistemological system developed in the *Critique of Pure Reason* (1781/1787)—and, perhaps, also in approaching the enigmas of media. In addition, however, Kant's elaboration of this schema also prompts questions regarding *how* he articulates problems at the extremities of conceptual understanding. It is this second, procedurally-oriented aspect that will guide the direction taken here, leaving interpretation of the

---

[1] Immanuel Kant, *Critique of Pure Reason*, trans. Werner S. Pluhar (Indianapolis; Cambridge: Hackett Publishing Company, 1996), pp. 210-211 (A138/B177).

[2] Ibid., p. 214 (A141/B180-181).

profundities briefly hinted at slightly earlier (i.e. *what* it is or means) to those more philosophically-minded.

One passage immediately preceding the admission of intractable secrecy will be the focus of interest. Here, Kant writes:

> A schema is, in itself, always only a product of the imagination. Yet, because here the imagination's synthesis aims not at an individual intuition but at unity in the determination of sensibility, a schema must be distinguished from an image. **Thus if I put five dots after one another, like this, ... , then this result is an image of the number five.** Suppose on the other hand, that I only think a number as such, which might then be five or a hundred. Then my thought is more the presentation of a method for presenting – in accordance with a certain concept – a multitude (e.g., a thousand) in an image, than this image itself. Indeed, in the case of a thousand I could hardly survey that image and compare it with the concept. Now, this presentation of a universal procedure of the imagination for providing a concept with its image I call the schema for that concept.[3]

Or, more precisely, one should say: *here, Kant's publisher, Johann Friedrich Hartknoch of Riga, prints*. For in this paragraph we readers are not just confronted with the abstract idea of a text, but also the presentation of actual traces on a surface. At the limits of reasoning in dealing with cognitive capacities, the more conventional tools of the philosopher are set aside to make room for a demonstration of mark-making. Kant (momentarily) abandons logical argumentation; instead he employs the typographer's press to stage a graphical performance.

If, as Friedrich Kittler has argued, "German poetry begins with a sigh"[4] (*ach!*), might it be added that German philosophy – and, possibly, even the entire modern Western philosophical tradition – is based on dots? That Kant's treatment of "mediating" operations may indeed be taken

---

[3] Ibid., pp. 212-213 (A140-141/B179-180); my emphasis.

[4] Friedrich Kittler, *Discourse Networks 1800/1900*, trans. Michael Meteer with Chris Cullens (Stanford, CA: Stanford University Press, 1985), p. 3.

as an intrusion of the problem of media into philosophical territory is most overtly corroborated by Samuel F.B. Morse's "system of signs for transmitting intelligence between distant points," an invention he named the "American Electro-Magnetic Telegraph."[5] Morse's code echoes Kant's transcendental idealism in declaring that a sequence of five dots results in "an image of the number five":

> Signs of numerals consist, first, of ten dots or punctures, made in measured distances of equal extent from each other, upon paper or any substitute for paper, and in number corresponding with the numeral desired to be represented. Thus one dot or puncture for the numeral 1, two dots or punctures for the numeral 2, three of the same for 3, four for 4, five for 5, six for 6, seven for 7, eight for 8, nine for 9, and ten for 0, as particularly represented on the annexed drawing marked Example 1, Mode 1.[6]

More generally, Kant's maneuver occupies what Bernhard Siegert has described as the problem of "sign-signal distinction."[7] In the *Critique of Pure Reason*, an Imaginary unity mediates the passage from Real *signals* to Symbolic *signs*: "the imagination's synthesis" transmits correspondence of "five for 5," as Morse puts it—the first "five" refers to a collection of actual dots (which are, in themselves, meaningless; i.e., a signal), whereas the referent in the latter "5" is a conceptually meaningful numeral (which does not exist except as an element in a semiotic system; i.e., a sign). Implementation of typographic methods inevitably affirms its medium, in that the physical materiality of the channel is not an extraneous dimension to be elided in a quest for underlying

---

[5] Samuel F. B. Morse, Improvement in the Mode of Communicating Information by Signals by the Application of Electro-Magnetism, US Patent 1647A, filed 7 April 1838, and issued 20 June 1840, https://patents.google.com/patent/US1647A/en, p. 1.

[6] Ibid.

[7] Bernhard Siegert, *Cultural Techniques: Grids, Filters, Doors, and Other Articulations of the Real*, trans. Geoffrey Winthrop-Young (New York: Fordham University Press, 2015), pp. 19-32.

meaning but the very site of transformations between sense and nonsense, signification and insignificance.

Were Kant to have his way, the faculty of the imagination would be reasonably well-secured under the rule of its schema, the mediating third. But discord between the pair is only barely suppressed. Already in the first *Critique*, Kant alludes to troubling possibilities. These would have to be approached with caution – or, better still, avoided altogether. And, should one proceed with insufficient prudence, an unyielding stream of nonsense was ready to overwhelm even the most resolute of minds.

One century later, Hermann Ebbinghaus found himself in precisely such an unfortunate state when investigating another of the so-called "inner senses," *Memory* (1885). Ebbinghaus described his method of choice as the construction of "series of nonsense syllables."[8] First, "all possible syllables" were constructed from combinations of "the simple consonants of the alphabet and our eleven vowels and diphthongs." Then, "these syllables, about 2,300 in number, were mixed together and then drawn out by chance and used to construct series of different length." Over two separate periods, each lasting more than a year (1879-1880 and 1883-1884), he immersed himself in "the nonsense material," undertaking the solitary mission of conducting (and himself completing) daily tests of memorization with these series. References to these trials invariably describe them as "heroic"; William James was even sufficiently inspired to conduct his own studies "*à là* Ebbinghaus on series of nonsense-syllables" (although, apparently, not adequately

---

[8] Hermann Ebbinghaus, *Memory: A Contribution to Experimental Psychology* (New York: Teachers College, Columbia University, 1913), p. 22.

enough to subject *himself* to the regimen: "I induced two of my students to perform that experiment also ...").[9]

Even more deliberately than Kant, Ebbinghaus was determined to evacuate his material of meaning and any connections between the syllables that might be provoked semantically. To achieve this, the use of "special associations of the mnemotechnik type" was prohibited, artificially limiting his abilities of recollection to "the influence of the mere repetitions upon the natural memory."[10] Thus could he answer such questions as, "What number of syllables can be correctly recited after only one reading?," with complete precision:

> For me the number is usually seven. Indeed I have often succeeded in reproducing eight syllables, but this has happened only at the beginning of the tests and in a decided minority of the cases. In the case of six syllables on the other hand a mistake almost never occurs; with them, therefore, a single attentive reading involves an unusually large expenditure of energy for an immediately following reproduction.[11]

When a more demanding task of repeating 12 syllables was set, Ebbinghaus required 16.6 readings to reproduce the series correctly; upon increasing that further to 16 syllables, he required 30.0 repetitions; 24 syllables required 44.0 repetitions; and, 36 syllables required 55.0 repetitions.

This method was such a departure from traditional doctrine of memory based on an association of images that Kittler has described it as a "shift in paradigms," arguing that "Ebbinghaus presupposed forgetfulness, rather than memory and its capacity, in order to place the medium of the soul against a background of emptiness or erosion."[12] Thus, in line with these

---

[9] William James, *Principles of Psychology*, vol. 1 (New York: Henry Holt, 1890), pp. 676-679 (on Ebbinghaus's experiments) and n. 24 (on James's re-staging).

[10] Ebbinghaus, *Memory*, p. 25.

[11] Ebbinghaus, *Memory*, p. 47.

[12] Kittler, *Discourse Networks*, p. 207.

revised presuppositions, Sigmund Freud's discussion of "Screen Memories" (1899), for example, would begin from the premise that "we are so much accustomed to this *lack of memory* of the impressions of childhood that we are apt to overlook the problem underlying it."[13] Freud would argue that "our childhood memories show us our earliest years not as they were but as they appeared at the later periods when the memories were aroused"[14]—such memories were mediated by a "screen" in two senses: (1) as the site for the projection of "mnemic images" (i.e., a display); but also, (2) as a filtering operation to impressions from the time of childhood "that have been suppressed" (i.e., a partition).[15]

One can't help but suspect that Ebbinghaus would have benefited from just such a screen; side-effects of his trials included "exhaustion, headache, and other symptoms."[16] Regardless of its epochal significance, his modestly named "contribution to experimental psychology" in any case exhumes that which the project of critical philosophy seemed intent on ignoring. Kant's attribution of synthesis as a function of the imagination takes interest in an ability to form complex wholes from simpler, nonsensical elements (or, "the act of putting various presentations with one another and of comprising their manifoldness in one cognition"[17]); Ebbinghaus shifts the emphasis onto *in*ability.

---

[13] Sigmund Freud, "Screen Memories," in *The Freud Reader*, ed. Peter Gay (New York; London: W. W. Norton, 1989), p. 117; my emphasis.

[14] Ibid., p. 126.

[15] For a more thorough study of this distinction, see Erkki Huhtamo, "Elements of Screenology: Toward an Archaeology of the Screen," *ICONICS: International Studies of the Modern Image* 7 (2004): 31-82.

[16] Ebbinghaus, *Memory*, p. 55.

[17] Kant, *Critique of Pure Reason*, p. 130 (A77/B103).

That is, given the findings of experimental psychology, one might with some confidence extend Kant's claim: if I put *seven* dots after one another, like this, ... , then this result is an image of the number *seven*. Should one push the matter further, however, with *twelve* dots, like this, ... , can the result still be said to be an image of the number *twelve*? And what of even lengthier series of 16, 24, or 36 dots? Worse, the open-ended sequence that Ebbinghaus initiates carries implications of true monstrosities: if presented with an extreme example, like this,

. . . .
. . . .
. . . .
. . . .
. . . .
. . . .
. . . .
. . . .
. . . .
. . . .
. . . .
. . . .
. . . .
. . . .
. . . .
. . . .

, how should the result be described? This possibility is anticipated in the *Critique of Pure Reason*: "in the case of a thousand I could hardly survey that image and compare it with the concept."[18] Kant, being a sensible philosopher, declined to wade into the murky abyss of such nonsense. For Ebbinghaus, it was unavoidable. Perhaps a line of 36 dots might strain the abilities of a particularly capable imagination (or an extremely dedicated experimental psychologist), but in the greatly exaggerated case of a thousand dots, one has surely crossed the threshold between the sublime and the ridiculous; it is uncertain if this can even be said to be an "image" at all, or if it is merely an indeterminate quantity of dots.

Can any synthesis be imagined here? What are the limits in making sense of dots? These questions might be more easily dismissed as caricatures of philosophical abstruseness—a modern equivalent of asking, "How many angels can dance on the head of a pin?"—were they not in fact central to the crisis of anthropological difference in the latter half of the twentieth century, becoming the factor through which humanity sought to distinguish itself from (or, equate itself to) information-processing machinery. Alan Turing's definition of a class of "computable numbers" (in 1936) had attracted little interest except within a highly-specialized circle of logicians, until the publication of his later paper (in 1950), which made the scandalous claim that the production of "intelligence" was adequately simulated by the processing of dots on an imaginary strip of paper.[19]

When the problem of counting "larger numbers" had been discussed earlier in the *Critique of Pure Reason*, it was described as "a *synthesis according to concepts*, because it is performed

---

[18] Ibid., p. 213 (A140/B179).

[19] See A. M. Turing, "On Computable Numbers, with an Application to the Entscheidungsproblem," *Proceedings of the London Mathematical Society* 42, n.s. (November 1937): 230–65; and "Computing Machinery and Intelligence." *Mind* 49, no. 236 (October 1950): 433-460.

according to a common basis of unity (such as the decimal system)"[20]—in other words, quantitative extravagance features in Kant's system only to signal a retreat into pure concepts ("i.e. without anything empirical"). It is difficult—after the telegraphic transmission of Morse's code; after the travails of Ebbinghaus; after our own attempted "survey" of a thousand dots—to find this convincing: such a condition might be described as shock, or even just plainly as modernity, but here we can simply say that being subject to "larger numbers" is not merely a conceptual pretense; it belongs to quotidian experience, and hence is very much a matter insisting on empirical interest. Kant's mediating third leaves one dyspeptic.

By contrast, in more properly media theoretical approaches, such as Siegert's, "the third precedes the second,"[21] explicitly confronting the intractability of nonsense rather than purporting to silence noise. It is not "a secret art" that bridges universally given faculties of the intellect and the senses, but the introjection of cultural techniques (including, but not limited to, Kant's preferred decimal system) which come before and condition the division of the two *as if* such a schema were "always only a product of the imagination." In other words, this media *a priori*, comparable with a Freudian approach to the trauma of childhood, screens the excess of Real dots prior to any possibility of Imaginary synthesis or Symbolic meaning; a history of such screen media is the subject of this chapter.

---

[20] Kant, *Critique of Pure Reason*, pp. 130-131 (A78/B104).

[21] Siegert, *Cultural Techniques*, p. 21.

§3.2: The Altair 8800: "Hackers"

Kant, Morse, and Turing were not alone in their appreciation of the humble dot. In fact, it features with surprising regularity as an operator of distinctions between sense and nonsense. The reversal of fortunes experienced by Turing's imaginary dot-processor was occasioned by the emergence of actual machines displaying comparable traits. His formalization of computability would come to be the standard reference in their assessment but cannot be taken as an exhaustive description; graphic traces are not easily reduced to clean logic.

Steven Levy's pop-nonfiction account of *Hackers* (1984) recounts the transformation of such technology into ubiquitous media. Departing from the ideals of critical rigor in Kantian philosophy, as well as the aspirations to precision that so deeply motivated Ebbinghaus, Levy's portraits are instead examples of what Roland Barthes termed, *myth*: "the mystification which transforms petit-bourgeois culture into a universal nature."[22] His protagonists are imbued with a set of uncontestable values—they are "adventurers, visionaries, risk-takers, artists."[23]

More precisely, the book seeks to elevate a subcultural group (rather than petit-bourgeois class) to paradigmatic status. Much of its interest arises from this tension between an aspiration to recognition and simultaneous deliberate self-marginalization from mainstream society, thus preserving the paradoxes of countercultural movements.[24] When appropriated by Levy, the designation, "hacker," maintained a decidedly pejorative connotation, "as a form of derision,

---

[22] Roland Barthes, *Mythologies*, trans. Annette Lavers (New York: Farrar, Straus & Giroux, 1991), p. 8.

[23] Steven Levy, *Hackers: Heroes of the Computer Revolution* (New York: Doubleday, 1984), p. ix, hereafter abbreviated *H*.

[24] On the associations between countercultural movements and subcultures of computing, see Fred Turner, *From Counterculture to Cyberculture: Stewart Brand, the Whole Earth Network, and the Rise of Digital Utopianism* (Chicago; London: University of Chicago Press, 2006), esp. pp. 132-140 for his discussion of Levy's *Hackers*.

implying that hackers were either nerdy social outcasts or 'unprofessional' programmers who wrote dirty, 'nonstandard' computer code" (*H*, p. ix). If these stereotypes remain familiar and even dominant to this day, it was at least in part cemented by the "Hacker Ethic" he outlined.[25] The normative reversal enacted in *Hackers* did not so much contest these evaluations, but performed a sort of dialectical reversal, enthusiastically adopting these negative traits as if they were virtues: by imposing simplistic binaries, an affirmation of "unprofessional" and "nonstandard" behavior became a means of indulging in the fantasy of bureaucratization's supposed other, unalienated engagement.

In Levy's narration, anti-corporatist sentiment was signified through an almost tactile craving for machinery. Desire for physical proximity is the primary measure in his structuring dichotomy between "planners" and "hackers." A planner was someone who worked on computers and did so to make life better, but "did not necessarily think that working on a computer would be the key element in making that life better" (*H*, p. 57); that is, a planner was a perfect specimen of alienated labor. The planner's favored tool was the IBM 704, which processed information in bulk and thus closed off any possibility of responding to the results of computation while the machinery was in operation. As such, the expensive equipment could be safely cordoned away from programmers, who would not even be allowed in the same room as the computers. This was unproblematic for planners, but of great frustration to a hacker who believed in unrestricted access: "Most of the rules were designed to keep crazy young computer fans like Samson and Kotok and Saunders physically distant from the machine itself. The most rigid rule of all was that no one should be able to actually touch or tamper with the machine itself" (*H*, p. 13). Needless to say,

---

[25] For a more nuanced take on the construction of the "hacker" stereotype, see Nathan Ensmenger, "'Beards, Sandals, and Other Signs of Rugged Individualism': Masculine Culture within the Computing Professions," *Osiris* 30, no. 1 (2015): 38-65.

such an arrangement provoked stern disapproval: "The epitome of the bureaucratic world was to be found at a very large company called International Business Machines—IBM. The reason its computers were batch-processed Hulking Giants was only partially because of vacuum tube technology. The real reason was that IBM was a clumsy, hulking company that did not understand the hacking impulse" (*H*, p. 30).

By contrast, a hacker adhered to what Levy called the "Hands-On Imperative": "Hackers believe that essential lessons can be learned about the systems—about the world—from taking things apart, seeing how they work, and using this knowledge to create new and even more interesting things. They resent any person, physical barrier, or law that tries to keep them from doing this" (*H*, p. 28). These archetypes built on the organizational division between "planning" and "coding" upon which the programming of computers had been founded, wherein the latter's "hands-on" work was considered to be mere implementation and hence of low prestige, subordinate to the former's detached theoretical analysis.[26] Inverting this hierarchy, the hacker celebrated an autonomy of manual activity.[27]

One episode from 1975 offers an especially evocative sketch of the obsessive *jouissance* characteristic of this "imperative" as a forceful compulsion.[28] In chronicles of the efflorescence of

---

[26] Herman H. Goldstine and John von Neumann, "Planning and Coding of Problems for an Electronic Computing Instrument: Report on the Mathematical and Logical Aspects of an Electronic Computing Instrument: Part II, Volume 1" (Princeton, NJ: Institute for Advanced Study, 1947).

[27] It is worth noting the distinct difference in gender coding between the "coder" (feminized labor) and "hacker" (masculine independence)—the hacker's ability to stake claims to a raise in the normative evaluation of his activities (i.e., his "innovation") is predicated on access to forms of social and cultural capital outside the reach of others (of which gender is perhaps the most notable and severe, but not sole basis—e.g., hacking's root as a hobbyist activity restricts entry to middle-class recreation, etc.). For an account of gender relations in labor and computing, see Jennifer S. Light, "When Computers Were Women," *Technology and Culture* 40, no. 3 (July 1999): 455-483.

[28] As Lorraine Daston and Katherine Park have shown, the "passion of wonder" has long been considered unscientific, a pathological excess over normative, disinterested curiosity. See Lorraine Daston and Katherine Park, *Wonders and the Order of Nature, 1150-1750* (New York: Zone Books, 1998).

microcomputing—the development and subsequent popularization of smaller, microprocessor-based computers which, unlike IBM's "Hulking Giants," one could "actually touch or tamper with"—the Altair 8800 holds a legendary standing, matched perhaps only by anecdotes about its early sites of adoption. Somewhat counterintuitively, the ideological construction of "personal" computing was not centered on individual toil, but the conjunction of such isolated dedication with equally immersive communitarian involvement: *Hackers* offers a redemptive tale of supposedly marginalized individuals finding quasi-religious communion with the like-minded. Levy's discussion of the Altair 8800 is anchored by a dramatic description of the Homebrew Computer Club's inaugural meeting, where Steve Dompier introduced his new machine:

> The meeting was held in a room on the second floor of the school, a huge, ancient wooden building straight out of *The Addams Family*. Dompier's Altair was, of course, the object of much adoration, and he was dying to show them the first documented application. But when Dompier tried to turn on the Altair, it wouldn't work. The electrical outlet was dead. The nearest working outlet was on the first floor of the building, and after locating an extension cord long enough to stretch from there to the second floor, Dompier finally had his Altair plugged in, though the cord was not quite long enough, and the machine had to stand a bit outside the doorway. Dompier began the long process of hitting the right switches to enter the song in octal code, and was just about finished when two kids who had been playing in the hallway accidentally tripped over the cord, pulling it out of the wall. This erased the contents of the computer memory, which Dompier had been entering bit by bit. He started over, and finally shushed everyone up in preparation for the first public demonstration of a working Altair application. (*H*, p. 205)

The performance exceeded expectations. Dompier had stumbled upon an unforeseen effect of radio interference that was generated when switching bits from one memory location in the Altair to another, taking advantage of this to chart a musical scale based on correspondence between address and sound: manipulating a bit at 075, for example, produced an F-sharp. When coupled with a low-frequency radio, the Altair could thus be used as a primitive musical instrument. If his preparatory work may be compared to monastic withdrawal into deep asceticism, the production's entry into public spectacle recalls the atmosphere of a cathedral instead: "the room of hackers—

normally abuzz with gossip about the latest chip—fell into an awed silence. ... They had just heard evidence that the dream they'd been sharing was real. A dream that only a few weeks before had seemed vague and distant" (*H*, p. 205).

Yet, this triumphant scene also preserves a rather less transcendent moment, as if the tinted lenses sorting hacker from coder had lost their hue and discerning any difference between independent wizard and administrative minion had all of a sudden become an insurmountable challenge. We witness the transformation of a so-called "hacker" into an engine of the machine. With great relish, Levy depicts a regression into creaturely abjection as Dompier, constrained by a leash prohibiting entry to the sacred space, assumes the role of data entry clerk, (twice) transcribing the contents of his program "bit by bit"—that is, dot by dot.

The necessity of such measures arose from the Altair 8800's input-output system (or relative lack thereof), described in vivid detail as well:

> It seems that the only option supplied by MITS [Microinstrumentation and Telemetry Systems, an electronics company based in Albuquerque, New Mexico] for those who actually finished building the machine was a machine language program that you could key into the machine only by the row of tiny switches on the front panel. It was a program which used the 8080 chip instructions LDA, MOV, ADD, STA, and JMP. If everything was right, the program would add two numbers together. You would be able to tell by mentally translating the code of the flashing LEDs out of their octal form and into a regular decimal number. You would feel like the first man stepping on the moon, a figure in history—you would have the answer to the question stumping mankind for centuries: What happens when you add six and two? Eight! "For an engineer who appreciates computers, that was an exciting event," early Altair owner and Homebrew Club member Harry Garland would later say, admitting that "you might have a hard time explaining to an outsider why it was exciting." To Steve Dompier it was thrilling. (*H*, pp. 203-204)

Despite Levy's rigorous attention to features, perhaps the most notable element in this construction figures through its conspicuous absence: the (missing) computer screen as a graphical interface. In its place was a panel of flashing dots, sited at the threshold between sense ("For an engineer who appreciates computers, that was an exciting event") and nonsense ("you might have a hard time explaining to an outsider why it was exciting"). One could even say that, in the Altair, screen technologies have been outsourced onto the techniques of hackers. Dompier embodies the interface, functioning as the medium to an otherworldly realm.

As Levy understands it, they were victims of their own success. He concludes with a tone of nostalgia: the age of the hacker lies in the past. In being "the ones who most clearly saw why the computer was a truly revolutionary tool" (*H*, p. ix), their "innocent wonder" (*H*, p. 453) was doomed to exploitation by "the values of the outside world" (*H*, p. 451). corrupting the possibilities afforded by these new technologies with impure motives. Microcomputers were no longer the exclusive toy of those thoroughly devoted, but a consumer good. Another enemy—another source of constitutive alterity—was on the horizon: the *user*.

In certain strands of media theoretical discourse, the user has acquired a suspect reputation, perhaps resulting from an allergic reaction to technophilic fantasies that had heralded its ascent in emancipatory terms of communicative transparency and universal accessibility. Kittler, aligning himself with the Hacker Ethic, condemns Intel's decision to split chip design into "Protected Mode" and "Real Mode," the former of which paternalistically shields users from themselves, creating restrictions over the manipulation of systems critical functions through a hierarchy of different privilege levels: access is impeded by default.[29] The user is engineered under a condition of "minority."[30] Similarly, Cornelia Vismann and Markus Krajewski define the user in opposition

---

[29] Friedrich Kittler, "Protected Mode," in *The Truth of the Technological World: Essays on the Genealogy of Presence*, trans. Erik Butler (Stanford, CA: Stanford University Press, 2013), pp. 209-218.

[30] In this regard, Kittler offers a comparable diagnosis to Bernard Stiegler's critique of "grammatisation" under hyperindustrial conditions. See Bernard Stiegler, "Die Aufklärung in the Age of Philosophical Engineering," trans. Daniel Ross, *Computational Culture* 2 (28 September 2012), http://computationalculture.net/die-aufklarung-in-the-age-of-philosophical-engineering/.

to competency. In particular, the graphical interface of screen technologies is allotted the responsibility of confining users to their seat of blissful ignorance. For these scholars, the "anthropomorphic face" of user-friendly desktops is read as a symptom of specular narcissism, an Imaginary misrecognition of the machine as a reflection of the self, presenting but the mere illusion of a "personified computer."[31] They are more attracted to the direct infusion of Symbolic code through a Command Line Interface, believed to express a more honest relationship to the imperative nature of programs. But, surely even better still would be a thorough entanglement with dots on a panel? Computing in Real Mode…

The impossibility of the so-called "Hacker Ethic" as a utopian ideal—its immediate demise upon widespread adoption—derives from its liminal situation between two contrasting modes of alienation. Perhaps this is also the source of its enduring appeal as a myth. More specifically, however, the hacker does not anticipate subsequent developments but is retrospectively written into historical narrative with an eye towards constructing a pedigree for then-current conditions, establishing an ancestry for the values of "hands-on" user-friendliness. The hacker precedes the user chronologically, but is logically posterior: as Levy himself admits, "it is an ethic seldom codified" (*H*, p. x)—that is to say, the grouping he pronounces is neither coherent in space nor time but forged by himself under the guise of a phantasmatic "dream they'd been sharing." In this way, the hacker is really nothing more than the user's uncanny double—a screen memory, Freud might say: a projection constructed in the present to explain gaps from a traumatic past.

If the inevitable path from "planner" to "user"—from corporate to consumer capitalism—is to be believed, the sole function of the "hacker" in this structural formation is as an intermediate

---

[31] Cornelia Vismann and Markus Krajewski, "Computer Juridisms," *Grey Room* 29 (Fall 2007): 96.

bridge linking the two given poles, justifying the preordained development of computing as subaltern associate of socioeconomic formations. But such hackneyed formulations as Levy's assertion of "why the computer was a truly revolutionary tool," characteristic of the naturalizing function of myth, completely miss the contingency involved in the social construction of technology. My interest here tarries with the moment of potential: unlike Levy—and unlike Kittler—I am reluctant to replace the planner and user by championing their ostensible other, the hacker; perhaps viable alternatives may be foraged even in these spaces.

Can Steve Dompier's investment in the Altair be read as an attempt at taking the computer's pulse? Levy's treatment herds his protagonists into an uncompromising stampede, depicting them trampling over established norms with a swagger of brash disregard; his hacker exudes the most toxic aspects of what has come to be the distinguishing traits of "tech": complete self-confidence manifest as obnoxious solipsism, desire for directness betraying a blunt incapacity for nuance, and community building efforts that lead towards a tendency of cult formation—each potentially worthy inclinations in need of pharmacological recalibration. But, I think, sufficient evidence remains to recode Dompier's efforts along lines that foreground the cultivation of sensitivity and responsibility;[32] another "Ethic," founded on affection. Although *Hackers* presents his construction of a musical scale as conquest—a bold pioneer taming the unruly wilderness—I find it hard to see anything other than the delicate composition of a provisional assemblage, a praxis of tuning oneself to another: not tactless and unrestrained proximity but considered adjacency.

---

[32] Or, as Donna Haraway puts it, "response-ability": a process of "becoming-with"; that is, not the forceful compulsion of a superegoic injunction (as perhaps more commonly meant when speaking of "being responsible"), but concrete engagement with alterity. See Donna J. Haraway, *Staying with the Trouble: Making Kin in the Chthulucene* (Durham, NC; London: Duke University Press, 2016).

Sphygmology—the study of the pulse (*sphygmos*)—requires a light touch, "applied with sufficient pressure to steady, but not to deform the artery."[33] The conditions of screen media implied here, adopting Dompier as the paradigmatic instance of such a medium, lead again towards the architectural sense of a partitioning screen—a break from excessive familiarity. Closer attention to the history of screening practices in computing shows that this is not an isolated anomaly; indeed, not even a rare specimen.

§3.3: The Charatron: "Real Mode"

Kittler expounds at length about "Protected Mode," but what is "Real Mode"? This should not be mistaken as relief from the former's restrictions. As all good Lacanians know, the Real is an index of danger; and, similarly, as all inept users are warned, operating in Real Mode opens the possibility of irreparable crash. The common (mis)characterization of Kittlerian media theory as hardware fundamentalism takes an overly literal reading, as hardware for Kittler is not a fundamental or definitive core that provides an explanatory framework for understanding technology: as a site of the Real, it *returns*. On the contrary, then, his infamous declaration—"There Is No Software"—entails a rejection of anthropocentrism without seeking recourse in a meta-discourse that grounds the consistency of the Symbolic order into which one is inscribed (Protected Mode), only finding nonsensical excess (Real Mode); there is no possibility of success in the escalating approximation of human reason through higher-level programming languages (software), only the persistent base materiality of senseless switching elements and threat of explosive ballistics (hardware).

---

[33] W. M. Ewart, *The Pulse-Sensations: A Study in Tactile Sphygmology* (New York: William Wood and Co., 1895), p. 18.

The techniques and technologies of screen media metabolize this problem. While certainly a device of Imaginary user-friendliness and Symbolic command, the screen is, of course, also a piece of hardware—a filter for channeling Real dots. In this sense, the computer's screen is one of an extended series of attempts to mediate the distinction between sense and nonsense, of which Kantian graphics is but another episode. Several are highlighted here as orienting coordinates.

For Albrecht Dürer, the transformation between a point and a dot—between an idealized bit and its materialization as graphic mark—was of foundational importance in implementing a pedagogical program which developed mental understanding through sensorial engagement. His manual on measurement, *Underweysung der Messung* (1525), offered a means of entry into the liberal art of geometry but was aimed at practitioners of artisanal vocation, a textbook intended "not only for painters, but also for goldsmiths, sculptors, stonemasons, carpenters, and all those for whom using measurement is useful."[34]

The treatise begins with an exercise of the imagination. Having established the authority of Euclid's canonical definition of the point as indivisible and occupying no space, Dürer continues with a presentation of the range of possibilities implied, displaying his virtuosity: "I may in my imagination throw a point high up in the air, or drop it into the depths where I cannot reach it with my body."[35] However, he also recognizes that for those "not skilled in this art," such speculative flights with abstract form might be too challenging. Thus, aid is offered by appealing to a more concrete mode of corporeality: "to make it plausible for the young in its everyday application, I

---

[34] Albrecht Dürer, *Underweysung der Messung* (Nuremberg, 1525), quoted in Noam Andrews, "Albrecht Dürer's personal *Underweysung der Messung*," *Word & Image* 32, no. 4 (2016): 409.

[35] Dürer, *Underweysung der Messung*, quoted in Caroline O. Fowler, *Drawing and the Senses: An Early Modern History* (Turnhout, Belgium: Brepols Publishers, 2016), p. 38.

shall draw a point as a dot and write the word 'point' next to it."[36] Likewise, when introducing the key concept of a line, Dürer again interrupts the flow of text to stage yet another performance of draftsmanship: "If, then, this point is connected from its source with another, it is called a line; and this line is a length of any thickness or width and can be drawn as long as desired. This line drawn here is with a pen and I mark it line."[37]

These are not mere embellishments of secondary concern in the pursuit of pure geometry; graphical interruptions are here literally embedded in—introjected into—the body of the text. They express a haptic sensibility that escalates in increasinly more complex examples over the course of the book. Drawing is a cultural technique that processes imaginative capacities. As Caroline Fowler explains, Dürer's commitments may be aligned to idealized Euclidean geometry, but the practical craft of "how things in the mind may be made extant as perceptible objects" was fundamental in attaining proficiency: "The point and the line are tools of the artist, but they are also intellectual ideals that become perceptible through the artisan. With the point and the line, Dürer introduced the student to the connection between 'inner understanding' and 'external exposition.' He recognized that illustrations are fundamental for the beginner because through these diagrams the student develops his own inner understanding."[38]

Although Kant adopts a similar technique of graphical demonstration, he maintained stronger affinity with another approach to the problem that we might think of as an accounting of pulsations. Aside from neglecting potential for the cultivation of sense (explained instead by the

---

[36] Ibid., p. 40.

[37] Ibid.

[38] Fowler, *Drawing and the Senses*, pp. 40-41.

"secret art" of a transcendental schema), his "five dots after one another" do not unfold into a line but are conceived of in terms of quantity. An unlikely pairing thus offers more resonance: Thomas Hobbes's *Leviathan* (1651) is more regularly read as a founding text of modern political philosophy, but also contains extensive elaboration of his metaphysical system, in which the "Artificiall Man" of political "Common-wealth" (i.e., the eponymous "great Leviathan") could be derived from "imitating that Rationall and most excellent worke of Nature, Man."[39] This metaphysics was, in turn, founded on what William Sacksteder has tactfully described as "his own special notion of geometry."[40]

That is, as Sacksteder elaborates, Hobbes's understanding of mathematics was "certainly eccentric to the important accomplishments of his own time": even more bluntly put, neither then nor now has Hobbesian geometry been considered an acceptable approach to the subject. Nevertheless, without hoping to contest such evaluations, it remains of interest as a depository of the problems that moved him to action and the plots that he embarked upon in response.[41] For Hobbes, the point was a central actant in his dispute over number, and Gordon Hull has even argued that "in this distinction [between the unity or divisibility of the point] lies the entirety of

---

[39] Thomas Hobbes, *Leviathan: Or The Matter, Forme and Power of a Commonwealth Ecclesiasticall and Civil* (Cambridge, UK: Cambridge University Press, 1991), p. 9.

[40] William Sacksteder has elaborated on Hobbes's geometry and the controversies it sparked with the Oxford professors in "Hobbes: The Art of the Geometrician," *Journal of the History of Philosophy* 18, no. 2 (April 1980): 131-146, here p. 131; and "Hobbes: Geometrical Objects," *Philosophy of Science* 48, no. 4 (December 1981): 573-590. My discussion of Hobbesian mathematics also draws on Gordon Hull, "Hobbes and the Premodern Geometry of Modern Political Thought," in *Arts of Calculation: Quantifying Thought in Early Modern Europe*, eds. David Glimp and Michelle R. Warren (New York: Palgrave Macmillan, 2004), pp. 115-135. Also noteworthy here, historians of science have directed attention towards the implications of Hobbes's ambitious epistemological system, perhaps most influentially in Steven Shapin and Simon Schaffer, *Leviathan and the Air-Pump: Hobbes, Boyle, and the Experimental Life* (Princeton, NJ: Princeton University Press, 1985).

[41] In this regard, I follow the principle that sociologists of knowledge have described as "symmetry": "the sociologist seeks theories which explain the beliefs which are in fact found, regardless of how the investigator evaluates them.... The same types of cause would explain, say, true and false beliefs" (David Bloor, *Knowledge and Social Imagery* [Chicago: University of Chicago Press, 1976], pp. 5-7).

Hobbes's debate with the algebraists."[42] Deviating from Euclidean orthodoxy, he altered the principle defining a point as "that of which there is no part" to instead claim that "a point is indeed divisible, but no part of it is to be considered in a demonstration," thus treating geometric objects as products of mental construction, created in the act of mathematical staging rather than based on abstract but pre-existent and indivisible units.[43]

In *Leviathan*, these concerns surface in Hobbes's chapter on speech, "the most noble and profitable invention of all other."[44] Concluding a discussion of the utility derived in "the imposing of *Names*, and the *Connexion* of them," he argues:

> But the use of words in registring our thoughts, is in nothing so evident as in Numbring. A naturall foole that could never learn by heart the order of numerall words, as *one*, *two*, and *three*, may observe every stroak of the Clock, and nod to it, or say one, one, one; but can never know what houre it strikes. And it seems, there was a time when those names of number were not in use; and men were fayn to apply their fingers of one or both hands, to those things they desired to keep account of; and that thence it proceeded, that now our numerall words are but ten, in any Nation, and in some but five, and then they begin again. And he that can tell ten, if he recite them out of order, will lose himselfe, and not know when he has done: Much lesse will he be able to adde, and subtract, and performe all other operations of Arithmetique. So that without words, there is no possibility of reckoning of Numbers; much lesse of Magnitudes, of Swiftnesse, of Force, and other things, the reckonings whereof are necessary to the being, or well-being of man-kind.[45]

---

[42] Hull, "Hobbes and Premodern Geometry," p. 120.

[43] Hull argues that "for Hobbes, but not for the Greeks, a demonstration creates the objects it demonstrates" ("Hobbes and Premodern Geometry," p. 122). Likewise, Sacksteder points out that, in Hobbes's mathematics, derivation of number "depends on 'motions of the mind,' rather than on motions imputed to an imagined point or magnitude-less body. For it is the act of discerning, a form of rational division or analysis, which supplies us with points which we may order or count" (Sacksteder, "Hobbes: Geometrical Objects," pp. 583-584).

[44] Hobbes, *Leviathan*, pp. 24-31, here p. 24.

[45] Ibid., p. 27.

Leviathan announces the arrival of modernity. Not only in political theory—its semiotic system, as well, is coherent with the modern linguistics of Ferdinand de Saussure in affirming the primacy of structural convention. Hobbesian signifiers are not defined by their direct correspondence to what is signified, but in relation to other signifiers as part of a system of language: the word, "*one*," does not acquire its meaning in repeating the "stroak of the Clock" (a procedure equally satisfactorily fulfilled by a nodding "foole"), but becomes an element of speech proper through the difference it maintains with other words, such as "*two*" and "*three*."

Hobbes is most radical in formulating the act of naming as a problem of "Numbring." As Hull notes, he "says not only that numbers are words, but that numeration is the paradigm case of signification through words."[46] While it had long been common, even in Aristotle's discussion of naming, to distinguish "inarticulate noises (of beasts, for instance)" from "a spoken sound significant by convention,"[47] this mode of interpreting speech was not extended to the realm of numerals. In Greek, medieval, and Renaissance traditions, "mathematicians treated numbers not as concepts but as things ontologically prior to their expression by signs."[48] *Leviathan*, by contrast, is written under exposure to the Hindu-Arabic notation system (widely used in Europe from the 1500s), and is thus inscribed into a culture that conceives of number in terms of place-value not as a multitude of (pre-existent and indivisible) "ones."[49]

---

[46] Hull, "Hobbes and Premodern Geometry," p. 128.

[47] Aristotle, "De Interpretatione," in *The Complete Works of Aristotle: The Revised Oxford Translation*, vol. 1, ed. Jonathan Barnes, trans. J. L. Ackrill (Princeton, NJ: Princeton University Press, 1984), pp. 25-26.

[48] Eugene Ostashevsky, "Crooked Figures: Zero and Hindu-Arabic Notation in Shakespeare's Henry V," in *Arts of Calculation*, p. 206.

[49] See Brian Rotman, *Signifying Nothing: The Semiotics of Zero* (Houndmills, Basingstoke, Hampshire: Macmillan, 1987).

In effect, well before Turing proposed his thought experiments, Hobbes diagrams symbolic being as a type of hardware, namely an *accumulator* (comparable, for instance, to those in the first electronic digital computer, the ENIAC, which unlike most of today's binary-based systems architectures "worked with decimal numbers, each communicated as a series of pulses. For example, eight would be transmitted as a succession of eight pulses"[50]). Less capable automata, such as the "naturall foole," lack the required memory to keep track of changes in state (between *"one"* and *"two"*; between *"two"* and *"three"*; etc.), and thus cannot even be considered finite-state machines (as Hobbes demands) much less claim to be Turing-complete (a class which possesses even greater powers of computation).

To be even more precise, however, Hobbes has not simply moved numbers from *things* (e.g., "every stroak of the Clock," "fingers") to *signs* (e.g., "numerall words" like *"one," "two," "three"*), but focuses his semiotics on processing the transformation between them. *Leviathan* discusses speech in terms of "the cultural techniques of sign-signal distinction."[51] As the audible materialization of a point in time, a "stroak of the Clock" preserves the possibility of failure in sense-making, leaving an irreducible gap to informatic purity; the succession of sonic dots poses a threat of noise impeding what Kant would call imaginative synthesis.

---

[50] Thomas Haigh, Mark Priestley, and Crispin Rope, *ENIAC in Action: Making and Remaking the Modern Computer* (Cambridge, MA: MIT Press, 2016), p. 223.

[51] In directing attention to "a time when those names of number were not in use; and men were fayn to apply their fingers of one or both hands," Hobbes addresses a seminal example Thomas Macho provides of fundamental cultural techniques: "that cultural techniques are always already older than their media and that they are certainly older than the terms which emerged from them.... Counting, too, is older than numbers. Most known cultures did, no doubt, count or perform certain mathematical operations, but they did not necessarily derive the notion of number from such operations" ("Second-Order Animals: Cultural Techniques of Identity and Identification," *Theory, Culture & Society* 30, no. 6, trans. Michael Wutz [November 2013], pp. 44-45).

Beyond the mathematical formalisms of abstract machines, Hobbes is concerned with the sublimation of messy counting techniques into semantically-rich speech. Inverting this procedure, communications engineers in the twentieth century sought to convert the complex wave forms transmitted over telephone into binary signals in which "information lies only in the presence or absence of the code pulses" based on "samples regularly taken from the speech signals."[52] Hardware limitations (i.e., the return of the Real) curtailed the implementation of such ambitions despite the issue having, in principle, attained theoretical (i.e., Symbolic) closure with Alec Harley Reeves's 1938 patent for an "Electric Signaling System" based on telegraph-like "code pulses" (i.e., pulse-code modulation)[53]; in 1948, further mathematical analysis determined that it even "offers greater improvement in signal-to-noise than other systems, such as FM, which also depend upon the use of wide bands."[54] Although "the idea of replacing the audio output from a microphone by pulse signals (pulse-width modulation, in fact) was first tried in 1924," it was only in the 1960s that digitization of civil telecommunications systems became an economic possibility following the development of semiconductor devices.[55]

Computational apparatuses display kinship with telegraphic systems in their shared duty of digesting a barrage of electrical impulses. Unlike the machines imagined by Turing, which are allowed to handle their dots as slowly as they please, hardware faces the further challenge of

---

[52] G. C. Hartley et al., *Techniques of Pulse-Code Modulation in Communication Networks* (Cambridge, UK: Cambridge University Press, 1967), p. 3. See also Bernhard Siegert, *Relays: Literature as an Epoch of the Postal System*, trans. Kevin Repp (Stanford, CA: Stanford University Press, 1999), pp. 258-264.

[53] Alec Harley Reeves, Electric Signaling System, US Patent 2,272,070, filed 22 November 1939, and issued 3 Feb 1942, https://patents.google.com/patent/US2272070A/en.

[54] B. M. Oliver, J. R. Pierce, C. E. Shannon, "The Philosophy of PCM," *Proceedings of the IRE* 36, no. 11 (November 1948): 1324-1331.

[55] Hartley et al., *Techniques of Pulse-Code Modulation*, pp. 1-4.

coping with speed. This factor is not confined to functions in arithmetic and logical processing units, but also matters in the workings of screens; at the porous border distinguishing computing from telegraphy, electronic imaging is rendered as sphygmographic practice.

Read against standard landmarks in histories of the computer screen, the Charactron is an especially intriguing artifact as it undermines the conventional dichotomy between "vector" and "raster" displays. Vector-based screens express the logic of Dürer's geometry, tracing lines across the screen's surface. As the master artisan from Nuremberg theorized, in these devices a "point is connected from its source with another." Dots mark the start and end of lines, if they can be said to exist at all; they are consumed within extension. Vector displays maintain a rather direct relationship to the internal workings of the cathode-ray tube (CRT), an instrument comprising an electron gun and a phosphorescent screen which momentarily luminesces where it is hit by emissions. In such line-based systems, graphics are inscribed by directing the gun towards the starting coordinates and tracing a "vector" with a stream of electrons as it is redirected to the endpoint.

It is less accurate to say that such screens have since been replaced by raster-based systems than that the procedures they execute are now largely subject to an additional layer of mediation, simulated through software rather than performed in hardware; computer "graphics" is quite appropriately named, as drawing remains the conditioning sensibility in its imaging operations. Computer displays today more typically project a grid (or, "raster") over the screen's surface, dividing the plane into addressable units of space. Each dot occupies one such block which, like those in the *Critique of Pure Reason*, is combined with others in the viewer's mind rather than explicated during the process of inscription: the Kantian image, unlike Dürer's, is formed by synthesizing a collection of pixels. Implemented in a cathode-ray tube, the raster is maintained through a regular sweep of the electron gun, which periodically scans and updates each dot; rasters can also, however, be staged on other devices, such as the liquid-crystal displays (LCDs) common today. In fact, neither vector nor raster need even be expressed electronically at all. From the perspective of dots (and the engineers responsible for their logistics), the processing performed by computer screens could easily be thought of as a subcategory of print.

The Charactron cannot be easily fit into either category. It was a "cathode-ray apparatus" which placed emphasis on visualizing "images having predetermined shapes, such as characters"[56] (hence, *Charact*-ron). A 1952 press release from its launch claims that it combined "electronics and dry photographic techniques for the first time to provide high-speed, automatic recording of intelligence at rates as high as 10,000 characters per second."[57] This was achieved through the addition of a stencil with character-shaped apertures interposed between the electron gun and display surface, resulting in what would be called a "shaped-beam tube." At this "matrix mask," raw signals were pre-screened, arriving on the viewing screen as high-resolution character images.

An early example of screening systems based on such technology was developed in 1954 as an interactive display for the Semi-Automatic Ground Environment (SAGE) Air Defense System, where legible presentation of "alphanumeric data such as flight number, speed and altitude"[58] affected the efficacy of radar operators working under the stress of time-sensitive and perceptually demanding conditions. With shaped-beam technology, pertinent symbolic

---

[56] Joseph T. McNaney, Cathode Ray Apparatus, US Patent 2,803,769, filed 7 July 1952, and issued 20 August 1957, https://patents.google.com/patent/US2803769A/en, p. 1.

[57] "Charactron hi-speed printer," *Journal of the Franklin Institute* 253, no. 5 (1952): 533.

[58] Peter A. Keller, *The Cathode-Ray Tube: Technology, History and Applications* (New York: Palisades Press, 1991), p. 77; see also, Keller's discussion of later examples of "data display cathode-ray tubes" based on the Charactron, pp. 196-197.

information could be clearly superimposed on a vector-drawn map. Subsequently, from 1959, another model without interactive capacities was commercially manufactured by Stromberg-Carlson as the S-C 4020 Microfilm Recorder. Zabet Patterson has shown how this variant of the Charactron has had a formative role in the development of computer art despite having been designed with more instrumental ends in mind, focusing on the products of just one particular S-C 4020. Installed at Bell Labs in 1961, it was (mis)used by participants of their artist-in-residence program, including Stan VanDerBeek and Lillian Schwartz; as she argues, "the machine made all kinds of previously invisible objects and processes suddenly, startlingly visible—and made previously impossible visualizations remarkably possible."[59]

Expanding Patterson's study, my account sets out in the other direction, burrowing into the Charactron's frayed genealogy rather than following its displaced legacies: What were its antecedents? Can other family resemblances be found? What led its creators to such a solution, so unfamiliar to us today—and why was it considered a compelling option? Adopting this vantage opens an alien landscape of graphical technologies that confounds expectations against what computer "graphics" has become. Historicization induces the vertiginous disorientation of perspectival shift: approached from this angle, the Charactron does not anticipate the inevitability of the way things have come to be, but the contingency of current circumstance. This artifact is, to my mind, most interesting not when taken as a forerunner to later practices, but if its radical alterity is affirmed, offered as a capsule condensing how things could otherwise be—that is, if it is dispensed as an antidote to user-based histories of the computer screen.

---

[59] Zabet Patterson, *Peripheral Vision: Bell Labs, the S-C 4020, and the Origins of Computer Art* (Cambridge, MA: MIT Press, 2015), p. xvi.

While common sense would suggest locating the origins of computer graphics at or after the origins of computers, doing so would foreclose the deep historical conditions of electronic imaging. These practices were not founded on a tabula rasa. More directly than the long shadows cast by Dürer, Hobbes, and Kant—distant percolations which may resume action without warning—situating its development in its immediate context of "pulse techniques" from communications systems clarifies the computer's earliest screening technologies as a filter of Real dots. In 1940, prior to the conception of the modern computers on which it would run, the engineer who would later develop the Charactron, Joseph T. McNaney, had filed a patent for a "Signaling System" offering a similar shaped-beam solution. His system introduced CRT technology to overcome obstacles faced by "teletype systems" as well as "in printing telegraphs," arguing:

> Heretofore, in systems of the general type to which my invention pertains, the limitation upon the speed of transmission and reception has been largely mechanical. That is to say, referring for example to teletype systems, the inertia of the moving parts at the receiver prevents ultra high speed and in printing telegraphs the same limitation appears.
>
> It is, accordingly, an object of my invention to provide a signaling system wherein the speed of transmission and reception is substantially unlimited, within reason, and a permanent record is formed.[60]

In other words, by 1940, Hobbes's "natural foole" had been joined by mechanical printers in suffering difficulties when attempting to screen a stream of nonsensical signals into sensible speech. Photoelectric devices (i.e., without any "moving parts") were enlisted with the goal of attaining a more sympathetic relation. McNaney explains: "Because of the fact that the cathode ray itself is devoid of inertia the speed of transmission is limited only by the rate at which the transmitting tape may be caused to move past the transmitting photo cells, the photo-sensitivity of

---

[60] Joseph T. McNaney, Signaling System, US Patent 2,283,383, filed 6 November 1940, and issued 19 May 1942, https://patents.google.com/patent/US2283383A/en, p. 1.

the record receiving material and the maximum speed at which the said material may be caused to pass through the apparatus."[61]

His attention was hardly peculiar; on the contrary, it would have been irregular had any major corporation with interests in signals equipment not made efforts at producing their own device "capable of translating incoming electrical impulses representing characters of a message into visible replicas of the said characters."[62] At Bell Labs, Harry A. Burgess developed a "High Speed Telegraph System" (1942) which included a circular "stenciled screen used in the cathode ray tube for producing the letters of the alphabet or other desired characters," which then "may be read on the fluorescent screen on a circle or may be optically recorded at high speed."[63] Engineers from the Hughes Aircraft Corporation and the Radio Corporation of America (RCA) retained McNaney's choice of a grid-based organization of apertures in their "matrix mask" CRTs.[64]

The Charactron belongs to this problem space. Its limitations conformed to standard practice in recording signals at the time, and only appears unorthodox in retrospect; "automatic printing-telegraphs," which output legible characters rather than raw dots, had similarly long worked via selection from a "type wheel" (a rotary movement perhaps most comparable to Burgess's cathode-ray system). Computer graphics is formed through the piecemeal ingestion of

---

[61] Ibid., p. 4. See also the earlier work on electronic (i.e., inertia-free) signal processing "flip flops" of W. H. Eccles and F. W. Jordan, "A Trigger Relay Utilizing Three-Electrode Thermionic Vacuum Tubes," *The Electrician* 83 (1919): 298.

[62] McNaney, Signaling System, p. 1.

[63] Harry A. Burgess, High-Speed Telegraph System, US Patent 2,379,880, filed 7 Oct 1942, and issued 10 July 1945, https://patents.google.com/patent/US2379880A/en, pp. 1-2.

[64] Charles J. Young, System for Character Code Signal Transmission and Electronic Character Selection and/or Printing, US Patent 2,759,045, filed 1 Mar 1951, and issued 14 August 1956, https://patents.google.com/patent/US2759045A/en; and, Henry M. Smith, Direct-Viewing Storage Tube with Character Writing Electron Gun, US Patent 2,728,872, filed 23 Oct 1953, and issued 27 December 1955, https://patents.google.com/patent/US2728872A/en.

these existing technologies. Especially noteworthy amongst telegraph printers, given the current prevalence of raster displays, Joseph N. Loop's "Apparatus for Printing Characters" (1937) took an electromechanical approach but was also "intended primarily for use in high speed telegraphic communication systems."[65] It minimized "lost motion" from its movable parts by printing marks through a grid of dots.

Symbolic data, as much as pictorial inscription taking less prescribed forms, would continue to be a chief concern in dot-based graphics; one might even speculate that its role as a relatively efficient "character generator" was the main advantage offered by raster scan devices, given that computational imaging was otherwise primarily concerned with plotting graphs, a task more appropriately fulfilled with vector-based hardware. Unlike the fancier affordances of shading and three-dimensional modeling more commonly associated with the rise of raster displays in computing, the visualization of alphanumeric information—that is, the conversion of an abstract idea of text into actual graphical marks—sought to minimize the resolution of images. Walter Griffin Paige, an assignor to Remington Rand, described the situation circa 1951 when staking claims to the novelty of his own "High-Speed Dot Printer":

> Printing mechanisms are known in which the outlines of the characters to be printed are formed by printing the appropriate dots of a dot grid which is of the same general size as the characters to be printed. Some machines of this type effect printing of the dots by passing electrical currents through minute areas of treated paper sheets. This sort of printing, however, is unsatisfactory because of the great expense of the treated paper. Other dot printing machines employ a character forming series of individually operable dot printing elements which are projected in combination simultaneously against an ink ribbon to effect printing of the whole character at once. This sort of machine is unsatisfactory in that the printing elements and their actuators are too bulky for machines to print a series of whole characters

---

[65] Joseph N. Loop, Apparatus for Printing Characters, US Patent 2,129,065, filed 6 July 1937, and issued 6 September 1938, https://patents.google.com/patent/US2129065A/en, p.1.

side by side. Further, such machines are slow in operation due to the masses of moving parts therein.

>The principle object of the invention is the provision of a mechanical dot printing mechanism which is operable at extremely high speed to print a series of characters side by side under control of electrical impulses.[66]

Perhaps most ironically, this symptom was also indicated in patient zero of the hacking outbreak. In Levy's *Hackers*, the PDP-1 is presented as an interactive alternative to IBM's "batch-processed Hulking Giants." Introduced in 1959, it is celebrated for its sixteen-inch "Precision CRT Display (Type 30)," a direct-viewing output device "useful for high speed presentation of graphs, diagrams, drawings, and alphanumerical information."[67] Equally cherished, an additional equipment option was the "Light Pen (Type 32)," which could be coupled with the Type 30 as a sort of cursor: "By 'writing' on the face of the CRT, stored or displayed information can be expanded, deleted or modified."[68]

The Type 32 could be used to manipulate "information," but of what kind? Less fanfare has greeted the "Symbol Generator (Type 33)," also developed for use with the Type 30. As its name suggests, "the Type 33 plots symbols on a 5 x 7, 35-dot matrix in one of four sizes"—it "greatly increases the Type 30's capacity for character and symbol generation. Plotting rate is increased approximately ten times: a total of 220 characters (based on an average character of 16 points) can be displayed flicker free. Any symbol compatible with a 5 x 7, 35-dot matrix can be

---

[66] Walter Griffin Paige, High-Speed Dot Printer, US Patent 2,694,362, filed 25 August 1951, and issued 16 November 1954, https://patents.google.com/patent/US2694362A/en, p.1.

[67] *Programmed Data Processor-1 Handbook* (Maynard, MA: Digital Equipment Corporation, 1963), p. 33.

[68] Ibid., p. 36.

displayed. The Type 33 includes a subscript control with adjustable offset and an increment control which spaces successive symbols one position to the right."[69]

In the PDP-1's *Handbook*, a picture accompanies the presentation of these peripherals. Lodged between sections on the Type 33 Symbol Generator and the Type 32 Light Pen, as if its allegiances were undecided, the computer screen proclaims, simply: "THE TYPE 30 DIGITAL DISPLAY AND TYPE 32 LIGHT PEN PROVIDE FAST MAN-MACHINE COMMUNICATION." One might discern in its "communication" a degree of cognitive dissonance between what Roman Jakobsen has termed the poetic and phatic functions of language. The *message* transmitted here expresses the PDP-1's screen as initiating a history of interactivity leading from the hacker to the user; the *channel* of transmission, on the other hand, performs the PDP-1's screen as part of a history of dot-handling. Beyond the Type 30's limit of 22 characters (or ~350 points), "fast man-machine communication" is conditioned by the unspoken and invisible function of the Type 33 Symbol Generator, and its ability to take—and make sense of—an electronic pulse.

§3.4: The IBM 740 and 780: "Hulking Giants"

Throughout the 1950s, the International Business Machines (IBM) Corporation systematically avoided referring to their new line of electronic products as *computers*, instead preferring such unwieldy terms as "Card Programmed Calculator," "Tape Processing Machine," "Electronic Data Processing Machine," "Magnetic Drum Calculator," and even "Defense Calculator." In a corporate animation they commissioned from the Office of Charles and Ray

---

[69] Ibid., p. 35.

Eames titled *The Information Machine* (1958), we are initially introduced to an "electronic calculator" before the film finally relents towards its end, eventually referring to it as "the computer": by the end of the decade, the device had already infected the popular imaginary, and—as if over the course of a single short film—defeat of the corporate juggernaut's censorship had become secured.

What could have been so horrific about "the computer" that even the ominous notion of a "Defense Calculator" was deemed preferable, even comforting?

Steven Levy disdainfully depicts IBM as the pantomime villain of computing, "the epitome of the bureaucratic world" (*H*, p. 30). His disappointment at the segregation of hacker from machine arises from the same concerns that led to their terminological insistence on "calculator" over "computer": as historians of computing have noted, this strange practice was motivated by anxieties "that the latter term, which had previously always referred to a human being, would raise the specter of technological unemployment."[70]

At IBM in the 1950s, ontological hygiene was implemented through an equally sanitized spatial partitioning—a policy of screening the computer. Scholars like Turing had playfully suggested that the human mind could be satisfactorily simulated by dot-processing machinery; corporate strategy, on the other hand, was dictated by the possibility of a public relations disaster. The former's provocations have perhaps been retained with more clarity in the afterimages of cultural memory, but the latter's schemes should not be underestimated. Aside from directly promoting the virtues of their products, it was also important that IBM emphasize the disagreeable

---

[70] Martin Campbell-Kelly et al., *Computer: A History of the Information Machine* (Boulder, CO: Westview Press, 2014), pp. 105.

nature of the laborious tasks they completed, demonizing clerical operations like bookkeeping, paper filing, and card punching as dehumanizing chores; that is, besides addressing the products themselves, IBM dug a (computer-sized) hole into which desire could be planted. Against the alternative of drowning in information, data processing equipment could be more favorably presented as a means of alleviating what their chief propagandists, the Eameses, would call "drudgery," thus allowing the corporate empire to position their products as a contribution towards visions of sublimated humanism. Their slogan succinctly captures this sentiment: *Think*.[71]

Above all, the tenets of humanistic bureaucracy ordained that even hackers should be isolated from their supposed other: dots, the emblem of pathological excess over distilled information. Levy is perhaps not entirely off the mark in contending that IBM's preference for batch-processing as a computational framework "was only partially because of vacuum tube technology"—the "hulking company" truly "did not understand the hacking impulse," and their calculators were shaped to reflect this. But IBM did not merely lack a comprehension of the Hacker Ethic; it was pursuing a deliberate agenda. As an agent of cultural-technological construction, computers were an apparatus enacting IBM's values and beliefs, imposing the corporation's normative worldview, and thus cannot be treated as a mute technological object only later imbued with cultural meanings from external media like the Eameses' films or Levy's myths. Maintaining a firm division between "planner" and "coder"—between Thinkers and technicians, between transcendence from matter and contact with machinery—ensured that intellectual endeavors could

---

[71] See also Ben Kafka, *The Demon of Writing: Powers and Failure of Paperwork* (New York: Zone Books, 2012), pp. 145-150. On IBM's role in the emergence of corporate design, see John Harwood, *The Interface: IBM and the Transformation of Corporate Design* (Minneapolis, MN; London: University of Minnesota Press, 2011).

be freed from the rule-bound necessity of embodied existence. The CRT as an implement of screening the computer is injected into this milieu.

Over the 1950s, IBM developed and consolidated its position as the dominant firm of the emerging computer industry. Most models of computers they designed in this period were not compatible with CRT (or, for that matter, any other electronic) displays. This was not only or even primarily due to technical deficiencies: Remington Rand's UNIVAC I, for example, could be equipped with a CRT produced by Tektronix, through which its operator could examine any memory location; IBM's competing product, the 701, lacked this function—as Levy gripes, it was not a technological, but cultural incompatibility.

Computers in IBM's "Data Systems Division," the largest machines leased for more than $10,000 per month, were produced under two distinct lines, geared towards target markets with different needs. The first (the IBM 701, 704, and 709) was intended for military-scientific research, including cryptanalysis, calculating ballistic trajectories, and running simulations. The other (the IBM 702 and 705) comprised of data processors for business computing, fulfilling tasks such as census collection, accounting, and corporate administration, thus extending IBM's traditional competence in punched-card machinery and tabulating equipment. Computers in the former line would typically perform a long and potentially complex sequence of operations on a relatively small set of data, taxing the central processor more heavily than input-output units. The latter required the opposite: a short sequence of operations on large quantities of data. Even the type of data differed in each domain. Scientific computing dealt with numbers over twenty digits long, necessitating a degree of precision superfluous in data processing. While machines from both lines were "universal" (i.e., capable, in theory, of simulating either style given sufficient time and memory), material constraints of hardware meant that actual machines had to be optimized for one or the other—in the alternating implementation of floating-point arithmetic and variable word lengths, one can find the structuring of social institutions wired into the minutiae of circuitry.

While models in the military-scientific line could be configured with an optional CRT attached (the IBM 740, available from 1954), this peripheral was not compatible with those designed for business data processing—there was simply no need for number crunchers to generate images. Electronic displays have become thoroughly naturalized as the de facto mode of visualizing computational output, effectively synonymous with the notion of a computer screen. Nick Montfort has criticized the tendency towards such "screen essentialism" customary in media studies, pointing out that "early interaction with computers happened largely on paper: on paper tape, on punchcards, and on print terminals and teletypewriters, with their scroll-like supplies of continuous paper for printing output and input both."[72] Seminal studies of the computer screen by Lev Manovich and Charlie Gere exemplify this disposition, absorbed within IBM's ideological campaign to associate computing with dematerialization.[73] Their assertion that its genealogy extends to the command-and-control systems of radar oscilloscopes rather than the supposedly more passive reception of television has become a presupposition of discourse on digital media. These accounts (Montfort included) *assume* the adoption of interactivity, rather than *explain* its construction; Manovich and Gere, in particular, are insensitive to the material specificities of the screen as an artifact and take little account of the conditions under which screening takes place. While largely in agreement with Montfort, I would push his point further: computing's early screen

---

[72] Nick Montfort, "Continuous Paper: The Early Materiality and Workings of Electronic Literature" (paper presented at ISEA 2004, Helsinki, 20 August 2004), http://nickm.com/writing/essays/continuous_paper_mla.html.

[73] See Lev Manovich, *The Language of New Media* (Cambridge, MA: MIT Press, 2001), pp. 94-115; and Charlie Gere, "Genealogy of the computer screen," *Visual Communication* 5, no. 2 (2006): 141-152.

media are developed as a form of print, and any "early interaction with the computer" is a function of capital seeking to maintain divisions in class through an exertion of idealist philosophy.

In computers of the 1950s, input-output and control mechanisms were print- and console-based. A 1953 manual for the IBM 701—that is, a catalog from just before the release of the 740, their CRT screen product—lists a limited range of options: punched cards, magnetic tapes and drums, as well as a rotary printer (the IBM Type 407 Accounting Machine, "equipped with 120 rotary wheels. Each wheel has 48 characters, including Arabic numerals, alphabetic symbols, and special characters").[74] Even after electronic screens were introduced at IBM, however, these were not used as "monitors"—that is, not instruments for *monitor*ing the computer's operations in so-called "real-time." Imaging was an *outcome* of computation (for example, charting the graph of an equation, an operation useful in the context of military-scientific research), not part of the *process* of usage; to speak of navigable cyberspace would be an anachronism.

Before 1959 (when both the PDP-1's Type 30 and Stromberg-Carlson's Charactron-based S-C 4020 were introduced), the IBM 740 had little (if any) commercial competition in the electronic imaging of computation. More properly, the device comprised of two separate screens: the IBM 740 CRT Output Recorder, a 7-inch screen used in conjunction with a camera to record computer-generated graphics on film, and the IBM 780 CRT Display, a larger 21-inch screen for inspection by the computer's operator. The latter opened the possibility of "decision making and possible intervention by the operator as the computation progressed,"[75] and thus might plausibly

---

[74] *Principles of Operation: Type 701 and Associated Equipment* (New York: International Business Machines Corporation, 1953), pp. 33-46 and 55-67, here p. 37.

[75] "IBM 740: Cathode ray tube output recorder," IBM Archives, http://www-03.ibm.com/ibm/history/exhibits/701/701_1415bx40.html.

be taken as a so-called forerunner to interactivity. A 1954 article in the *Wall Street Journal* announcing the new product emphasizes this affordance, comparing it to "windows" in which "the big calculators' 'thoughts' will be pictured on the tubes in the form of graphs, geometrical figures, engineering symbols, or in words and numbers, just as they might show up on a television screen."[76]

Yet, the smaller screen—and the encounter it stages between computation and celluloid—is of equal if not greater significance. When computer-generated imagery was printed on film, this was not a secondary procedure derivative to the production and viewing of that image on an electronic screen, but the opposite. If direct viewing was at all involved in the imaging process, it was only so in a provisional capacity, with a view towards a final, fixed, *printed* product. Inscribing graphical output photographically allowed it to act as what Bruno Latour has called an "immutable mobile."[77] At a time when computers were rare and bulky, when access to them was limited and processing time precious, the physical stability of celluloid made it possible for the products of computing to be circulated and distributed. Screening the computer in this manner (through film projection or further printing) endowed it with qualities that enabled it to have a wider influence, as its results could travel over space (not remain constrained to the computer's lab), as well as be preserved over time (viewed repeatedly, at will, rather than glimpsed briefly on an ephemeral display). The prevalence of formats like the PDF suggest that even in today's cultures, effects like durability and reproducibility remain vital.[78]

---

[76] "'Windows' for Computers," *Wall Street Journal*, 18 November 1954, p. 10.

[77] Bruno Latour, "Drawing Things Together," in *Representation in Scientific Activity*, ed. Michael Lynch and Steve Woolgar (Cambridge, MA; London: MIT Press, 1990), pp. 19-68.

[78] See further, Lisa Gitelman, *Paper Knowledge: Toward a Media History of Documents* (Durham, NC; London: Duke University Press, 2014), esp. "Chapter Four—Near Print and Beyond Paper: Knowing by *.pdf," pp. 111-135.

I do not find it compelling to make a categorical distinction between printing and screening, much less pose a teleological advance from former to latter: CRT screens were themselves printers. In this, the IBM 740 is indicative of the norm. In addition to the sixteen-inch Type 30 "Precision CRT Display," the PDP-1 offered the Type 31, a 5-inch "Ultra-Precision CRT Display" similar to the Type 30, but with "resolution, accuracy, and stability ... much more suitable for the accurate, photographic recording of data."[79] Stromberg-Carlson's S-C 4020 reverses conventional narratives of technological progression from print to screen, redeveloping the Charactron tube as a microfilm printer after it was earlier configured for direct-viewing in the unique environment of the SAGE Air Defense System. I prefer to align myself with the perspective of dots, which are agnostic on this matter, expressing themselves as whatever is most suitable; as McNaney states in his 1952 patent for a "Cathode Ray Apparatus" primarily intended "to provide a printed record of the displayed information": "If desired, the apparatus may be arranged to provide a display which is suitable for direct visual observation."[80] In fact, IBM's division for printer development made an attempt at developing their own version of the proprietary Charactron using technology from RCA's competing shaped-beam tube named the Compositron.[81] The project, however, did not lead to a successful line of products: "Upper management was distracted by an offer by Stromberg-Carlson to provide its printer under a special contract—one that, after acceptance by IBM, was not fulfilled on schedule by Stromberg-Carlson. After reevaluating the market, IBM dropped its

---

[79] *PDP-1 Handbook*, p. 36.

[80] McNaney, Cathode Ray Apparatus, p. 1.

[81] The Compositron was "a developmental character-printing tube for use in non-mechanical high-speed printers for computers and data-processing machines. This tube is capable of writing several thousand characters per second. Because the characters are generated photoelectrically by projection of a lantern slide upon a photo-cathode, type styles may be changed at will" (R. J. Kistler, "The Compositron—A Developmental Printing Tube For Computer Output," *IRE Transactions on Electron Devices* 5, no. 2 [April 1958]: 112).

microfilm printer, although a single machine using transistor circuits was delivered to the Social Security Administration offices in Baltimore. It operated there quite satisfactorily for many years, but as replacement components such as the Compositron tube became difficult to obtain, the machine was displaced by printers from Stromberg-Carlson"[82] (which, of course, had since independently marketed the S-C 4020, such a Charactron-based printer).

In short, IBM re-programmed the scientific researcher in the image of a corporate executive: just as decision-making faculties of higher-level management would not wish to concern themselves with the petty details of tabulating equipment (*just the summary, please!*), knowledge production in disembodied form would be screened from internal processes. As Paul Ceruzzi explains, contact with hardware was a residual task left to the menial labor of assistants, specifically the computer's operator, whose "job consisted of mounting and demounting tapes, pressing a button to start a job every now and then, occasionally inserting decks of cards into a reader, and reading status information from a printer. It was not a particularly interesting or high-status job, though to the uninitiated it looked impressive."[83] Ceruzzi further elaborates that for others, such as the planners programming the machine, "a typical transaction began by submitting a deck of cards to an operator through a window (to preserve the climate control of the computer room)." This "window"—rather than those of Microsoft's graphical interface—is indicative of the prophylactic tendencies in computing of that era, designed to minimize rather than encourage interaction. Contra Manovich and Gere, the comparison that the *Wall Street Journal* made to television is apt, as the "window" the article refers to functioned like Steve Dompier, as a screen

---

[82] Charles J. Bashe et al., *IBM's Early Computers* (Cambridge, MA: MIT Press, 1986), pp. 488-489.

[83] Paul E. Ceruzzi, *A History of Modern Computing* (Cambridge, MA: MIT Press, 1998), p. 73.

medium across a spatiotemporal threshold rather than as an instrument of control: it could be said "to let engineers and scientists see what goes on inside its giant electronic computers."[84]

In this regard, perhaps the proliferation of names assigned by IBM over the 1950s could also be interpreted as a sort of return of the repressed: with the exception of the "Defense Calculator" (bespeaking another kind of trauma), each model refers to the raw ingredients through which abstract information remained bound to fleshy existence—"*Card* Programmed Calculator," "*Tape* Processing Machine," "*Electronic* Data Processing Machine," "*Magnetic Drum* Calculator."

While IBM may have attempted to instigate an era of transcendence (*Think!*), their production also betrays a compulsive sensitivity to base matter. It is unsurprising, given these contradictions, that their take on screening the computer was doomed to fail. Absent the possibility of completely avoiding its technics, other forms of screening would have to suffice: at this juncture, one might resume the more familiar myths of interactivity that lead computer displays from the hacker to the user; I intend to pursue another path through the deep histories of the graphical method.

§3.5: The Sphygmograph and the Capillary Electrometer: Rheotomic Physiology

Graphics, as Latour suggests, process the creation of publics. They inscribe connections between sociotechnical nodes, "drawing things together." But more, they mediate relations: in producing visibility, Joseph Vogl argues, media "also have a tendency to erase themselves and

---

[84] "'Windows' for Computers," p. 10.

their constitutive sensory function, making themselves imperceptible and 'anesthetic.'"[85] Indeed, in Dürer's articulation of drawing as a cultural technique, the pedagogical impact of illustrations persists even when they are no longer actual actants in a network; they become schematic.

In this, graphic procedures maintain a deep affinity with the role computation acquired by the end of the 1950s. As Peter Galison has shown, in the postwar era, computer simulations functioned as a "trading zone" between scientists from varied and potentially irreconcilable disciplines, making it possible for them to engage in exchange by providing a space of exception from the specific commitments that they might otherwise be beholden to. Instead of a shared framework of laws or ontology, Galison argues that "they held a new cluster of skills in common, a new mode of producing scientific knowledge that was rich enough to coordinate highly diverse subject matter."[86] Treating computing in such mercantile terms—as a *middle*man of trade—means that it works in-between, rather than at the center; it makes no claims to the status of meta-discursivity.

When does the computer cease to be content with its subordinate role as a simple calculator and instead aspire to the station of media? In this capacity, rather than at the spectacles of interactivity, computation transmits the conditions of reality whilst erasing traces of itself, becoming the mediator of knowledge production—it subtends the belief that isolated subcultures are participants in a shared project.

---

[85] Joseph Vogl, "Becoming-media: Galileo's Telescope," *Grey Room* 29 (Winter 2008): 16.

[86] Peter Galison, "Computer Simulations and the Trading Zone," in *The Disunity of Science: Boundaries, Contexts, and Power*, eds. Peter Galison and David J. Stump (Stanford, CA: Stanford University Press, 1996), p. 119.

Over a series of articles published between 1957 and 1962, physicians Hebbel E. Hoff and Leslie A. Geddes describe the long histories of graphical techniques in similar terms.[87] Although their accounts lack Galison's more nuanced approach towards divergences and discrepancies, unfortunately instead preferring a harmonious picture of scientific progress, it is emphasized that they understand mark-marking as a disturbance to territorial sovereignty over fiefdoms of knowledge. These practices engender a zone "where sciences have overlapped."[88] On this point, they concur with their predecessor, physiologist Étienne-Jules Marey, whom they describe as "the great French exponent of the graphic method" and cite approvingly: "in the field of rigorous experimentation all the sciences give a hand to each other. Whatever is the object of his studies, he who measures a force, a movement, an electrical state or a temperature, whether he is a physicist, chemist, or physiologist, must have recourse to the same method and employs the same instruments."[89] In Marey's estimation, any scientific inquiry must contend with the problem of hardware; the graphical method underwrites his conception of scientific community.

Hoff and Geddes take the history of their profession beyond the boundaries of medical research. Key landmarks indicating a shift in sensibility are not viewed in isolation but arise out of methodological commerce. For them, Carl Ludwig's invention of the kymograph, typically

---

[87] H. E. Hoff and L. A. Geddes, "The Rheotome and its Prehistory: A Study in the Historical Interrelation of Electro-Physiology and Electromechanics," *Bulletin of the History of Medicine* 31 (1957): 212-234 and 327-347; "Graphic Registration before Ludwig," *Isis* 50, no. 1 (March 1959): 5-21; "Ballistics and the Instrumentation of Physiology: The Velocity of the Projectile and of the Nerve Impulse," *Journal of the History of Medicine* 15, issue 2 (April 1960): 133-146; "The Technological Background of Physiological Discovery: Ballistics and the Graphic Method," *Journal of the History of Medicine* 15, issue 4 (October 1960): 345-363; "The Capillary Electrometer: The First Graphic Recorder of Bioelectric Signals," *Archives internationale d'histoire des sciences* 14 (1961): 275-290; "The Beginnings of Graphic Recording," *Isis* 53, no. 3 (September 1962): 287-324.

[88] Hoff and Geddes, "The Beginnings of Graphic Recording," p. 287.

[89] Étienne-Jules Marey, *La methode graphique dans les sciences expérimentale et principalement en physiologie et en médecine* (Paris: G. Masson, 1874), quoted in and trans. Hoff and Geddes, "The Beginnings of Graphic Recording," p. 287.

considered to have introduced graphical techniques into the study of physiology, is situated within a complex intersection of research around charting the time course of short-duration bioelectric signals (i.e., the characteristic waveforms of the "action potential"), including "a chain of events linking ballistics and neurophysiology and culminating in one of the latter's most important experiments, the measurement of the velocity of the nerve impulse."[90] This coupling of early studies into electrophysiology and electromechanics in the aftermath of Luigi Galvani's experiments with bioelectricity is exemplary of epistemic flux, an instance "when, for a time, physics and physiology, electricity and neurophysiology occupied common fields": as Hoff and Geddes elaborate, "it was not always clear what was physiological and what was physical, and many a physicist found in the frog the most convenient galvanometer."[91]

That is, the blending of sciences was defined by difficulties in finding appropriate instruments; perhaps this challenge accounts for the keen attention Hoff and Geddes afford it, finding cases where inscription does not proceed smoothly as the modular implementation of a pre-constituted framework. Hermann von Helmholtz, who in 1850 had successfully timed the conduction of the nerve impulse, described the problem as one involving "the Methods of Measuring very Small Portions of Time," with particular concern (in his case) towards "their application to Physiological Purposes."[92] At the time of his experiments, it had been observed that muscular activity may be induced through the stimulation of nerves, but understanding of details in the process through which this excitation is propagated remained limited; in fact, the so-called

---

[90] Hoff and Geddes, "Ballistics and the Instrumentation of Physiology," p. 133.

[91] Hoff and Geddes, "The Rheotome and its Prehistory," p. 212.

[92] Hermann von Helmholtz, "On the Methods of Measuring very Small Portions of Time, and their application to Physiological Purpose," *The London, Edinburgh and Dublin Philosophical Magazine and Journal of Science*, series 4, vol. 6, no. 40 (November 1853): 313-325.

"rheoscopic frog" (a severed frog's leg used to indicate the presence or absence of an electric current; *rheo*: "flow") was for a time more sensitive than any artificially constructed galvanometer. How, then, was one to measure such phenomena when they were themselves the conditioning apparatus of research? In setting the premises of his investigation, Helmholtz stressed the challenge it poses to immediate experience:

> In the living body the muscle receives the excitation to activity from the threads of nerves which ramify through it; these, in turn, from the brain. Here the mysterious influence of the will imparts an excitation whose nature is unknown, which propagates itself throughout the entire length of the fibres, and arriving at the muscle excites it to action. If we modernize the comparison of Menenius Agrippa, who pacified the starving plebeians by wisely likening the state to the human body, then the nervous fibres might be compared with the wires of the electric telegraph, which in an instant transmit intelligence from the extremities of the land to the governing centre, and then in like manner communicate the will of the ruling power to every distinct portion of the land. The principal question I have sought to answer is the following:—In the transmission of such intelligence, is a measurable time necessary for the ends of the nerves to communicate to the brain the impression made upon them; and on the other hand, is time required for the conveyance of the commands of the will from the brain to a distant muscle?
>
> This, perhaps, appears improbable; in our own case we have never perhaps experienced anything similar. When, however, we reflect on the limited accuracy of our perceptions, and that we naturally cannot perceive more quickly than our nerves, which are the necessary media of all our perceptions, transmit impressions, it is easy to see that the expression of our own experience can give us no information here.[93]

Earlier in the paper, he had explained the inadequacy of intuitive accounts in the task of measuring "Small Portions of Time," offering several examples where the senses display their limitations:

> When we see two flashes of light appear one after the other in the same place, we perceive them as double, if the time of interruption amount to the tenth part of a second; if the time between both flashes be smaller, then both the latter melt into one, as is illustrated by the common experiment of the continuous circle of fire when a glowing coal is swung speedily round. The ear perceives successive taps either as separate noises, or, when more than thirty-two such taps occur in the

---

[93] Ibid., pp. 320-321.

second, as a uniform and continuous tone, which increases in pitch with the speed at which the taps follow each other.[94]

As a further introduction, Helmholtz detailed how instruments devised for the purposes of artillery (where accurate knowledge of the ball's velocity was necessary in calculating its path) had been applied to measuring the velocity of light (which also evade immediate grasp through the unaided senses). These, in turn, were used in his own experiments on the velocity of the nerve impulse.

Rather than elaborating on the results and implications of this seminal experiment, Hoff and Geddes expand on the procedural lineage Helmholtz placed himself within, both narrating its transmission in greater depth, as well as broadening its context to show that principles behind the ballistic galvanometer were also mobilized in other electrophysiological investigations; the plane of discursivity addressed in their media archaeology (so to speak) of "very Small Portions of Time" is not the positivity of *statements* (i.e., *what* Helmholtz could say) but cuts across a collection of *practices* (i.e., *how* Helmholtz could work).

Specifically, this problem hinged—quite literally—on the galvanometer's tardy response. Although adequate in gauging continuous currents, mechanical galvanometers were poor indicators of rapid changes due to their lag in reaction. Both physiologists (who sought to plot graphs of transient electrical activity in nerves and muscles on the order of fractions of a millisecond) as well as physicists (facing the increasing industrial importance of systems based on alternating current oscillating at a high frequency) were ill supported by measuring instruments usually requiring a period between 10 to 60 seconds before reaching a terminal reading.

---

[94] Ibid., p. 314.

"It is known," Marey would write when addressing the topic "Of Electricity in Animals" in his book on *Animal Mechanism*, "that the needle of a galvanometer subjected to a frequently-interrupted current, takes a fixed position intermediate between zero and the extreme point which it would have occupied if the current had been continuous."[95] Emil DuBois-Reymond had recognized this phenomenon in his analysis of the situation he encountered, noting the undesirable "inertia" of electromechanical graphic registration in reflecting "instantaneous currents":

> The galvanometer, in truth is an instrument eminently adapted to detect the presence of continuous electric currents, as well as the variations of the intensity of these currents when these variations last a sufficiently long time in comparison with an oscillation of the needle. But if it is a question of instantaneous currents, or even of variations in the intensity of continuous currents, that are extremely short with respect to the duration of an oscillation, when these variations take place singly or are repeated continuously at more or less short intervals, the galvanometer then ceases to be of value. In fact, the inertia of the needle permits it only to perceive the sum of all the electrodynamic actions exerted during the passage of the current, and prevents it from following in its movements the rapid changes that one can impress, in one direction or another, upon the intensity curve. The galvanometer, in this case, no longer is capable of faithful indication of what occurs at every instant in the circuit of which it is a part, and instantaneous currents, if not very strong, traverse it without creating easily appreciable effects.[96]

This interstitial space—the symbolically vacant passage between off and on, between "zero" and an accurate terminal reading—would be mobilized as a crucial component in time sampling methods to circumventing these difficulties. Strategies taking this approach could be described as having adopted an inverted sensibility towards the frictions of instrumentation, seeking not so much to mitigate artifacts from the measurement process as to repurpose the impediments from

---

[95] Étienne-Jules Marey, *Animal Mechanism: A Treatise on Terrestrial and Aerial Locomotion* (New York: D. Appleton and Co., 1874), pp. 50-51.

[96] Emil DuBois-Reymond, quoted in and trans. Hoff and Geddes, "The Rheotome and its Prehistory," p. 231.

these in-between spaces into the very medium through which phenomena could be expressed; the deficiency of a needle's inertia was dealt with as an asset.

Claude Servais Pouillet's ballistic galvanometer had established the principle on which such responses were modelled. Useful in the precise measurement of short intervals of time, Pouillet's instrument had been so named for its redeployment of a schema familiar from the ballistic pendulum.[97] Measurements of projectile velocity had proceeded by applying the well-known law of momentum conversation: given two objects of known masses—one small and in motion (a bullet), the other relatively large but stationary (the pendulum's bob)—the velocity at which the former strikes the latter may be derived from the results of impact, namely from the amplitude of the pendulum's deflection (which increases proportionately with the bullet's velocity). Of course, discharging this procedure is easier in principle than with hardware. Hoff and Geddes recount numerous contraptions from gunnery science preceding Pouillet, specifically their difficulties in marking the pendulum's deflection.[98]

Pouillet's electromechanical adaptation relied on an analogy between a projectile pushing a resistant bob and an electric current rousing a galvanometer's sluggish indicator needle into movement. Just as the pendulum's resistance made the imperceptibly fast movement of a bullet legible, the inertia in the galvanometer afforded a means of determining the exact length of timespans even below the threshold of an observer's reaction. As only prolonged stimulation would effect the terminal reading in a galvanometer, the extent of its needle's partial deflection from a brief shock could be used as an index for the measurement of time, longer durations of

---

[97] See Hoff and Geddes, "Ballistics and the Instrumentation of Physiology."

[98] See Hoff and Geddes, "The Technological Background of Physiological Discovery."

contact resulting in a stronger reading (akin to the wider amplitude of a pendulum struck by a faster bullet). In other words, the ballistic galvanometer worked by leeching on the latencies of instrumentation, reflecting not an apparatus's perfection in measurement but its degree of failure at attaining this accuracy; it operated in the space of noise.

To Kittler's oft-cited characterization of media as a product of the "misuse of military equipment,"[99] it might thus be added that the calculation of ballistic velocities itself channels a principle of "misuse," perverting the intended application of a galvanometer. In this way, nerve impulses—"the necessary media of all our perceptions" according to Helmholtz—lose their immediacy neither as presence nor absence. They became a discernible object only as an artifact of the excluded middle between on and off, amidst the latency of graphical inertia.[100]

Readings obtained in this manner were calibrated against a controlled range of output generated by an instrument designed specifically to periodically break a continuous electric current, the rheotome—literally, "flow slicer." Hoff and Geddes foreground the role of a rheotomic principle in their account of the development of curve tracing technologies, deeming it indispensable to Emil Lenz's early solution to plotting the variation in intensity over a cycle of alternating current. Lenz's setup involved a modified commutator, refashioned such that unlike regular commutators it would not convert alternating current to direct current, but rather would deliver a train of short-duration pulses indicative of the intensity at a given phase in each cycle. By isolating these slices of current, Lenz was able to further tap on the indicator needle's inertia

---

[99] Friedrich Kittler, "Rock Music: A Misuse of Military Equipment," in *The Truth of the Technological World*, pp. 152-164.

[100] See Henning Schmidgen, *The Helmholtz Curves: Tracing Lost Time*, trans. Nils F. Schott (New York: Fordham University Press, 2014): "In this regime, *what was measured was produced by the measurement*" (p. 4).

to his advantage, exploiting the symmetry in its latency. In the same way that the presence of electricity was registered slowly, its absence likewise only took full effect at a delay. Thus, sampling of a single phase from multiple pulses could yield a cumulative impact leading to a terminal reading due to the persistence of effects registered from previous samples of that same phase: as DuBois-Reymond put it, when presented with "instantaneous" electric currents, "the inertia of the needle permits it only to perceive the sum of all the electrodynamic actions exerted during the passage of the current." This process would be repeated for each phase in the cycle of oscillation, making it possible to assemble a reconstruction of the curve of alternating current from a collection of discrete readings.

Although Lenz did not himself use the term, it is compelling to follow Hoff and Geddes in describing his commutator as a sort of rheotome: it operated by delivering *slices* of a continuous *flow*. This association is clearer still in an apparatus designed by DuBois-Reymond's student, Julius Bernstein, to graph the time course of bioelectric intensities following excitation, named the differential rheotome. Inspired by Lenz's success, Bernstein's solution worked along similar lines, but instead was adapted to the needs of physiological research by periodically delivering a stimulus before taking a brief sample after an interval of time. Insofar as this method relied on artificially inducing responses in a predictable rhythm comparable to a series of oscillations, it in effect worked by turning physiological specimens into circuits of alternating current. As in Lenz's commutator, a legible reading of a single phase would be built up on the tardy galvanometer over multiple instantiations through repeated stimulation. Subsequently, by replicating this process across a range of interval lengths between stimulus and sample, the entire waveform of the action potential could be scanned.

It would be difficult to appreciate the strong spurs Marey had to leave the relative solidity of his regular graphic implements without recognizing the difficulties of operation encountered in research into electrophysiology. His recourse to photographic technology was prompted by the limitations that time sampling methods like Bernstein's had imposed, such as their inability to investigate spontaneously arising bioelectric events due to the need for repeated stimulation of tissue. The capillary electrometer, developed by Marey in collaboration with the physicist Gabriel Lippmann, was unlike prior approaches in that it did not exacerbate the effects of friction but, perhaps more intuitively, sought to overcome it. Lippmann's research into electrocapillarity—specifically, into variables associated with effects on the surface tension at an interface between mercury and dilute sulfuric acid resulting from changes in the electric potential between them—had led to a promising basis for an electrometer. Variation in the shape of the mercury meniscus in response to fluctuations in the electric current passed through it occurred relatively swiftly and thus, unlike existing electromechanical rheoscopes (i.e., galvanometers), could be used to indicate rapid shifts in the current's intensity. Further, unlike the not-quite-docile bodies of physiological rheoscopes (i.e., severed and skinned frog legs), it was possible to derive quantitative magnitudes from its measurements. In Marey's words, the resulting instrument was "so marvelously sensitive that it was capable of registering the slightest electrical variation that occurred in living tissues."[101]

Unfortunately, he continued, its effects took place at such an "exceedingly fine" scale that its "movements had to be observed under the microscope."[102] Photography was a compromise given this unwieldy situation, light standing in for more cumbersome mechanical inscription tools. As with computer graphics of the 1950s, the assemblage of electrometer and photography

---

[101] Étienne-Jules Marey, *Movement*, trans. Eric Pritchard (London: William Heinemann, 1895), p. 49.

[102] Ibid.

functioned as an immutable mobile, mediating the production of sense by traversing space and time. Indeed, it does not require too far a stretch of the imagination to grasp the analogous relation between the capillary and cathode-ray tubes, both agents of the translation from imperceptible flow into visible form.

Marey constructed two setups for chronophotographic recording, both involving an illuminated capillary electrometer, a photosensitive plate, and a narrow vertical slit placed between the two to mediate their relation, funneling light into a measurement on the y-axis. In the first setup, the slit was moved horizontally over time, registering duration elapsed on the x-axis; in the other, the plate was moved, with the same result. "In effect," Marey reported to the Académie des sciences in July 1876, "the opacity of the mercury column was used to obscure, at a varying height [based on the current's change], a slit through which a beam of light would be painted on the photographic plate (*l'écran photographique*)."[103]

Or, translated more literally, "painted on the photographic *screen*." This crude interpretation is perhaps more appropriate as, for Marey, photography is introduced into his graphic method as an operation of distillation through which a material "beam" is filtered—that is, *screened*—through a "slit" and subsequently projected onto a light-sensitive surface, a procedure no different in principle than tracing inscriptions with any other stylus. Marta Braun has pointed out that Marey's initial apathy to this particular medium stemmed from this practical equivalence of its results with other chronographic procedures, as "the camera was only translating the phases of a rectilinear movement as a function of time, just as the graphing inscriptors did—

---

[103] Étienne-Jules Marey, "Inscription photographique des indications de l'électromètre de Lippmann," *Comptes rendus hebdomadaires des séances de l'Académie des sciences* 83 (1876): "En effet, on utilisait l'opacité de la colonne de mercure pour obturer, dans une éntendue à chaque instant variable, une fente à travers laquelle passait un faisceau de lumière qui allait se peindre sur l'écran photographique" (p. 279).

no more, no less."[104] Perhaps it was necessary to fiddle with messy and slow wet-collodion processes given the exigencies of this situation, wherein the surface tension of mercury in a fine capillary tube ("scarcely $\frac{1}{20}$ of a millimeter"[105]!) could hardly be expected to summon sufficient force to power a mechanical marker, but why else bother? The severe abstraction of lines against a void achieved here would continue to be the ideal to which his later work would aspire, emphasizing the indexicality of photography over iconicity. As Noam Elcott argues, chronophotography was an apparatus through which "humans were transposed into graphic notations"[106]—it functioned as a semiotic purifier, swallowing the nonsensical excess of Real bodies, inscribing their movements within a Symbolic regime.

Instead of a continuous exposure, the chronophotographic apparatus was illuminated by "a series of flashes from an induction coil furnished with a condenser. This intermittent illumination disturbed the continuity of the images, and thus a series of bright lines of unequal length was produced."[107] An advantage of discrete readings, rather than unfurling the line into a solid band, was that each mark also indicated a temporal interval. The resulting (photo-)graph could thus be described through the somewhat paradoxical notion of an immanent grid: the structuring raster is not superimposed over an innocent object but is internalized within its expression. What had for Lenz and Bernstein been a necessary compromise became, in Marey's image processing, a useful trait, mobilizing time sampling as a formal device. Opacity and photosensitivity work in parallel

---

[104] Marta Braun, *Picturing Time: The Work of Étienne-Jules Marey (1830-1904)* (Chicago; London: University of Chicago Press, 1992), p. 47.

[105] Marey, "Inscription photographique," p. 279.

[106] Noam M. Elcott, *Artificial Darkness: An Obscure History of Modern Art and Media* (Chicago; London: University of Chicago Press, 2016), pp. 18-28, here p. 27.

[107] Marey, *Movement*, p. 50.

with insulation and conductivity; an epistemology of interruption—a rheotomic principle, one could say—pervades Marey's technique.

Curve tracing and flow slicing are coupled operations that stage the visual culture of what Bernhard Siegert has termed the "passage of the digital." In Siegert's account, Pouillet and Helmholtz herald the conclusion of an episteme rooted paradigmatically in the spatial organization of central perspective and the gravitational dynamics of attraction and repulsion, introducing another regime, conditioned instead by "rotational or oscillatory movement."[108] Subjective response could hence instead be adequately simulated as a circuit of alternating current, as indicated by Bernstein's differential rheotome—and the production of moving imagery post-Marey. Over the course of Marey's career, an expanded range of pulse techniques adjust the stakes of distinct fluctuations in flow, putting the palpation of arterial pressure in touch with the analysis of electric signals, the latter of which would become known as communications or signals engineering.

Even before directing attention to the capillary electrometer, Marey had been familiar with the problem of curve tracing. The first device for which he would attain widespread recognition was an improvement to Karl Vierordt's sphygmograph, used to obtain traces of the pulse. Ludwig's pioneering kymograph, which Hoff and Geddes take care to place in the broader context of graphical recording, made use of a mercury manometer attached directly to the artery, producing inscriptions on a rotating drum through indicative movements of a stylus. The sphygmograph was

---

[108] Bernhard Siegert, *Passage des Digitalen* (Berlin: Brinkmann & Bose, 2003): "Was ist, erscheint nicht mehr unter den Bedingungen eines zentralperspektivisch konstruierten Raumes, dessen Nullpunkt die Spitze der Sehpyramide ist. Es erscheint auch nicht unter den Bedingungen eines dynamisch von Anziehung und Abstoßung konstruierten Raumes, dessen Nullpunkt das Gravitationszentrum ist. Was ist, erscheint vielmehr nur unter der Bedingung, daß das, was Bedingung der Möglichkeit von Wahrnehmung ist, das Subjekt, in einer Rotations- oder Schwingungsbewegung exsistiert. Und da, streng nach Ritter, alles, was sich ereignet, sich oszillatorisch ereignet, gilt dieser Satz nicht weniger allgemein als die Bedingungen der Zentralperspektive im 17. Jahrhundert" (p. 366).

an instrument that allowed for similar examination of changes in arterial pressure, but noninvasively; Marey's amendments to Vierordt's initial bulky design resulted in a portable device which was lightweight (220 grams) and reliable (fabricated by the esteemed watchmaking house Breguet), making utilization in clinical practice viable.

Interest in examining the pulse was not unique to modern physiology. The practice has an extended and venerable history stretching back millennia; it cannot be limited to the emergence of biopolitical regimes taking the body as an object of study. To again leech off Kittlerian media theory as an orienting cue, if music and mathematics are especially important spheres to the study of cultural techniques (as suggested in his later writings), such an assessment is epitomized in the practices of sphygmology—on this, the Alexandrian physician Herophilus is said to have declared: "To detect its exact harmony in relation to age and disease one needs to be a musician and even a mathematician to understand the pulse."[109]

An association between the tempo of music and the beat of a pulse was especially pervasive in the sphygmograph's genealogical pedigree. Avicenna asserted that "the nature of music is found in pulse," a claim based on Galen's analysis of cardiac rhythms as musical ratios which, Nancy Siraisi notes, "distinguished at least twenty-seven varieties of pulse." These authorities were affirmed by other widely read accounts, such as those of Averroes and Giles de Corbeil.[110] When polymath Athanasius Kircher addressed the topic, not only was the pulse discussed in a chapter

---

[109] Herophilus, quoted and trans. in Kenneth D. Keele, *The Evolution of Clinical Methods in Medicine* (London: Pitman Medical Publishing Co, 1963), pp. 16-17.

[110] See Peter Pesic, "Music, Mechanism, and the 'Sonic Turn' in Physical Diagnosis," *Journal of the History of Medicine and Allied Sciences* 71, no. 2 (April 2016): 144-172, quoting Avicenna on p. 146; and Nancy G. Siraisi, "The Music of Pulse in the Writings of Italian Academic Physicians (Fourteenth and Fifteenth Centuries)," *Speculum* 50, no. 4 (Oct. 1975): 696-697. See also Leofranc Holford-Strevens, "The Harmonious Pulse," *The Classical Quarterly* 43, no. 2 (1993): 475-479; and Laurinda S. Dixon, *Perilous Chastity: Women and Illness in Pre-Enlightenment Art and Medicine* (Ithaca, NY; London: Cornell University Press, 1995), pp. 180-185.

from his writings on music, *Musurgia Universalis* (1650), its various proportions were charted according to a graphical system derived from musical notation.[111] Likely the most extensively elaborated graphic typology of this sort was constructed by François-Nicolas Marquet, a physician from Nancy who proposed an easy and curious new method of knowing the human pulse by musical notes, *Nouvelle méthode facile et curieuse pour apprendre par les notes de musique à connoître le pous de l'Homme* (1747).[112] Marquet's thorough mapping of the pulse through an accumulation of discrete moments was mocked by proponents of vitalism such as Joseph-Jacques Ménuret de Chambaud, whose article on the pulse in Diderot's influential *Encyclopédie* (1765) singled out Marquet's undertaking for ridicule: "The doctrine which he [Marquet] establishes on the differences, the causes, and the omens of the pulse is but an absurd and strange mixture of the dogmas of the Galenists, the Mechanists, and the Chemists."[113] Early theories on the circulation of blood, as initially championed in the seventeenth century by William Harvey and his contemporaries like Robert Fludd, had been motivated less by modern scientific methodology than introduced as part of a cyclical cosmology based on a metaphysics of fluidity. It is thus unsurprising that sympathizers to vitalist philosophies, including Menuret, would similarly favor a harmonics of disposition based on an interpretation of Chinese pulse theory, considering Marquet's quantitative measures mechanical and reductive.[114]

---

[111] Athanasius Kircher, *Musurgia Universalis, sive Ars Magna Consoni et Dissoni*, vol. 2 (Romae: Typis Luouici Grignani, 1650), pp. 413-422.

[112] François-Nicolas Marquet, *Nouvelle méthode facile et curieuse, Pour apprendre par les Notes de Musique à connoître le Pous de l'Homme* (Nancy: N. Baltazard, 1747).

[113] Jean-Joseph Menuret, "Pouls," in *Encyclopédie, ou dictionnaire raisonné des sciences, des arts et des métiers, etc.*, vol. 13, ed. Denis Diderot (Neufchastel: Samuel Faulche, 1765), p. 220.

[114] See Walter Pagel, "William Harvey and the Purpose of Circulation," *Isis* 42, no. 1 (April 1951): 22-38; and Allen G. Debus, "Robert Fludd and the Circulation of the Blood," *Journal of the History of Medicine and Allied Sciences* 16, no. 4 (October 1961): 374-393.

Contextualizing Marey's graphical method within this longer historical trajectory complicates prevailing readings of his deployment of instrumentation which characterize it as a process that "allowed objective, verifiable examination as well as exact measurement,"[115] dispensing with the role of subjective judgment. Marey himself had encouraged just such an understanding, affirming that graphical output expressed the "language of phenomena themselves" and that its adoption as method would allow scientific inquiry to "proceed in the manner of geometers whose demonstrations are not discussed."[116] But his claims should be approached with caution.

Marey's graphic instrument was, like other instances from the history of sphygmology, a machine for making publics, defining directions of shared sensibility. With it, fleeting indications could be affixed in durable form; made visible on paper, diagnosis of the pulse could be compared and regulated. Rheotomes, their scientists, and the drawings they yielded formed a powerful actor-network against vitalist strands of thought that objected to their use of interruption, consigning any remnants of the latter to marginal curiosity. Of course, well after controversy over instrumentation had subsided, Marey's colleague at the Collège de France, Henri Bergson, would continue to protest the discretization engendered by what he referred to as the "cinematographical mechanism." Although his objections to the practice of rheotomic sampling were articulated in the vocabulary of a photographic imaginary, Bergson's arguments belong to and extend a vitalist tradition already substantially developed more than a century earlier in Menuret's snarky attack

---

[115] François Dagognet, *Étienne-Jules Marey: A Passion for the Trace* (New York: Zone Books, 1992), p. 29. Likewise, Marta Braun notes that "Marey's instrument helped demonstrate that objective science could replace the eminently personal art of medical touch" (*Picturing Time*, p. 34). See also Soraya de Chadarevian, "Graphical Method and Discipline: Self-Recording Instruments in Nineteenth-Century Physiology," *Studies in the History and Philosophy of Science* 24, no. 2 (1993): 267-291.

[116] Marey, *La méthode graphique*, p. iii and p. vi.

on Marquet's graphic schema. For Bergson, this "contrivance of the cinematograph" mirrors "that of our knowledge":

> Instead of attaching ourselves to the inner becoming of things, we place ourselves outside them in order to recompose their becoming artificially. We take snapshots, as it were, of the passing reality, and, as these are characteristic of the reality, we have only to string them on a becoming, abstract, uniform and invisible, situated at the back of the apparatus of knowledge, in order to imitate what there is that is characteristic in this becoming itself.[117]

His concerns—like those of Menuret—centered precisely on the *flow slicing* operations that "solidify into discontinuous images" and thus fail to respect the integrity of "the fluid continuity of the real."[118]

At stake in these incessant skirmishes was the basis for rendering the Real signals of a pulse within Symbolic definition. As a cultural technique, sphygmology is such a constitutive procedure of sense-making. Commenting on the differences between the Greek and Chinese traditions of pulse taking, Shigehisa Kuriyama has described these alternatives as "paths of perceptual education," maintaining that like any other cultural activity, "the apprehension of the body also requires the cultivation of special sensibilities":

> What I propose is that we consider this and other such statements about the transformational potential of sites [presented by the more topologically inclined Chinese approach to the pulse] in much the same way that we consider expressions such as "Bordeaux wines of 1935 are distinguished by their chicory bouquet" or "Steinway pianos have a baroque timbre." That is, I urge that they are statements of fact of a special kind. In stating what is the case, they neither call for nor permit critical examination, rejection, or assent. Rather, they define directions of learning: they invite us to develop our sensibility in such a way as to discern the realities described. For the untrained individual the *k'an* proclivities of the north may seem as unreal or at least as meaningless as "chicory bouquet" and "baroque timbre" are for those unversed in wine-tasting or music; but for the cultivated palate, to take

---

[117] Henri Bergson, *Creative Evolution*, trans. Arthur Mitchell (New York: Modern Library, 1944), p. 332.

[118] Ibid, p. 328.

just one example, the chicory bouquet is a fact of immediate experience. To accept the statement "North is *k'an*, the site of water," thus, means nothing more or less than engaging oneself in a process of self-transformation.... The inquiry into history is an inquiry into the possible realms of human experience.[119]

G. E. R. Lloyd has contended that, in contrast to an attunement to site appreciated in Chinese sphygmology, music offered a model for "the successful mathematisation of harmonics" within the more metrically-inclined Greek lineage of Galen, an association to it displaying "the evident *ambition* to make the inquiry an exact one": "If the main concords are expressible in terms of simple numerical relationships, why not also the main ratios between the dilations and contractions of the arteries?"[120]

Conversely, the pulse also presented the possibility that it might remain irrecuperable to legibility. Working in the Herophilian tradition, Rufus of Ephesus remarked on the threatening possibility that nonsense would prevail: "The pulse of newborn children, then, is completely short and not distinct in its contraction and dilation. Herophilus says this pulse is constituted 'without definable ratios' (*a-logos*; 'irrational'). He calls the pulse which is without a 'relation to some ratio' (*ana-logia*) a pulse 'without definable ratios', for it has neither a double ratio, nor a ratio of one and a half to one, nor any other proportion (*logos*), but rather is completely short, and we observe it to be similar in size to the prick of a needle."[121]

---

[119] Shigehisa Kuriyama, "Pulse Diagnosis in the Greek and Chinese Traditions" in *Beyond the Body Proper: Reading the Anthropology of Material Life*, eds. Margaret Lock and Judith Farquhar (Durham, NC; London: Duke University Press, 2007), p. 607 and pp. 600-601.

[120] G. E. R. Lloyd, *The Revolutions of Wisdom: Studies in the Claims and Practices of Ancient Greek Science* (Berkeley, CA; Los Angeles; Oxford: University of California Press, 1995), p. 284.

[121] Rufus Ephesius, quoted in *Herophilus: The Art of Medicine in Early Alexandria*, ed. and trans. Heinrich von Staden (Cambridge: Cambridge University Press, 1989), p. 351.

It is easy to see why there was cause for alarm. Appreciation of the pulse was a form of connoisseurship typically associated with the testing (i.e., tasting) of urine. These decidedly sensuous modes of gathering knowledge presented "non-verbal signs accessible to the doctor's senses," diagnostic indicators that Faith Wallis argues were "emblems of the rational physician's ability to see the invisible inner workings of the body" even beyond what the patient could express in speech—that is, sphygmology belonged to the untamed realm beyond *logos*.[122] Carlo Ginzburg has suggested that "there could be no greater contrast than between the Galileian physicist, professionally deaf to sounds and forbidden to taste or smell, and the physician of the same period, who ventured his diagnosis after listening to a wheezy chest, or sniffing faeces, or tasting urine"; he further advocates for a sympathetic relation between historiographic praxis and "medical semiotics" rooted in the examination of "concrete" signs, explaining that "the historian's knowledge, like the doctor's, is indirect, based on signs and scraps of evidence, conjectural."[123]

When addressing the topic of pressure in his book on the circulation of blood, *La circulation du sang* (1881), Marey explained that "any act exerted in order to overcome a resistance is necessarily limited by the strength of that resistance itself," a basic principle from which no organ was exempt:

> The heart also regulates its effort on the resistance it experiences, that is, on the pressure to which the blood is subjected in the arteries. However, since this pressure varies, at every moment, under all sorts of influences, nothing is more variable than the strength that the heart will deploy under these diverse conditions.... Thus, the strength actualized by the heart is, like that of any muscle, proportionate to the resistance that the ventricle must overcome.

---

[122] Faith Wallis, "Signs and Senses: Diagnosis and Prognosis in Early Medieval Pulse and Urine Texts," *Social History of Medicine* 13, no. 2 (December 2000): 267-268.

[123] Carlo Ginzburg, "Morelli, Freud and Sherlock Holmes: Clues and Scientific Method," trans. Anna Davin, *History Workshop* 9 (Spring 1980): 15-16.

> If the ventricle found an increasing resistance in front of it, the effort of its systole would increase proportionately. Finally, if blood exiting the ventricle were opposed by an absolute obstacle, the effort developed by the walls of this organ would be raised to the limit of their muscular power, and would thus be the measure of the heart's greatest *possible strength*.[124]

As Marey argues, the study of flow cannot proceed without the incorporation of an impediment; interference is not just a possibility of corruption, distorting an untouched ideal of circulation, but a constitutive condition of sampling. Even in noninvasive procedures where arterial pressure is externally gauged, supplementary resistance is necessary to make the strength of pulsations palpable: Vierordt's sphygmograph used a weight to maintain pressure; Marey's design replaced this cumbersome counterforce with a spring; traditionally, compression would be performed manually.

This factor featured prominently in nineteenth-century studies. William H. Broadbent argued in his elucidation of *The Pulse* (1890) that "to feel the pulsation in an artery, or to take a sphygmographic trace, a certain degree of pressure must be applied to the vessel, and, as is well known, there must be a bone behind it against which it can be compressed": the pulse

> is not, as commonly understood, an expansion of the artery. This, at any rate, is not what we feel or what is recorded by the sphygmograph. A moment's reflection as to the volume of blood discharged by the left ventricle into the aorta, and a comparison of this with the capacity of the entire arterial system, will convince us that it is altogether inadequate to produce any such expansion of the smaller arteries as will be appreciable to the touch.... In the intervals between the pulsations, when

---

[124] Étienne-Jules Marey, *La circulation du sang: a l'état physiologique et dans les maladies* (Paris: G. Masson, 1881): "Tout acte qui s'exerce dans le but de surmonter une résistance a nécessairement pour limite la valeur de cette résistance elle-même....
Le coeur aussi règle son effort sur la résistance qu'il éprouve, c'est-à-dire sur la pression à laquelle le sang est soumis dans les artères. Or, comme cette pression varie, à chaque instant, sous toutes sortes d'influences, rien n'est plus variable que la force que déploiera le coeur dans ces diverses conditions.... Ainsi, la force actuelle du coeur est, comme celle d'un muscle quelconque, proportionnelle à la résistance que le ventricule doit vaincre.
Si le ventricule trouvait au-devant de lui une résistance croissante, on verrait croître proportionnellement l'effort de sa systole. Enfin, si l'on opposait à la sortie du sang du ventricule un obstacle absolu, l'effort développé par les parois de cet organe s'élèverait jusqu'à la limite de leur puissance musculaire, ce serait la mesure de la plus grande *force possible* du coeur" (pp. 68-69).

the resistance by the contained blood is at its lowest, the tube of the artery is more or less flattened by the pressure of the finger upon it; then comes the so-called wave of blood propelled by the systole of the left ventricle, or, to speak more accurately, the fluid pressure in the vessel is increased, and this forces the artery back into the circular form. It is this change of shape from the flattened condition impressed upon the vessel by the finger, or by the sphygmographic lever, to the round cylindrical shape, which it assumes under the distending force of the blood within it which constitutes for us the pulse. Such a pulsation can be felt on a large scale by placing the foot on the inelastic leather hose of a fire-engine in action, in which there can be no expansion, or shown in a schema of the circulation with inelastic vessels. It is not, then, an increase in the diameter of the vessel, but an increase of the blood-pressure within it, created by the systole of the ventricle of the heart, which constitutes the pulse.[125]

Broadbent's description of pulse taking technique construes it as an active intervention into the circulation of blood, hindering and manipulating its passage: "pressure is made till the wave is arrested, so as not to be felt by the other fingers, or, if necessary, two fingers are employed to extinguish the pulsation. In this way, by the degree of pressure required, and by varying the pressure with one, two, or all three fingers, an idea is obtained of the force with which the heart is propelling the blood onwards."[126]

As a pulse reflects the shape rather than the size of an artery, indicating a change in pressure not volume, its effect is contingent on the deformation introduced by a measuring tool. In other words, when taking a pulse, the apprehending sensor is also the source of its beat. William M. Ewart was particularly emphatic on this point, even going so far as to label the pulse "factitious" in his book on *The Pulse-Sensations* (1895): "The pulse cannot be felt with efficiency without putting upon the artery a degree of pressure sufficient to partly flatten it. The tactile pulse is, more

---

[125] William H. Broadbent, *The Pulse* (London; Paris; New York; Melbourne: Cassell & Co., 1890), p. 19. Marey made the same analogy with a rubber tube in *La circulation du sang*, pp. 207-208.

[126] Broadbent, *The Pulse*, p. 41.

often than not, a modified, and in that sense, a manufactured pulse."[127] Without this leverage of resistance, the result would not be an undistorted pulse, but no discernable pulse at all; for sphygmologists of the nineteenth century, there was no pure channel prior to the introduction of noise.

The primacy of interference in sphygmology perhaps accounts for the difficulties practitioners of the time had in reconciling the sphygmograph with the virtues of abnegation that its inventor had sought to imbue it with. It sets the techniques of pulse taking at odds with models of mechanistic knowledge at a distance and further suggests that its practice might have had stronger resonance with "parasitic" modes of knowledge.[128]

Despite Marey's efforts at promoting the practicality of his invention—it was, after all, a patented product to be marketed commercially—others remained unconvinced by the sphygmograph's utility for clinical practice. Their doubts did not concern its capacity for accurate transcription, but rather involved the degree of familiarity required for effective use, especially amongst practitioners whose usage was infrequent. These critics noted precisely a continued need for trained operators, emphasizing subjective competency not its removal. In Broadbent's disparaging assessment,

> it is not every student who can thoroughly familiarize himself with this instrument and acquire the requisite skill for bringing out its indications, and the busy practitioner has still less chance of doing this; nor has he the time to employ it constantly, while without constant use the results are untrustworthy. ... The indications obtained from it are not, like those of the thermometer, independent of the observer. Skill and practice are required in applying it; judgment is called for in determining the position and pressure which give the best trace, and indeed in deciding which of the traces obtainable is the best representative of the particular

---

[127] Ewart, *The Pulse-Sensations*, p. 24 and p. 19.

[128] See Michel Serres, *The Parasite*, trans. Lawrence R. Schehr (Baltimore: Johns Hopkins University Press, 1982).

pulse; the personal equation of the observer, therefore, comes in, and if any special result is expected or wished for, an enthusiastic investigator can obtain it, and may, without the least conscious intention, twist facts in the desired direction. ... [A] sphygmogram does not speak for itself, but requires interpretation.[129]

His opinion was echoed by Ewart, who added that a sphygmogram "needs interpretation, and it also needs correction."[130] On the other hand, for proponents of the sphygmograph, its "defects" meant that "modifications" to its setup were recommended prior to effective use—even Marey's allies acknowledged the indispensable role of tweaks to the mechanism based on a physician's judgment, wasting little effort maintaining the pretense of independent measurement.[131]

Where the sphygmograph was appreciated, this was not because it supplanted the authority of an experienced practitioner. Instead, Marey's product was considered most useful as a pedagogical aid. It might thus be said, following Kuriyama, that the sphygmograph opened "paths of perceptual education": such instruments "invite us to develop our sensibility in such a way as to discern the realities described." Against his broader misgivings, Broadbent conceded that this technological appendage "is invaluable as a means of educating the sense of touch and of cultivating the faculty of observation."[132] Insofar as its direct employment in clinical practice was limited, then, interest in the sphygmograph did not derive from actual day-to-day application but from its ability to transform the particular into the general, extracting idealized specimens that were legible within inherited regimes of classification. The instrument was less a rupture from earlier conventions of symbolic notation but owed its limited success to a relative interpretative

---

[129] Broadbent, *The Pulse*, pp. 31-34.

[130] Ewart, *The Pulse-Sensations*, pp. 10-11.

[131] John Burdon Sanderson, *Handbook of the Sphygmograph* (London: Robert Hardwicke, 1867), pp. 5-11.

[132] Broadbent, *The Pulse*, p. 34.

flexibility that allowed its curves to conform to, be incorporated within, and contribute towards the maintenance of existing standards of a "cultivated palate."

Practices of the pulse are inadequately characterized in terms of disciplinary interrogation, suggesting the possibility of readings that depart from the stereotypes of normativity that Marey's studies are invariably associated with. As even a cursory scan through his chronophotographic imagery attests, Marey's graphical method is thoroughly stylized, inexistent without the incursions of a diagnostician. An epistemic culture expressed by sphygmography does not celebrate the observer's objectivity, but a process of intersubjective attunement. Bodies here insist on their fluidity, necessitating postures of responsiveness and approximation; as a figure of haptic affection, the sphymographer remains a medium of screening—that is, a site of projection and reception.

§1.6: Crookes's Tubes: Projections of Radiant Matter

Marey's posthumous reputation is largely tied to his role within (or at the fringes of) the history of cinema, but reading it alongside the materialities of sphygmography suggests that his efforts might also be situated amidst the development of electronic imaging. The capillary electrometer is a structural equivalent of cathode-ray displays, registering fluctuations in an imperceptible flow as luminescent form; Marey's photographic apparatus adds a horizontal dimension to the capillary tube's vertical axis.

In fact, like Lippmann's electrometer, the standard configuration of Karl Ferdinand Braun's initial design of the cathode-ray tube only modulated its light spot vertically, a single electromagnetic coil deflecting the stream of electrons up or down relative to the intensity and direction of an electric current. Introduced in an article on a method of demonstrating and studying the time dependence of variable currents, "Ueber ein Verfahren zur Demonstration und zum Studium des zeitlichen Verlaufes variabler Ströme" (1897), the first version of the Braun tube featured an external rotating mirror, an optical mechanism commonly used in the visualization of waveforms during the nineteenth century.[133] Horizontal expansion in this primitive CRT occurred only in the virtual image reflected, based on variations in the mirror's angle, thus tracing a curve of changes in current over the course of rotation.

When Braun made use of a secondary indicator coil, taking advantage of the screen as a two-dimensional surface, it was not in order to spatialize duration but to add a second current against which the first could be charted in relation to; both coils expressed the states of *dependent* variables. Redeploying its horizontal dimension as an indicator of time (i.e., using the CRT as an oscilloscope by internalizing the process of unfolding waves into visible form) entailed a conceptual revaluation rather than technical improvements to the electromagnetic deflector, applying one coil as an *independent* variable instead. Finally, adapting the CRT for image transmission further extends this to both coils, regarding both x- and y-axes as components of an

---

[133] Karl Ferdinand Braun, "Ueber ein Verfahren zur Demonstration und zum Studium des zeitlichen Verlaufes variabler Ströme," *Annalen der Physik und Chemie* 296, issue 3 (1897): 552-559. Braun refers to the use of a "König mirror," a device introduced by Rudolph Koenig in collaboration with Hermann von Helmholtz. See Rudolph Koenig, "On Manometric Flames," *The London, Edinburg, and Dublin Philosophical Magazine and Journal of Science* 45, series 4, issue 297 (Jan 1873): 1-18; and *Quelques expériences d'acoustique* (Paris, 1882), 47-83. This device was particularly influential in the visualization of acoustics. Helmholtz discussed it in this context, emphasizing the mirror's ability to make public, a recurring concern in nineteenth-century curve tracing: "to recognize the beats of two tones reinforced by the resonator, it is enough to look at the flame and observe how it alternates between its forms of rest and of oscillation. But to see the separate oscillations the flames should be viewed in a rotating glass, in which the flame at rest appears to be drawn out into a long uniform ribbon, while the oscillating flame appears as a series of separate images of flames. It is thus possible to allow a large number of persons at once to determine whether or not a given tone is reinforced by the resonator" (*On the Sensation of Tone as a Physiological Basis for the Theory of Music*, trans. Alexander J. Ellis [London: Longmans, Green, and Co., 1885], p. 374).

addressable location (i.e., ordinal positions: *first, second, third*, etc.), rather than as an index of value (i.e., cardinal magnitudes: *one, two, three*, etc.).

Braun's biographers somewhat gleefully recount the indifferent response that his tube—"a device whose numbers on the American continent alone were destined to run into hundreds of millions, in television receivers, oscilloscopes, radars, and instruments"—provoked upon its North American debut, noting that "at the time Braun's invention did not cause a great stir."[134] His contemporaries were instead more impressed by Edward B. Rosa's attempt at "An Electric Curve Tracer" (1898), just one of numerous efforts to surmount what seemed to be the limits of representation.[135] Amongst these, George J. Burch, a physicist who worked with the physiologist John Burdon-Sanderson on applications and calibration of capillary electrometers, demonstrated how the Lippmann-Marey apparatus could be used to produce chronophotographs of an alternating current's waveform.[136] Despite Burch's vigorous efforts at promoting the merits of this instrument, however, it does not appear to have attracted much interest outside of the specialization of electrophysiology—oscillography was a competitive field.[137]

---

[134] Friedrich Kurlyo and Charles Susskind, *Ferdinand Braun: A Life of the Nobel Prizewinner and Inventor of the Cathode-Ray Oscilloscope* (Cambridge, MA: MIT Press, 1981), p. 95.

[135] See Edward B. Rosa, "An Electric Curve Tracer," *The Physical Review* 6, no. 1 (January 1898): 17-42.

[136] George J. Burch, "The Capillary Electrometer in Theory and Practice," *The Electrician* 37 (August 1896): 532-535.

[137] Further examples of such instruments include: A. E. Blondel, "Oscillographs for the Investigation of Slow Electric Oscillations," *The Electrician* (March 1893): 571-572; E. J. Hotchkiss and F. E. Millis, "A Galvanometer for Photographing Alternating Current Curves," *Physical Review* 3, no. 1 (1895): 49-62; and, E. Hospitalier, "The Slow Registration of Rapid Phenomena by Strobographic Methods: The 'Ondographe' and the 'Pusisancegraphe' (Wave-Recorder and Power-Recorder)," *Journal of the Institution of Electrical Engineers* 33 (1903): 75-97. For an overview of the development of early oscillography, see Vivian J. Phillips, *Waveforms: A History of Early Oscillography* (Bristol: Adam Hilger, 1987).

With the benefit (or delusions) of hindsight, it is easier to dismiss devices such as Rosa's, an alternative to the CRT incapable even of following oscillations faster than 30 cycles per second. Braun's biographers offer several excuses for its lack of immediate acclaim:

> It was no real competition for Braun's tube, but under the unfavorable circumstances—the large audience, insufficient darkening of the room, frequency mismatch, and insufficient vacuum—even professional observers could scarcely be blamed for failing to recognize the superiority of Braun's cathode-ray tube over electromechanical recording systems.[138]

Yet the disadvantages in Braun's apparatus cannot be attributed to accidents of circumstance alone. For example, whereas the virtual image of movement on a mirror would have to be manually transcribed, Rosa's curve tracer was an automatic recording mechanism, leaving durable dots of pencil on paper. These traits of the CRT as a display system would continue to necessitate (photographic) a supplementa even decades later when the device was later adopted in the context of computing technologies. Most strikingly, in an article on the direct inscription of variable currents, "Sur l'inscription directe des courants variables" (1900), André Blondel—himself a designer of a successful oscillograph—deemed Braun's tube "the most imperfect method thus far for practical use" amongst the methods he reviewed, citing numerous deficiencies ("the very complicated equipment it requires, the lack of precision of the trace, the low sensitivity, the difficulty of the mode of operation, etc.").[139]

---

[138] Kurlyo and Susskind, *Ferdinand Braun*, p. 96.

[139] André Blondel, "Sur l'inscription directe des courants variable," in *Électro-optique et ionisation. Applications. Physique cosmique. Physique biologique.*, vol. 3 of *Rapports présentés au congrès international de physique réuni à Paris en 1900 sous les auspices de la Société française de physique*, eds. Charles-Édouard Guillaume and Lucien Poincaré (Paris: Gauthier-Villars, 1900): "La méthode la plus imparfaite jusqu'ici comme emploi pratique est la méthode oscilloradiographique, à cause du matériel très compliqué qu'elle exige, du manque de précision du tracé, de la faible sensibilité, de la difficulté du mode opératoire, etc. ; à ces divers points de vue, il semble difficile de la perfectionner, à moins que l'on ne puisse remplacer les rayons cathodiques par ceux du radium ou d'un corps très actif" (p. 295).

By way of contextualizing his contribution, Rosa outlined two "general methods" commonly used for tracing electric current curves: (1) the *"instantaneous method"* involving the reflection of a modulated light source (e.g., "Fröhlich mounted a light mirror excentrically upon the diaphragm of a telephone and caused a beam of light reflected from it to fall upon a series of revolving mirror in such a way as to get a upon a screen a stationary wave, representing the current which passed through the coil of telephone"); and, (2) the *"step-by-step method"* which scanned a sequence of average readings from discrete phases of the wave's curve (as already achieved by Lenz's modified commutator in 1854).[140] He considered his own mechanism a contribution to the latter method, with an emphasis on alleviating the "slow and laborious" task of reconstructing the curves: "The scale readings must all be taken and recorded, and finally the curve plotted out carefully by hand. One does this very willingly for a while, but if one must take a good many curves, each of a hundred or more points, the work becomes a burden."[141] Braun's tube, on the other hand, could be understood as one example—amongst many—of the former approach. Vivian J. Phillips's study of early oscillography argues, "the early cathode ray tube was seen as just a natural development of other deflecting instruments."[142]

Unlike in more typical accounts of the social construction of technology, the eventual familiarity of the CRT does not result from its successful negotiation of closure against such a range of competing alternatives. Instead, it proceeded through deviations, as a traveler into other domains; not shutting out rivals but opening channels of passage. Hence, it is more appropriate to discuss its development in terms of cultural-technical displacements, i.e., sequences of "misuse"

---

[140] Rosa, "An Electric Curve Tracer," pp. 18-19.

[141] Ibid., p. 21.

[142] Phillips, *Waveforms*, p. 242.

which cannot be contained within local spheres of interest but emerge out of provisional moments of contact in-between. Placing Marey's work in this expanded frame is not intended as a frivolous hagiographic exercise, assigning him credit for innovation. Rather, this realignment is a means of reconstructing the complex space of potential that conditioned the imaging of movement toward the end of the nineteenth century. Curve tracing was a participant in the parasitic traffic between incongruous subcultures: here, the professionalization of disciplinary expertise coincides with popular pictorial vernaculars, and the industrialization of infrastructure does not dispel but relies on artisanal fabrication.

In late 1895, as Auguste and Louis Lumière were repurposing Marey's decomposition of durational continuity as mass spectacle, Wilhelm Röntgen was publishing his observations on a new kind of rays, "Ueber eine neue Art von Strahlen," claiming that they displayed the hitherto unheard-of capacity to penetrate opaque matter. His article provoked widespread astonishment amongst scientists. Röntgen himself assumed a cautious or even perplexed tone, unsure of how to conceive of this aberration (and well aware that mistakenly promulgating such farfetched accounts would ruin his credibility). A footnote tentatively adopted algebraic convention for signifying an unknown variable, proposing: "For the sake of brevity, I would like to use the term 'rays' and the name 'X-rays' to distinguish it from others."[143] Soon, wooden crates from the Bonn workshop of Franz Müller marked "Caution! Glass" were arriving at the University of Strasbourg's Physics Institute, where Professor Braun and his assistants would investigate the unbelievable phenomenon themselves.

---

[143] W. C. Röntgen, "Ueber eine neue Art von Strahlen," *Sitzungsberichte der Physikalisch-medizinischen Gesellschaft zu Wuerzburg* 29 (1895): "Der Kürze halber möchte ich den Ausdruck 'Strahlen' und zwar zur Unterscheidung von anderen den Namen 'X-Strahlen' gebrauchen."

Müller was a successor to Heinrich Geissler, the physicist and glassblower who had in 1855 devised a vacuum pump crucial in the fabrication of evacuated glass bulbs useful for the study of electrical discharge through low pressure gases. Amongst the many environments they would inhabit, such gas discharge tubes were the primary actors in Röntgen's experiments; later, in the 1930s they would be developed as neon lamps and fluorescent lights. Prior to these episodes, they had been the subject of scientific interest for several decades. In 1859, Julius Plücker had observed that the glass walls of Geissler tubes would fluoresce and that the cathode's emissions in these tubes were deflected by magnetic fields, phenomena which did not occur under higher pressures. Following Plücker, Eugen Goldstein developed a concave cathode that focused the rays produced, coining the term *kathodenstrahlen* (cathode rays) in 1876 to describe them. Röntgen's article on X-rays made reference to the tubes of Johann Hittorf and Philipp Lenard, as well as those of William Crookes, who preferred to refer to the atmospheric conditions in the evacuated tube (rather than the emitted rays themselves), adopting Michael Faraday's expression: *radiant matter*.[144] The new rays Röntgen noticed differed from the cathode-rays identified by previous

---

[144] Crooke uses the term "radiant matter" to refer to a fourth state of matter, beyond solid, liquid, and gas—what today would more commonly be referred to as plasma. He explains his insistence on the irreducible materiality of low pressure conditions which might be mistaken for a procedure of dematerialization: "It may be objected that it is hardly consistent to attach primary importance to the presence of *matter*, when I have taken extraordinary pains to remove as much matter as possible from these bulbs and these tubes, and have succeeded so far as to leave only about the one millionth of an atmosphere in them. At its ordinary pressure the atmosphere is not very dense, and its recognition as a constituent of the world of matter is quite a modern notion. It would seem that, when divided by a million, so little matter will necessarily be left that we may justifiably neglect the trifling residue, and apply the term *vacuum* to space from which the air has bee so nearly removed. To do so, however, would be a great error, attributable to our limited faculties being unable to grasp high numbers. It is generally taken for granted that when a number is divided by a million the quotient must necessarily be small, whereas it may happen that the original number is so large that its division by a million seems to make little impression on it. According to the best authorities, a bulb of the size of the one before you (13.5 centimetres in diameter) contains more than 1,000000,000000,000000,000000 (a quadrillion) molecules. Now, when the exhausted to a millionth of an atmosphere we shall still have a trillion molecules left in the bulb – a number quite sufficient to justify me in speaking of the residue as *matter*" (William Crookes, "On Radiant Matter," *Popular Science Monthly* 16 [November 1879]: 165-166). Note: Crookes uses the terms "quadrillion" and "trillion" to refer respectively to 10^{24} and 10^{18} as standard in his time, rather than 10^{15} and 10^{12} conventional today. On variants of the cathode-ray tube before Braun, see Keller, *Cathode-Ray Tube*, pp. 45-54.

studies in several ways: they dispersed rather than travelled in straight lines, were not susceptible to the influence of magnetism—and, of course, were not screened by the glass enclosure of the apparatus, nor for that matter by what had previously been thought solid and impenetrable.

Braun's response to the sudden extreme prominence of vacuum tubes did not build on Röntgen's findings but returned to the more established effects of cathode-rays, instrumentalizing their responsiveness to magnetism (and frustrating any residual desire historians might retain for clean lines of narrative causality). When coupled with a rotating mirror and one of Müller's tubes, the alternating current output by Strasbourg's generating station presented itself as a perfect sine wave, generating an electromagnetic field that fluctuated in proportion to the flow of electricity, thus deflecting the stream of electrons accordingly. At this coincidence between multiple historical vectors, the (soon-to-be) CRT's instability and indeterminacy as an object is especially vivid, suggesting other trajectories of graphics. Crookes's description of the emissions from the tube's cathode as "the projection of molecular rays" is particularly evocative, indicating that the function of electronic screening exceeds the Imaginary reflection of virtual curves and the addressable Symbolic coordinates of signification; it further foregrounds the senseless propulsion of radiant matter—a Real *projectile*:

> Radiant matter comes from the pole in straight lines, and does not merely permeate all parts of the tube and fill it with light, as would be the case were the exhaustion less good. Where there is nothing in the way the rays strike the screen and produce phosphorescence, and where solid matter intervenes they are obstructed by it, and a shadow is thrown on the screen. In this pear-shaped bulb the negative pole (*a*) is at the pointed end. In the middle is a cross (*b*) cut out of sheet-aluminium, so that the rays from the negative pole projected along the tube will be partly intercepted by the aluminium cross, and will project an image of it on the hemispherical end of the tube which is phosphorescent. I turn on the coil, and you will all see the black shadow of the cross on the luminous end of the bulb (*c*, *d*).[145]

---

[145] William Crookes, "On Radiant Matter," pp. 23-24.

In his demonstration, the linear path taken by electronic rays was visualized through the projection of an obstacle's shadow against the screen, utilizing a stencil-effect later resuscitated in shaped-beam tubes like the Charactron. The glass screen of these tubes work as a sieve, exposed to the impact of "molecular bombardment." This approach towards electronic screening did not result in a flat surface of pictorial representation but encompassed volumetric shapes of glowing objects maintaining a quasi-sculptural presence.

Crookes would continue working with such screen media even beyond the realms of radiant matter. His 1903 study of "The Emanations of Radium" described the flashes of light, or "scintillations," made visible on zinc sulfide screens exposed to radioactivity:

> A solid piece of radium nitrate is slowly brought near the screen. The general phosphorescence of the screen as visible to the naked eye varies according to the distance of the radium from it. On now examining the surface with the pocket lens, the radium being far off and the screen faintly luminous, the scintillating spots are sparsely scattered over the surface. On bringing the radium nearer the screen the scintillations become more numerous and brighter, until when close together the flashes follow each other so quickly that the surface looks like a turbulent luminous sea. When the scintillating points are few there is no residual phosphorescence to be seen, and the sparks succeeding each other appear like stars on a black sky. When, however, the bombardment exceeds a certain intensity, the residual phosphorescent glow spreads over the screen, without, however, interfering with the scintillations....
>
> During these experiments the fingers soon become soiled with radium, and produce phosphorescence when brought near the screen. On turning the lens [of a microscope] to the, apparently, uniformly lighted edge of the screen close to the finger, the scintillations are seen to be closer and more numerous; what to the naked eye appears like a uniform "milky way," under the lens is a multitude of stellar points, flashing over the whole surface. A clean finger does not show any effect, but a touch with a soiled finger is sufficient to confer on it the property. Washing the fingers stops their action.[146]

---

[146] William Crookes, "The Emanations of Radium," *Proceedings of the Royal Society of London* 71 (March 1903): 406-407.

Until Geiger-Müller counters offered an acceptable alternative, visual inspection was for around twenty years a standard means of quantifying emanations.[147] Ernest Rutherford and his assistant Hans Geiger (who would later work on electrical counting devices with his own assistant, Walther Müller) note in their study of α-particles: "In considering a possible method of counting the number of α-particles, their well-known property of producing scintillations in a preparation of phosphorescent zinc sulphide at once suggests itself. With the aid of a microscope, it is not very difficult to count the number of scintillations appearing per second on a screen of known area when exposed to a source of α-rays."[148] These graphic procedures were precursors to what Peter Galison has termed the "logic tradition" in research on microphysics, which based evidence on relations in statistical aggregates rather than in details of individual events.[149] Given their distinct epistemic presuppositions, they were not markedly affected by Braun's retreat into cathode rays, thus yielding a mode of electronic screening that implied a sensibility towards computer graphics and digital imaging alien in comparison to the traditions familiar today.

Indeed, Crookes's peculiarly haptic conception of the digital screen—i.e., "touch with a soiled *finger*"—stages a form of experimentation that would not be out of place if presented as a form of experimental video, resonating with the work of artists like Aldo Tambellini and Nam June Paik who took more interest in the electromagnetism of signals than the specular clarity of an image. In the early twentieth century, the production of logical abstraction was never far

---

[147] On the development of the Geiger-Müller counter, see Thaddeus J. Trenn, "The Geiger-Müller Counter of 1928," *Annals of Science* 43, no. 2 (Mar 1986): 111-135; and Sebastian Korff, "How the Geiger Counter started to crackle: Electrical counting methods in early radioactivity research," *Annalen der Physik* 525, no. 6 (2013), A88-A92.

[148] Ernst Rutherford and Hans Geiger, "An Electrical Method of Counting the Number of α-particles from Radio-active Substances," *Proceedings of the Royal Society of London* 81, issue 546 (August 1908): 141.

[149] Peter Galison, *Image and Logic: A Material Culture of Microphysics* (Chicago; London: University of Chicago Press, 1997), esp. pp. 438-454 on early practices using zinc sulfide scintillation screens.

removed from the stress of embodied existence. Rutherford and Geiger described the demanding conditions an "optical" method entailed:

> In our experiments a microscope of magnification 50 was used. The small area of screen, struck by the α-particles, covered only about one-half of the field of view. The experiments were made at night in a dark room. As Regener suggests, it is advisable to illuminate the screen slightly by artificial light, in order to keep the eye focused on the screen. The distance and intensity of the source were adjusted so that from 20 to 60 scintillations were observed per minute. It is difficult to continue counting for more than two minutes at a time, as the eye becomes fatigued.[150]

Adolf Theodor Krebs, who (like Geiger) developed an instrument to replace physiological counters, confirmed these sentiments in his reflections on the challenges encountered:

> Rapid fatigue of the observers and other subjective influences make it necessary to change observers frequently. They can only observe for thirty seconds to a minute, need to make long pauses between observations, and cannot make reliable observations for more than two hours a week. The efficiency of the method is poor; good, useful counts are to be had only at rates of 20 to 40 scintillations per minute.[151]

To achieve the purity associated with statistical reasoning, these scintillations would be screened further, their signals more thoroughly filtered into legible signs.

The resultant technologies of electronic counters and techniques of pulse control are not just distant relations of modern computers. As Galison notes, "the link is direct":

> On 3 August 191, John W. Mauchly, one of the builders of the first electronic general purpose computer, the ENIAC, recorded in his notes his first explorations of the digital electronic calculator. That same day, he jotted down references to the physicist Thomas Johnson's 1938 *Review of Scientific Instruments* cosmic ray article, "Circuits for the Control of Geiger-Muller Counters and for Scaling and

---

[150] Rutherford and Geiger, "An Electrical Method," p.157.

[151] A. T. Krebs, "Szintillationszähler," *Ergebnisse der exakten Naturwissenschaften* 27 (1953): 362, quoted in and trans. Hans-Jörg Rheinberger, *An Epistemology of the Concrete: Twentieth-Century Histories of Life* (Durham: Duke University Press, 2010), p. 174.

Recording their Impulses," a move made without the slightest visible interest in cosmic rays.[152]

Ensconced in a transcendent realm and relieved from the task of providing an index of radiation, an imperceptible relay of electronic pulses could give the impression of the sublimation of information, a condition of digitization far removed from fingers covered in radium and scintillations of zinc sulfide screens. That sort of "hands-on imperative" might have been appealing to amateur computing hobbyists like Steve Dompier, for whom—like a cinephile transfixed to an avant-garde film—the prospect of attentively examining flickers of light in a darkened room could be a source of excitement. But, of course, the etiquette of screening makes all of this unnecessary, and although it is tempting here to grieve the shrouding of dots, I doubt they'd really notice either way.

---

[152] Galison, *Image and Logic*, p. 454. See also, on the electronic counter of another assistant of Rutherford's, C. E. Wynn-Williams, and the early computers of Bletchley Park, Siegert, *Passage des Digitalen*, pp. 409-414.

www.ingramcontent.com/pod-product-compliance
Lightning Source LLC
LaVergne TN
LVHW011931070526
838202LV00054B/4592